in quiet desperation

Understanding the Challenge of Same-Gender Attraction

Fred Matis and Marilyn Matis
.
Ty Mansfield

DESERET BOOK

Salt Lake City, Utah

Visit us at deseretbook.com

Library of Congress Cataloging-in-Publication Data

Matis, Fred.
  In quiet desperation : understanding the challenge of same-gender
attraction / Fred Matis, Marilyn Matis, Ty Mansfield.
      p. cm.
  Includes bibliographical references and index.
  ISBN 1-59038-331-1 (pbk.)
  1. Homosexuality—Religious aspects—Church of Jesus Christ of Latter-day
Saints. 2. Matis, Stuart, 1967–2000. 3. Mormon gays. I. Matis, Marilyn.
II. Mansfield, Ty. III. Title.
  BX8643.H65M38 2004
  261.8'35766—dc22
                          2004013047

Printed in the United States of America   21239
Edwards Brothers Inc., Ann Arbor, MI

10   9   8   7   6   5   4   3   2   1

For Stuart
and all who strive to find
purpose and peace

The Refiner's Fire

Some time ago, a few women met in a certain city to study the scriptures. While reading Malachi 3, they came upon a remarkable expression in the third verse:

"And he shall sit as a refiner and purifier of silver" (Malachi 3:3).

One woman proposed to visit a silversmith and report to them on what he said about the subject. She went accordingly, and without telling the object of her errand, begged the silversmith to tell her about the process of refining silver. After he had fully described it to her, she asked, "But sir, do you sit while the work of refining is going on?"

"Oh, yes, madam," replied the silversmith. "I must sit with my eye steadily fixed on the furnace, for if the time necessary for refining be exceeded in the slightest degree, the silver will be injured."

The woman at once saw the beauty and comfort in the expression, "He shall sit as a refiner and purifier of silver." God sees it needful to put his children into a furnace. His eye is steadily intent on the work of purifying, and his wisdom and love are both engaged in the best manner for us. Our trials do not come at random, and he will not let us be tested beyond what we can endure.

Before she left, the woman asked one final question. "When do you know the process is complete?"

"Why, that is quite simple," replied the silversmith. "When I can see my own image in the silver, the refining process is finished."

Author Unknown

Contents

Contents

Publisher's Preface

This sensitive and significant book has been written by individuals who feel and know things that many of us do not comprehend. All three of the authors are dedicated Latter-day Saints who have a deep conviction of the truthfulness of the restored gospel and an unyielding faith in the person and power of Jesus the Christ. They are in complete agreement with the doctrines and principles set forth in the Proclamation on the Family.

As a publisher, Deseret Book Company is committed to providing books and other products that will help strengthen individuals, families, and the larger society. Like the living Church that is its owner, Deseret Book Company seeks to respond to changing needs and circumstances. This book has been prepared to help readers understand some of the struggles and crosses of those who experience same-gender attraction.

Those who have felt such attractions themselves will find valuable insights into the hearts and minds of two young men who have wrestled with feelings of worth and have sought to live balanced, faithful lives. In one case, the struggle proved to be insurmountable. In the other, the struggle continues, but the young man moves forward with a lively hope that in and through the atoning power of the Savior both strength and change will, in the due time of the Lord, come to pass.

Those who do not understand the nature of same-gender attraction and who either shake their head as if at a mystery or clench their fist in anger will likewise find within these pages understanding and reasons for compassion. Jesus Christ has called upon us all, particularly those of us who count ourselves his disciples, to lift up the hands that hang down, to strengthen the feeble knees, and to succor the weak (D&C 81:5). In a world where the hearts of too many have failed them and love has waxed cold (D&C 45:26–27), there is a pressing need for us who are of the household of faith to undergo the change of heart that would equip us to love as the Master loves and to reach out to those who yearn for fellowship and understanding. The Prophet Joseph Smith observed: "It is one evidence that men are unacquainted with the principles of godliness to behold the contraction of affectionate feelings and lack of charity in the world. The power and glory of godliness is spread out on a broad principle to throw out the mantle of charity. . . . The nearer we get to our heavenly Father, the more we are disposed to look with compassion on perishing souls; we feel that we want to take them upon our shoulders. . . . if you would have God have mercy on you, have mercy on one another" (*Teachings of the Prophet Joseph Smith,* 240–41).

Those who are teachers, advisors, and priesthood leaders will also find this book especially helpful. Our Eternal Father and his Beloved Son Jesus Christ are in the business of people. Their work and glory are to bring to pass the immortality and eternal life of man (Moses 1:39). Baptism into the Lord's Church initiates us into a service society as we are summoned to bear one another's burdens, mourn with those that mourn, and comfort those who stand in need of comfort (Mosiah 18:8–9). We are to be undershepherds to the flock of Christ. None of us desires to "do wrong in the sight of God" (Mosiah 26:13) when it comes to working with people, because only "fools will trifle with the souls of men" (*Teachings of the Prophet Joseph Smith,* 137). All of us called to instruct or lead or counsel with others want to do so the best we can. This book provides us with distinctive insights into a crucial issue of our times as it enables us to open our hearts more spontaneously to those who struggle with it.

This is not a self-help book. It is not a clinical text: it does not set forth theories or postulate why or how same-gender attraction occurs.

Rather, it is an effort to share feelings—deep and perceptive feelings—about one of the most difficult and perplexing challenges of our time. In the pages that follow, you will look into the heart and mind of a mother and father who did all they could to assist their son to bear an almost unbearable burden and face life in the best way he possibly could. In addition, you will read the reflections and impressions of another young man who presently wrestles with same-gender attraction. It will become obvious that he has spent hundreds of hours on his knees, in counsel with priesthood leaders, and in deep and pondering study of the holy scriptures in an effort to cope with feelings of attraction that he did not choose. And though these experiences come from the perspectives of men who have feelings of same-gender attraction and their friends and family who love them, the gospel principles and their application discussed here are equally applicable in the lives of women who have this challenge.

In fact, this book can teach all of us, through real-life experiences, how to draw closer to the Lord, no matter what our circumstances or burdens may be. President Howard W. Hunter once said tenderly: "Whatever Jesus lays his hands upon lives. If Jesus lays his hands upon a marriage, it lives. If he is allowed to lay his hands upon the family, it lives" (Conference Report, October 1979, 93). There is power in the blood of Christ, power not only to create worlds and part the Red Sea but also to still the storms of the human heart. There is power in Christ to bring about a sudden and miraculous change in a person's life and also the power to bear one's burdens with dignity and strength until one's mortal life is finished. God alone knows why some who suffer are delivered immediately from their suffering, why others pass away, and why yet others continue on earth to face the traumas of this second estate. We cling to the supernal promise from Him who is the Peacegiver, the Balm of Gilead, that He will heal us, whether here or hereafter. "For since the beginning of the world men have not heard, nor perceived by the ear, neither hath the eye seen, O God, beside thee, what he hath prepared for him [or her] that waiteth for him" (Isaiah 64:4).

Each of us wrestles with something. Perhaps it is our complexion, the shape of our bodies, our intellectual challenges, or same-gender attraction. To attempt to compare crosses is both unwise and counterproductive, for only He who knows all things can discern the depths of the individual human soul. We have not been promised a stress-free existence or a life of leisure. We have, however, the unimpeachable testimony of One who descended below all things and thus who knows what is in the heart of each of us that relief is real, that deliverance is definite. The Master beckons to us: "Come unto me, all ye that labour and are heavy laden, and I will give you rest. Take my yoke upon you, and learn of me; for I am meek and lowly in heart: and ye shall find rest unto your souls. For my yoke is easy, and my burden is light" (Matthew 11:28–30).

Part 1

A Parent's Spiritual Journey toward Understanding

.

Chapter 1

Introduction

In the musical *1776,* John Adams struggles with the Continental Congress to pass the Declaration of Independence. After one very heated debate, the Congress leaves for the day, and Adams remains alone on the stage. He is frustrated that few seem to understand the need to pass the Declaration of Independence. He is discouraged because he feels that he alone sees the vision of a great nation no longer in bondage to another country. In his loneliness he plaintively asks the audience, "Is anybody there? Does anybody care? Does anybody see what I see?"

Although I have not had to battle with the Congress, there have been many times when, as the mother of a child who battled valiantly with his feelings of same-gender attraction, I asked those same questions. I too felt frustrated, discouraged, and above all, so painfully alone. I frequently asked my husband, "Is there anybody who cares? Or even understands?"

You may wonder who I am and what led me to ask these questions. More to the point, you may wonder what prompted me to write a book about a subject that so many people feel uncomfortable discussing.

I wrote this book because when our son Stuart told me that he had feelings of same-gender attraction, I knew absolutely nothing on the subject. I felt completely lost and alone, and I really did not know where to turn for help.

For this reason, I want to reach out to families who have a loved one who faces the challenge of same-gender orientation. I want to help families understand what Stuart called "the true nature of homosexuality." I want families to know how important it is for them to love and understand a child or sibling who experiences this challenge. I want to bring comfort to such families, and I want them to know that they are *not* alone.

In addition, I pray that we as a society will become better informed about same-gender attraction. As we do become more educated about this issue, the more loving and supportive and less judgmental we will become. If in any way I can bring knowledge and comfort to families who have a family member with same-gender attraction and also assist society to better understand homosexuals, then this book will have value.

Let me explain, too, why I use the term *same-gender attraction* to describe the challenge Stuart had. He told me that he did not like the term *homosexual,* nor did he like the term *same-sex attraction.* He felt that both had a sexual meaning. He preferred the term *gay,* and yet the term *gay,* to most people, connotes sexual activity. Because feelings of same-gender attraction do not have to lead to sexual activity, I use the term *same-gender attraction.* It is vitally important to distinguish between the feelings of attraction and the choice to act—or refrain from acting—on those feelings.

As to my background, I am an active Latter-day Saint. In repeated prayers, I have acknowledged to Heavenly Father that as a mother I have made many mistakes, but I truly have always tried to do my best. I have always loved to read the scriptures, and so, as a new mother I read Book of Mormon and Bible stories to my babies. Reading scriptures to my children became a pattern. We held family home evening each Monday night. We had family prayer twice a day. My husband, Fred, and I faithfully attended the temple.

Fred has served as a bishop twice, as a stake mission president, as a counselor in a stake presidency, and, several times, as a member of a high council. I have served as a ward Primary president, ward Young Women president, counselor in a stake Relief Society presidency, Gospel Doctrine teacher in Sunday School, and an early-morning seminary teacher for many years. Fred and I both served missions. We married when I was twenty-eight and he was thirty. We became the parents of five children: three girls and two boys. Both sons and one daughter filled honorable missions for the Church. All of our children graduated from Brigham Young University—as did my husband and I. And all of our children, except for our son who died, were married in the temple.

In other words, we are a typical, average Latter-day Saint family. We love our Savior and his gospel, and in spite of the weakness of the flesh, we strive to do our best (see Matthew 26:41).

As you read our story and the story of our son Stuart, will you pray for a willing heart to guide you to a better understanding of a great challenge experienced by some Latter-day Saints, many of whom are active in the Church and faithful to the truths of the gospel of Christ they hold dear?

Chapter 2

"Yes, Mother, I'm Gay"

Upon waking early on a Friday morning in late February 2000, I turned to my husband and said, "Stuart had a restless night. I heard him pacing in his room until 4:30 this morning."

Fred went immediately to Stuart's room. On his bed was a letter: "Mother, Dad, and Family: I have committed suicide. These words are difficult to write, and I imagine they are more difficult to read . . ."

It is humbling to recognize how Heavenly Father prepares us for events about to take place in our lives. During the two years before Stuart's death, I had an unsettled feeling that I needed to gain a deeper understanding of the Atonement. Intellectually, I thought I had a good understanding of it—I had taught it in church classes many times—but I also felt I had not really internalized it.

Thus, the odyssey began. After a year of searching, serving, fasting, and praying, I felt no closer to achieving my desire to more fully understand the Atonement than I had the previous year. And so, I fell upon my knees and in tears begged Heavenly Father to tell me what he wanted me to do. Whatever it was, I told Him, I would do it.

Two weeks after I offered this prayer, Heavenly Father set my feet on a path that in all my wildest dreams I had never imagined I would travel. The path began with a poignant conversation with Stuart. It was a path filled with anguish and sorrow; and yet, it was a path that I am grateful to have traveled. I feel deep gratitude to my Heavenly Father for the blessings I have received while on this journey. I am grateful to Him for sending Stuart into our family circle.

Let me say simply that Stuart struggled with feelings of same-gender attraction, but he kept his feelings a secret from the whole world, including his family, nearly his entire life. Not until he was thirty-two years old did he tell us about the cross he was carrying. Our other children at various times had asked me if I thought Stuart were gay, but each time, upset they would ask such a question, I answered, "Just because he doesn't date doesn't mean he's gay!"

Eventually, I decided I must ask him myself. Stuart had just flown home to California from New York the night before and was sitting at his computer in his bedroom when I approached him. It was January 29, 1999. As I stumbled around trying to ask my questions, Stuart responded, "What you're trying to ask me, Mother, is—am I gay? Yes, Mother, I am."

Although I had tried to ask the question, I was completely unprepared to handle his answer. It was as though lightning went through my entire body. I had to hold onto the door handle because I could feel my legs giving out underneath me. How could he be gay? He had a temple recommend in his pocket!

When Stuart informed me that he sometimes was attracted to another man, I thought, "Who taught that to you?" As if he had read my mind, he said to me, "Mother, I didn't learn this attraction from anyone. And why would I teach someone else to be gay so they could be as miserable as I am?"

I soon learned how misinformed I was. A steep learning curve lay ahead of me.

Shortly before Stuart told us about the burden he was carrying, the media carried the story of Matthew Shepherd, a young man who was brutally beaten to death because he was gay. As Stuart told me about his own challenge, my thoughts bounced all over the place. It terrified me to think that someone might hurt or even kill Stuart if it became known that he experienced same-gender attraction. I wondered what his life would be like with no family of his own. Would he find friends who would understand his challenge? What had caused this challenge? Were his father and I to blame? Could Stuart change his orientation?

For the next two hours Stuart told me the saddest story I have ever heard. He described how at age seven he had a crush on a little boy in his school class and how his good friend had a crush on a little girl. He thought his friend's having a crush on a little girl was the strangest thing he had ever heard of, and he couldn't comprehend how that could be.

At age twelve, when Stuart received the Aaronic Priesthood, he thought his same-gender attraction would change. It did not. And then he thought when he received his patriarchal blessing, his same-gender feelings would change. They did not.

Surely his feelings would change when he attended the temple for the first time and then went on his mission. They did not. When he returned from his mission, he was called to be an elders quorum president. Now, he thought, God approved of his life, and his challenge would be taken away. Once again he was disappointed.

Stuart told me that as a child he would deny himself watching his favorite television programs or going to a party as self-punishment for being attracted to other boys. After his mission, when he returned to Brigham Young University, he went fasting and praying to the temple every week, seeking for the power to alter his attraction orientation. Night after night, he wept as he prayed the entire night—begging and pleading with God to change him. He began experiencing panic attacks because he was terrified that someone would guess his secret. And yet, Stuart had become a master at hiding his feelings.

He stayed two years longer than he needed to at Brigham Young University because he was so afraid to leave an environment that seemed relatively safe to him. He felt that once he left, he would lose all hope of being able to change his same-gender attraction. Finally, he reluctantly returned home to California and began to work for a consulting firm, traveling back and forth across the nation, living on airplanes and in hotels.

His hectic, lonely life began to take its toll. As his parents, Fred and I could tell that Stuart was stressed, but we assumed the stress was related to his work. We did not realize that he was having suicidal thoughts because he felt that God had abandoned him.

Stuart's entire life was spent striving for perfection. He reasoned that if he were perfect, then he would find God's approval. His efforts became a never-ending cycle: effort—perceived failure—effort—perceived failure. The harder Stuart strove for perfection, the more he hated himself. He hated his feelings of same-gender attraction, and he hated being unable to change his orientation because he believed that he not only *could* change but *should* change.

When no change in his feelings occurred, no matter how hard he worked at it, he came to the conclusion that he was not worthy and that God did not accept his efforts. His self-loathing became so intense that it began to affect his entire life. He lost confidence not only in himself but in God. Once Stuart said to me, "Mother, all my life I have tried to do what is right. I just can't pass the test."

Because other family members were visiting at our home when Stuart told me of his challenge, it was not convenient for me to talk with Fred immediately. At church on Sunday, I asked our bishop if I could talk with him. He invited me into his office, and after our conversation, he gave me a blessing, which gave me great comfort. Later that day our visitors left, and Stuart flew back to New York City.

When my husband and I were finally alone, I told him all that Stuart had told me. With tears of compassion in his eyes, he replied in his quiet, understated way, "Well, it isn't what I had hoped for Stuart's life." How grateful I was that he was so accepting of our son's situation.

Chapter 3

My Quest to Understand Same-Gender Attraction

Because I had absolutely no understanding of same-gender attraction, I read voraciously every book I could find on the subject. But as a result of all that reading, I became more confused than ever. Each author had a different opinion of what caused same-gender attraction, and each author had a different opinion of how to handle the situation.

After much reading, and after talking to many "experts," I have discovered that to date there is no solid scientific evidence pointing with any certainty to the cause of same-gender attraction. Science is still trying to determine whether something happens in individuals' lives to confuse their gender orientation, or whether individuals are simply born with factors that influence the attraction. Until we have a definitive understanding of what causes same-gender attraction, all therapy becomes a guessing game.

Occasionally, I have been asked if I thought someone could choose to have same-gender attraction. My answer is always the same: "I have never met, nor have I ever heard about or read about someone who has chosen the challenge, but I suppose there are individuals who have been curious and have experimented with same-gender sexual activity. I believe, however, that they are the rare exception."

In addition to my quest to understand same-gender attraction, I discovered that every man and woman I learned about who experienced same-gender attraction suffered great emotional pain. A substantial number of these individuals had repeated thoughts of suicide.

Many people who have same-gender attraction are in denial. Stuart told me that because he was a Christian, he thought he could never be gay. He therefore did all in his power to deny his feelings. He constantly tried to convince himself that he was not really attracted to other males.

In addition, he was always afraid to look another man in the eye because he didn't know how men looked at each other. He was always afraid that if he looked too long or had the wrong expression on his face, the man to whom he was speaking would wonder what was wrong with him.

When Stuart was thirty-two years old, he finally accepted his feelings of attraction to other men. He said he cried all night long when he realized his feelings of attraction had not gone away—nor had they diminished in any way since he had first recognized them. He said that he knew what it felt like to go in one day from being a first-class citizen everyone liked to being a third-class citizen everyone would hate if they knew his secret. Stuart was gone during the week on work assignments, but he flew home every Friday night. After he told me of his same-gender attraction, he would spend weekends in long hours of conversation with his father and me. He would cry as he told us of the deep emotional pain he was experiencing and had experienced over the past twenty years of his life.

"Trust in the Lord"

When I first learned about Stuart's challenge, sleep did not come easily for me. I would lie awake for countless hours at night, trying to make some sense out of what was happening to our family. I eventually learned that the easiest way to achieve sleep was to repeat the scripture "Trust in the Lord with all thine heart; and lean not unto thine own understanding" (Proverbs 3:5). As I would say the scripture over and over in my mind, sleep gradually would come.

During the last year of Stuart's life, I called twenty temples across the United States every two weeks to put his name on the prayer rolls. As time went on, we became increasingly aware of our son's desire to end his life. As a result, three times I fasted three days and nights, going without any food or water. And though I do not suggest that others do as I did, it was necessary for my own peace of mind to do so. We also had family fasts. Most important, I was trying desperately to do everything I could so that my son could be saved, both temporally and spiritually.

Shortly after we learned about Stuart's struggle, Fred and I went with him for counseling. Stuart had never told us that he loved us, and we had always wondered why. After one counseling session he told us, "The reason I have never told you I love you is that I haven't allowed myself to express feelings for anyone." He broke down and wept, and for the first time since he was a little boy, he hugged us and told us he loved us.

Family and Friends

Gradually we began to inform our family and close friends of Stuart's pain—and Stuart began to tell his friends. Our family members were all very kind and supportive. Some of Stuart's friends were supportive; others were not. It was difficult for Stuart to tell his friends. The friends who rejected him brought more anguish into his life. There were a few friends, however, with whom Stuart was afraid to share his challenge. After Stuart's death, it was sad to find that the friends Stuart had chosen not to tell were the very friends who had guessed his secret but said nothing to him about it. These friends were waiting for him to bring up the subject. They said that they wanted so badly to tell Stuart that his attraction orientation was not important to them because they knew what a noble spirit he had. These were the very friends who were the most understanding and kind.

As we told family and friends, some suggested that we not tell any others. I soon realized that some people felt very uncomfortable talking about homosexuality. At first, I took the advice and stopped telling anyone. Then, when I prayed about what to do, I felt that the only way that other members of our Church, our neighbors, our family, and our friends would begin to understand the challenge of homosexuality was to talk about it. As I resumed telling family members and friends about Stuart's challenge, I soon recognized that some individuals were willing to understand and others were so closed-minded that no matter what I said, I could not even begin to change their lack of understanding.

Stuart's Bishop

Eventually, Stuart went to his bishop, Bishop Russell Hancock of the Stanford singles ward in Palo Alto, California. In Stuart's time of greatest anxiety and despair, his bishop picked him up emotionally and carried him when he could no longer carry himself. His bishop also listened patiently, counseled, and gave blessings. Stuart leaned heavily on him for comfort and support.

Bishop Hancock asked Stuart if his parents would like to talk with him. Fred and I were grateful for the opportunity. We found the bishop compassionate and very knowledgeable on the subject of same-gender attraction. He told us that several other ward members experienced the same challenge.

Stuart's bishop asked us what he could do to help our son. We talked to him about how much Stuart loved to teach the gospel. The next week Stuart was asked to be a Gospel Doctrine teacher.

Bishop Hancock told us that he would always be there for Stuart whenever Stuart needed to talk with him. During the last two months of Stuart's life, he e-mailed his bishop many times, and Bishop Hancock always replied to him.

Chapter 4

An Overwhelming Peace

On a Sunday evening near the end of October 1999, Stuart asked me if we could talk. My husband was attending a stake meeting at church, and Stuart and I were alone. When we sat down, Stuart told me that he had purchased a gun, and he was waiting the required ten days before he could get it. Naturally, I became upset and told him all the reasons I could think of why he should not carry out this terrible deed. I spoke of the eternal consequences of his choice. Nothing I said seemed to have any effect upon his decision, and yet after he and I had talked a while, I felt peace overwhelm me. I could not understand why or how I could feel so peaceful about our conversation.

When Fred returned from his meeting, I told him about Stuart's conversation with me, but I did not tell him about my feeling of peace. The next morning when he awoke, Fred went into his office and knelt in prayer. In time he came back into our bedroom, weeping. He told me that he had begged Heavenly Father to tell us what we could do to keep our son from taking his life. He said, "While I was praying, I began crying so hard I could no longer speak. And then, a great feeling of peace came over me. I don't know what the feeling means. I don't know if Heavenly Father was saying that Stuart wouldn't try to take his life—or if it meant that Stuart's challenge would be taken away. All I know is that Stuart is in Heavenly Father's hands."

It was then that I told Fred about my feeling of peace the previous night.

Our other children later asked me why Stuart had told me about his plan to take his life. I answered that I had learned that when someone thinks about taking his life, frequently he will talk to someone about the decision. The suicidal person is sending a plea for help—a plea with the hope that there will be a reason to live.

Two days after Stuart came to me with his decision to end his life, one of his good friends, Paul (not his real name), tried for the fifth time to take his own life. When he failed, Paul begged Stuart not to try to end his own life.

Stuart and Paul met when they were both serving in the Rome Italy Mission. In fact, Paul was Stuart's district leader, and Stuart wanted very much to be the kind of missionary that Paul was. Although baptisms did not come easily in Italy, Paul would go into towns that hadn't had baptisms in years, and through his work many would join the Church. Paul was not only a gospel scholar but a humble, dedicated, hard-working elder.

After graduating from high school, Paul received scholarships to several universities, but he decided to attend Brigham Young University. At the end of his freshman year, Paul called his family, who belonged to another faith, and said there was something he needed to discuss with them. He had joined The Church of Jesus Christ of Latter-day Saints earlier in the school year, and now he wanted to go on a mission for the Church.

Upon returning home from their missions and then graduating from BYU, Paul and Stuart went their separate ways. Paul went away to law school, and Stuart returned to the Bay Area in California. Then one day, Stuart received a phone call from Paul, saying he had taken a job in San Francisco. They resumed their friendship.

One day they went shopping together for a gift for our first grandson. Stuart found a stuffed animal and said, "I think I'll buy Mickey Mouse for my nephew."

Paul responded, "Then I'll give him Minnie Mouse."

Stuart exclaimed, "What? You want him to grow up to be gay?"

Suddenly, Paul became very quiet and withdrawn. Stuart wondered what had happened to make his friend react in such a way. When he returned home, he found a message from Paul on e-mail. The message read: "Stuart, there is something you need to know about me. I'm gay." Stuart quickly responded: "So am I."

In his discouragement with the hurtful attitude of some Church members, Paul had stopped going to church, but otherwise he strove to be faithful to his temple covenants. Stuart encouraged Paul to come back to church, and Paul tried to keep Stuart from trying to take his own life. And yet, Paul was even more suicidal than Stuart.

After Paul's fifth failed attempt at taking his life, we were dismayed when we received a phone call from a friend telling us that Paul had tried for the sixth time—and again had failed. It was the Saturday following Thanksgiving. Stuart was devastated.

Early in December 1999, a knock came at our bedroom door at two in the morning. Stuart wanted to talk with his father. The two of them went into Fred's office and talked for a while. Fred came back into our bedroom and said, "Stuart wants a blessing. Come be with us." In the blessing Stuart was told that he did indeed have same-gender attraction and that the attraction would not be removed in this life. The blessing further declared that the Lord knew who Stuart was, that He loved him, and that He accepted his efforts. After the blessing, Stuart said, "That's the same blessing my bishop gave me!" It was as though the entire world had been taken off his shoulders.

Before knocking on our bedroom door, Stuart had stood at the front door of our home ready to leave and take his life. After the blessing he was happy and joking. We had our son back! That was our last Christmas with Stuart. It was a gift from Heavenly Father. And it was one of our happiest Christmases.

Chapter 5

There Must Needs Be Opposition in All Things

During the last few months of Stuart's life, voters in California were campaigning against same-gender marriages. The Church asked its members in California to assist in that campaign, and they were anxious to do what was asked of them. The problem came when some Church members, completely lacking in understanding the plight of a person with same-gender attraction, went beyond what was asked of them and became hostile and unkind in their remarks and attitude during church meetings.

As a result of the hostility of some of the Church members, Stuart began to have panic attacks at church meetings. He was terrified that someone would guess the secret that he had kept for twenty years. His bishop, realizing the pain Stuart was suffering, suggested to him that he refrain from attending church meetings until the election was over.

It was also difficult for me to attend church meetings during this politically heated time. Frequently I returned home in tears. The media was also in a political frenzy. Newspapers, television news and commercials, as well as talk-radio programs, were filled with anger and hate. Finally, I told my husband that I needed to get away from California for a while. We decided to visit our daughter in Colorado and begged Stuart to go with us. He told us that he couldn't go.

Our Temple Experience

Fred and I were gone for a week, and the day after we returned, we prepared to attend the temple in Oakland. Stuart asked if he could talk to us. He informed us that the gun was now in his possession. He told us not to look for it in his bedroom, because it was not there—but it was in a safe place where he could get it when he needed it. I could scarcely talk. When he finished with what he wanted to tell us, we knelt with him in prayer. We told Heavenly Father how much we loved Stuart and how grateful we were for him in our lives. Upon rising from prayer, we hugged and kissed Stuart and told him once again how much we loved him. And then we drove to the temple. All the way I kept saying to Fred, "I don't know how you can drive. I have no strength at all!"

During the temple session, I had difficulty concentrating. Fred, on the other hand, kept trying very hard to find something in the session that we could say to Stuart when we returned home. During the session, Fred received the personal revelation he was seeking. The experience was a sacred one. All I can say is that he received the strong impression not to worry about Stuart, because he would be all right.

When we were together in the celestial room, Fred drew me into a quiet corner where we could be alone. He described what had happened. We held hands, said a prayer together, and turned Stuart over to Heavenly Father. When we arrived home, he was still there. That was Tuesday.

Three days later, on Friday, we found Stuart's last letter to us on his bed.

A Letter to the Family

"Mother, Dad and Family,

"I have committed suicide. These words are difficult to write, and I imagine they are more difficult to read. I am sure you know the reasons why I have chosen this course of action. Throughout my life, despite all the pain that I endured, I always trusted in God and hoped for the best. This hope fed my desire to live. Now, however, I have become convinced that my anxieties will never be resolved. Furthermore, my anxieties will increase as I continue to deteriorate. As I am incapable of resolving them myself, I have decided to end them in the only way I know will work. I must remove the chains of my mortality.

"I am free, I am no longer in pain, and I no longer hate myself. Can you take comfort in the knowledge that my pain has been eliminated?

"I was convinced that my desire to change my sexual identity was a divinely inspired desire. As it turns out, God never intended my orientation to change in this lifetime. I had engaged my mind in a false dilemma: either one is gay or one is Christian. As I believed that I was a Christian, I believed that I could never be gay.

"The same dilemma now faces you. You all believe that the choice of life is good and the choice of death is not. . . . my life was actually killed long ago. Perhaps your action to help others understand the true nature of homosexuality might help to save many young people's lives.

"As you know, I have been suicidal for years, and in the past year, I have been vocal about my feelings. After a year of expressing my grief to you, I've realized that there is nothing that any of you could do to attenuate my pain. Thus, I decided not to burden you with my feelings these past several weeks. I'm sure that this note has come as a complete surprise, because I've done my best to conceal my feelings. Inside, however, I have been a complete mess, and the only comfort that allowed me to remain upbeat was the knowledge that I would soon end my life.

"Please be assured that in no way did you contribute anything to my depression, anxiety and inferiority complex. Thus, you have no responsibility for my decisions. Again, I want you to unequivocally realize that you both have been dear and loving. I couldn't have asked for better or more loving parents and siblings. Nevertheless, I simply could not live another day choking on my own feelings of inferiority. For the first time in over twenty years, I am free from my pains.

"I love you all. I really do. I didn't want to make any final speeches to you, or hug and kiss you because it would have been too difficult for me. I am sure that you realize that I do truly love and adore all of you. You have been remarkably loving and accepting of me this past year, and I applaud your love. Until we see each other again, I leave you with happy memories.

"Love,

"Stuart."

When Fred began to read Stuart's last letter, I could hear him cry, "No! No! No!" I was in another room, but I knew immediately what had happened. When Stuart wrote that he was sure his suicide would come as a surprise, he was mistaken. I knew he would eventually take his life. I had even discussed with Paul what we could do to stop Stuart from carrying out his plan. Paul told me there was nothing we could do—he said that if we were to turn Stuart in for help, he would be put into a mental hospital. Paul added, "Then Stuart will hate you, and nothing you can do will stop him. You will only delay the inevitable."

I had watched Stuart carefully his last month. His body language was a vivid warning of his frame of mind. I remember watching him walk down the hallway to his bedroom. His walk was deliberate, his hands tucked into his pockets, his shoulders slumped, his head bowed down. Frequently, I heard him pacing in his room. Each time I knew he was having another panic attack—and the panic attacks became a nightly occurrence.

The most pointed warning to me was finding Stuart's scriptures in the hallway by his bedroom door a few weeks before he took his life. I had never read my children's journals or their mail, but I sometimes checked the marker in their scriptures. As long as the marker was being moved forward, I took comfort in the thought that our children were walking a spiritual path. Stuart's scriptures in the hallway told me that he had completely given up fighting his anxiety and depression.

Many times in the middle of the night I got out of bed to see if his car was still there. When it was, I cried with relief. And yet, when the final morning came and Stuart's car was gone, the tears that came were not tears of grief. They were tears born of peace, for I knew that he was no longer suffering with emotional turmoil.

Although losing our son was difficult, it has been comforting to know that he was faithful to his temple covenants. In addition, Fred and I each had an indescribable feeling of peace that lasted for several weeks after Stuart's death. Fred remarked during this time of peace, "If this is the feeling that we have in the celestial kingdom, then I want to make certain I do all I can to get there."

One month after Stuart's death, Paul tried for the seventh time to take his own life. This time he succeeded.

Chapter 6

The Son We Did Not Know

I did not really know my son until after his death, and the days following his death were a revelation to me. As the news of Stuart's death spread by telephone calls, e-mails, and newspapers, we began to receive phone calls from people all across the nation who had crossed his path. Those who called sobbed uncontrollably as they expressed their love for Stuart. I did my best to comfort them. Some of these people had met him only once or twice, but they were profoundly influenced by his kindness and his efforts to assist them in a time of need.

A consistent theme mentioned by all who called was Stuart's great passion for life. One roommate said that *passion* was Stuart's favorite word. Everyone who called said that no matter what he was doing, he did it with passion and intensity.

They all said that Stuart was the kindest person that they had ever met. That did not surprise us. As his family, we were aware of his tenderness and kindness. I had always joked that when I became old and gray, it would be Stuart who would hold my hand.

The callers all said that Stuart was the most nearly perfect person they had ever met. Some of his former roommates would sit around their apartment talking about Stuart and ask each other how he had become so perfect. Because of his excessive zeal to achieve perfection and his continued obsession with trying to change his feelings of same-gender attraction, life just became more than he felt he could endure.

In addition to his last letter, Stuart had left a note to us asking us not to have a funeral. He wanted to be remembered as the "living" Stuart—he did not want us to dwell on his death. As people came to our home to comfort us, however, they told us that we needed to have a memorial for Stuart and to use it as a "teaching moment." After some thought, we consented. Stuart died on a Friday. The memorial was planned for the following Wednesday.

Because Stuart had gone to the steps of our stake center in Los Altos, California, to take his life, and because of the political climate in California at the time of his death, by Wednesday morning the media was picking up on Stuart's death. Early Wednesday morning phone calls from media people from New York to San Francisco began pouring in. We received so many calls that by midday I became concerned about having Stuart's memorial service, fearing that it would be turned into a media circus. Because of my concern, I knelt in prayer and asked for Heavenly Father's guidance. The phone continued to ring. I continued in prayer, seeking to know Heavenly Father's will. The phone was still ringing when Fred and I were ready to leave for our chapel. Once again we knelt in prayer.

When we arrived at the church, television vans, camera crews, and reporters were waiting for us. It was necessary to post security guards at all the doors to prevent the camera crews from coming into the church. Fred and I expressed our concern to our stake president, President David L. Lowe, and he suggested that we kneel together and pray one more time for guidance. When we arose from the prayer, our president said, "It is the Lord's will that this memorial service be held."

People Are There! People Do Care!

As we walked into the chapel, we could see that both the chapel and the cultural hall were filled with friends and loved ones. When it was my turn to speak to the congregation, I was overwhelmed to see and feel so much love for Stuart and for our family. After the service was over, we stood in a receiving line for more than an hour as people spoke with us and thanked us for helping them better understand the challenge of same-gender attraction. Many people apologized for unkind comments they had made in the past about homosexuals. Two stake patriarchs told us that they had learned more in Stuart's two-hour memorial service than they had in the past twenty years. Several people also remarked that they had sensed a major shift in the understanding of same-gender attraction take place at the service.

I have never witnessed a pentecostal event, but the Spirit was so strong during the service that I am certain the feeling of the meeting was very close to the Day of Pentecost. At that point I knew that people did care! My heart was brimming with gratitude for my Savior and the goodness of family and friends.

We flew to Utah the day after the memorial service. We had already planned to move to Utah in another three months, and so we decided to bury Stuart in a cemetery near our new home. The news of his death seemed as prevalent in Utah as it had been in California. Fred became concerned about another invasion of the media and asked the city police to assist us. How grateful we were for their response. When we arrived at the cemetery on Friday morning with the casket, we were once again met with television crews and newspaper reporters.

A reporter who spoke with me after the graveside service said with tears in his eyes, "I wish my parents were as loving and understanding as you are." I looked into his eyes and asked, "Are you gay?" He hugged me and whispered, "Yes."

Stuart was buried the day after his thirty-third birthday.

On the night of his burial, the television news showed a picture of our family and friends at the graveside service. I felt so violated. As we flew back to California, I turned to my husband and said, "Let's pray that the invasion of our privacy is over. What more does the press want?" Little did I know what lay before us.

Because it was Sunday, we went directly from the airport in San Jose, California, to our family ward chapel. After Relief Society, a friend said to me, "They say that gays don't teach it to you, but I know they do!" I looked at her in amazement. Later the same day, another friend said that

Stuart had to have been lying to us, because Heavenly Father would never have allowed Stuart to be a homosexual. Surely, he said, Stuart must have done something wrong to cause this challenge.

I could not believe that these friends harbored such erroneous thoughts. I could only think that they were still learning.

Truth Mingled with Fiction

When we arrived home following our church meetings, we found our mailbox stuffed with cards from reporters asking for interviews. The media so persistently invaded our privacy that the Church assigned a sister in our stake to take all phone calls directed to us. We did not answer the phone for more than a month.

Later, we learned that *Time* and *Newsweek* magazines were asking for interviews. We declined. Soon, however, we discovered that *Newsweek* had gone to some of Stuart's friends for an interview. We also learned that *Newsweek* planned to approach our younger son, Bill, who was a student at Brigham Young University at the time.

We called Bill and told him that although the decision was his, we preferred that he not give any interviews to the media. He chose to be interviewed. When the reporter interviewed him, he asked to take a photo of Bill in front of the Salt Lake Temple. Bill declined but agreed that a photo could be taken out in the hills someplace.

As Bill posed for the picture, the photographer kept saying, "Don't smile," or "Your smile is too big." Bill kept insisting that he wasn't smiling. Finally, a photo was taken with Bill looking angry. That photo was published next to a photo of the Salt Lake Temple.

What concerned me even more was a statement attributed to me. The article read: "Stuart's mother wrote to the leaders of the Mormon Church, asking them to change their position on homosexuals." I have never made such a request, nor will I ever do so.

As I reflected on the events of the preceding year, I concluded that the most difficult part was the media invasion of our privacy. It was difficult to see how the media misrepresented Stuart's life, particularly for political purposes. The most hurtful were statements Stuart supposedly had made. One such statement claimed that Stuart had said he wanted to have a loving relationship with a male like the relationship his parents had with each other. Stuart never made such a statement. In fact, Stuart and I had discussed that very subject several times. Each time he said, "Mother, I would never allow any such relationship to happen. I would kill it before it ever got started!"

Chapter 7

"Be Faithful to the Things You Know to Be True"

Before Stuart died, there was a time when many voices were pulling at me. Each voice tried to get me to accept a different philosophy of why Stuart was the way he was and what he should do. As a result, I fell upon my knees and cried to Heavenly Father, "I don't know what is right! I don't know what is wrong! I only know that Jesus is the Christ, the Atonement is real, Joseph Smith was a prophet of God, the Book of Mormon is true, and President Gordon B. Hinckley is a modern-day prophet of God!" Just as I finished exclaiming my testimony, the thought came ringing into my mind, *Be faithful to the things you know to be true.* It is equally important for those who are struggling because of same-gender attraction to be faithful to the things they know to be true!

Since Stuart's death, we have learned about and met many devoted Latter-day Saints who have the same challenge as Stuart's and who are faithfully serving in the Church. Because of the homophobia that prevails in society, they have lived secretive lives of quiet desperation.

A cross has been laid upon those who have feelings of same-gender attraction. We need to help them by loving them, having compassion, and trying to understand them. We need to help them to carry their cross and to know that they can make a joyful contribution to the kingdom of God. One of Stuart's favorite sayings when he was asked to serve was, "If I don't do it, who will?" The same applies to us. If we don't help our brothers and sisters who are in need, who will? So many who suffer do not have even family and friends to love and support them. Where are they to turn for understanding and love—to us in the Savior's Church or to the world? As parents of a child who suffered as a result of this difficult challenge, Fred and I pray that we, as members of the Savior's Church, will help all who earnestly strive to stay centered on Christ. We need to help those who are hurting listen to God's wisdom and not to the wisdom of the world.

During Stuart's last year with us, there were times when the grief we experienced seemed so unbearable I could scarcely breathe. Yet time has shown us the great blessings the Lord had in store for us. And as challenging as the last year of Stuart's life was, there were loving notes along the way from our Heavenly Father to let us know that we did not walk the path alone. We knew that our Savior had also walked this path for us, and He did indeed know how to succor us.

After Stuart died, I sent my testimony in a letter to a family member. I wrote, "At Stuart's death we felt the Comforter strengthening us and carrying us in our time of need. And in our extremity, we found our Savior and knew Him as we had never known Him before. Our testimony of the gospel became more precious to us. Our understanding of the Atonement became more clearly defined, and our love for our Savior became more reverent and profound. Our lives will never be the same. Who we are today, we owe to Stuart and all that we learned through the last year of his life. Stuart's life was and continues to be a schoolmaster for us. How grateful we are for his integrity and courage to remain faithful!"

Chapter 8

Letters of Comfort

After his memorial service, the city of San Francisco set aside a day in memory of Stuart, and radio stations dedicated songs to him. Nevertheless, the most meaningful tributes to Stuart were the letters of great comfort that flooded into our home. We received letters from family and friends and also from people we had never met.

"Dear Fred and Marilyn,

"We just returned home from Stuart's memorial service, and I felt the need to write a note to you. I never met Stuart, as far as I know. I wish that I had known him—and look forward to that opportunity on the other side of the veil. I was deeply touched by what you both shared with us tonight. I appreciate so much your willingness to help us better understand Stuart's struggles. I realize how much I have yet to learn about the Atonement and the extent of the Savior's love for us. Your obvious love for Stuart and for one another is a blessing for us and for all that attended this evening.

"I expect that Stuart's life and death will provide hope and direction for many of us. He provided me a service that I appreciate in that I better recognize the need to love and to serve Heavenly Father's children—all of them.

"On the way out, I noted the TV truck outside the building cranking up their antennae to send their report of the service. I so hope that they can capture the spirit and love that was there in abundance.

"May the Lord bless you and your family. Thank you for this evening of understanding."

"Dear Fred & Marilyn—

"When I heard of the death of your son Stuart, I wanted to come and see you and talk with you. But I knew you would have a house full of guests and family, and I did not want to talk to you on the phone. I probably could not have gotten through anyway. I thought I would come at a later date so I would not have to impose on you. I thought, I'll see them at the memorial.

"Your daughter Katharine appropriately sang a beautiful song that opened a very tender, stirring service. I never knew any of your children, but I do know they come from a home of a very loving mother and father.

"I do not know the feeling of losing a child, but I do know your grief is very deep. I have always held homosexuality at a very low level and have been very adamant in my expressions about it and have held a low tolerance for it. But your talk, Marilyn, has gotten me to thinking, and I have taken a different direction on my attitude towards it. I know your remarks were inspired of the Lord, and they put a whole different meaning on my approach to this subject.

"I do not know whether I can change my thinking or not, but I certainly will look at it in a different view. I do know that regardless of what our children do or become, the mother's love is a deep and ingrained feeling, and I certainly respect your love for Stuart. I know he had to be a special person because of the friends he had, the mission he completed when he was an emissary of the Lord, his work habits, and his love for his fellowmen.

"I can only say that I would find it very hard to handle this area as well and as lovingly and concisely as you two have. My thoughts and actions have a long way to go before I can reach that level, but I certainly will work and strive for it. I know the Lord will bless and comfort you. As you said, 'We will see him and have him again.'

"The gospel is for all, and those of us that have it are blessed. The gospel is true. May the Lord bless you at this time of sorrow."

"Dearest Matis Family,

"My intent was to send this sympathy card prior to Stuart's memorial. However, I was so greatly affected by what was said that I wasn't sure how to word the feelings of my heart, much less how to express them to you.

"It was obvious that the Spirit of the Lord, and your own personal efforts to handle this latest trial in your lives, had prepared you. It was also obvious that this trial is going to serve a purpose for not only yourselves but also others around you and those who are yet to become acquainted with you and be touched by your lives.

"I was greatly saddened to learn of this personal tragedy. The first and biggest question that formulated readily in my mind was, 'How could this happen?' Then to find out Stuart was gay was equally as disturbing, because it was an added burden for you as his family. My next thought was, 'How did he become gay?'

"I haven't spent time trying to learn about this issue, as life is so full of challenges for each of us that we only seem to deal with those that are forced upon us. I truly did not expect such a learning experience when I attended the memorial. I had tried to rationalize my not going by saying that the Matises don't really know me that well, they won't miss me, as I am only one person.

"I want you to know that I felt privileged to be at this memorial service, and I truly felt that I was on sacred ground in being there. The power with which you memorialized Stuart was such a spiritual experience. I have known and admired your great testimonies for years. However, it was more than your personal testimonies that were being borne to those in attendance. I truly felt and saw the power of the Lord with you as you delivered your memorial to your gay son.

"Thank you for your courage to share that with us. The most powerful message was that being gay with same-gender attraction was very different from being active in a gay or lesbian relationship. What a terrible burden and struggle was Stuart's for so many years.

"The third issue that troubled me was how could he be so faithful in not giving into these sexual drives, yet commit suicide and not be saved because of the act of suicide alone. The power with which all three of these issues became clear was a real testimony to me. I cannot believe that everyone in attendance was not touched similarly. I know you were prepared as 'noble parents' to handle this trial and challenge. I also know that it is not over for you and that it will be a big burden to carry as you endure to the end in a just cause.

"Although the newspapers and gay activists would have it reflect negatively on the Church, I know you will have a big role to play as you move forward in your cause to help Church members understand this issue and our responsibility to society and to the Lord.

"My prayers are with you. I admire and love you for what you are doing. I am blessed to have been in attendance at this memorial service. I know it was not easy. But with the Spirit of the Lord on your side, anything is possible."

"Dear Brother and Sister Matis,

"I served with Stuart as a missionary some eleven years ago in two cities. I have just learned of his passing this last weekend while reading the article in *Newsweek* magazine. I cried as I read the details. The memories of serving with him have flooded my mind. He was one of the best missionaries I knew. He was always happy and ready with a smile and a laugh. He knew the gospel and taught it well. He worked hard and was well respected by those he taught as well as by other missionaries. I am sorry for his struggle. I just felt compelled to write to you and tell you how much your son meant to me and let you know I am sorry for your loss. I will always remember him as someone I admired greatly."

"Dear Fred, Marilyn and Family,

"I was so saddened and grieved to hear of Stuart's passing. I wish I could have attended his memorial in Sunnyvale, but I found out about it after the fact. I have often thought about Stuart this past year after learning of the turmoil he's been going through most of his life. I remember him as such a conscientious and intent person. I'll never forget when I taught Stuart in Sunday School when he was quite young. I received a call from Fred one day after church. I guess there was some discussion or concern on Stuart's part about the lesson I had taught that day. I don't recall what the lesson was about, but Fred asked that I give Stuart a call and tell him something to the effect that we didn't have to be perfect, we just had to try our best. I was very impressed by that experience that at such a young age Stuart took very seriously those things that he was taught. I can't imagine the pain Stuart had to suffer, but it's comforting to know he's receiving the love and comfort that he needs. We love you and pray that your pain will be lifted and that you will receive peace and comfort."

"Dear Matis Family,

"I went to the church Wednesday night to take my son to Cub Scouts, and I sat in the foyer while your son's funeral went on. What I heard from 'Mom' and 'Dad' really touched my heart and taught me so much about myself. I gained a renewed faith in this gospel. I want to thank you, 'Mom,' for reading the letter your beautiful son wrote to you. I have been fighting my own affliction all my life and never really knew it until maybe three years ago. I was touched by how openly you spoke of your son's sexual orientation and how willingly you were trying to understand it all. You see, my affliction is sexual, as well, although homosexuality is not my affliction. My affliction came to me through no fault of my own.

"I feel so very close to your son and his agony and self-hatred that he went through, for I have lived with these very same feelings for forty-one years. I have never been able to speak of them before, for the shame that it brought to me. I know of shame, and I know how it can cut right to the core of a person. That's why I feel so close to your son, because I understand the shame that he's lived with for almost all of his life. Would you believe that I feel so blessed to have been given my particular affliction rather than the one your son was blessed with? Yes, I did say 'blessed with.' Before I explain this to you, let me tell you a little about my affliction.

"My father was abusive. He yelled and screamed at us, and I spent most of my days before I was five hiding in my mother's kitchen cupboard when he came home. My mother finally kicked my father out after fifteen and a half years and six kids. My father was a very proud man and loved to tell me how he was the right hand of God. He gave me the impression that I was lucky he let me listen to him, and I believed it.

"Then after my father left the house, a new abuse took its place. You see, my father always had the attitude that women were for one thing, and that was sex. Sex was everything to him, and we all knew it, even as young children. I should say that my father treated all his children, four sons and two daughters, exactly the same, so we all got the same abuse. The sons came to understand that girls were for one thing only, and the girls came to understand that same thing. So after my father left, my older brothers sexually abused me for years. And like every other child on this planet who is abused by parents or other family members, sexually abused, I thought it was all my fault.

"I came to hate this affliction I was living with. I hated life and found no joy in anything, and I was just waiting for someone to kill me, because I believed that I was one of the daughters who had followed Satan and was cast out but had found a way to get past God and find a body. Can you believe that? But those are the feelings that my father taught me, and the sexual abuse cemented that belief. When we went to church or anywhere outside the house, he was the nicest, smilingest guy you could meet. He had a way to contend and argue with people sometimes, but no one would ever believe me when I told him how my father was at home. So, I came to understand that when you go home and shut that door, dads turn into monsters, and so do men and husbands. And I came to understand that these men who are taller than you can and will hurt you and even kill you. Bad, bad, bad feelings.

"But after I had left the funeral of your beautiful son, I felt so blessed and so favored by God, especially after listening to 'Mom' and 'Dad' talk!

The Lord has been letting me know that I am about to take a new journey and face the feelings I have had since my father and brothers began to abuse me and to learn to forgive. That's the reason for this new journey, so I can learn to forgive and begin the healing process. After I left the church last night, and even now, my heart and mind are in a stupor as to how much harder your son's affliction was for him to live with!

"I now have come to understand that I could tell someone about what happened to me, and they would give me love and sympathy and understanding and kindness. How grateful I am for this understanding.

"I felt such sympathy and pain for your son whom I have never known or met! My heart went out to him, and I can truly and honestly understand why he would take his life. I have gone through a year of having the very same thoughts, of trying to find the easiest way to do this that would hurt my family the least. I became so caught up in this idea to take my life that I was actually making plans. At some point, I came to understand how serious I was in my suicide plans, and it shook me up to the point that I began to tell people about my plans. I went to the psychologist I was seeing and told him about my horrible, ugly feelings and how I always thought I was a sinner because of what had happened to me as a child. And then, what affected me the most from the words at your son's funeral was that what had happened to me as a child *was not my fault!* Nor was your son's orientation his fault!

"I felt the sense of hopelessness your son must have felt, but I think there's one thing he must have not understood, and that is, that he was gay through no fault of his own! And that is the most sacred difference that the Lord seems to make between a weakness or affliction and someone who seeks out sin. When 'Dad' said, 'The Savior's atoning sacrifice is far-reaching,' I knew it was true! I didn't just believe it—I knew it! I knew it was far enough reaching for your son, and how I did rejoice for this special boy whom I had never known! I felt so blessed and privileged to have gotten to know your family and most especially your son this way.

"Your son was a righteous boy who grew into a righteous man. I feel so blessed to have 'known him' in this way! Your son's affliction and how he handled it have given me strength and courage to go on in my journey—to let the Lord work his miracles and heal me, because he has promised me that he will heal me. This I know. This I believe.

"I cannot express to you in words how this experience has touched my heart and changed my life forever. I want to thank you for being so open and honest at his funeral and giving me a reason to rejoice in my easy afflictions when I compared them to your son! For wherever he went in society, he would find opposition, anger, and even hatred, and very few kind words. I have never in my life understood homosexuality as I now understand it, and it is my most earnest prayer that I never forget this lesson the Lord has taught me through the two of you, 'Mom and Dad,' and through your son's wonderful example.

"I cannot help but wonder what wonders our Savior shall be working right now, through your son, both on this earth and beyond the veil. I sincerely thank you for this experience and your love for your son. You've changed my life forever, and for the good. I would go on thanking you over and over because I just can't seem to say it enough, words just can't express my true feelings. I have asked the Lord to show you, through the Holy Ghost, how I truly feel, and I pray that it will be so."

"Dear Matis Family,

"I have been wanting to send you a letter ever since I heard of Stuart's death. We were in the same BYU ward for some time. He served as our Gospel Doctrine teacher. When he taught—*everyone* listened! There was never a 'hall crowd' when Stuart taught! His testimony was always evident, not just in the way he was able to share his knowledge with me and our ward but the way he made others feel!

"Stuart and I have lost contact over the last couple of years, but whenever I think of great teachers and friends, Stuart Matis is on that list for me and so many others! I feel honored and blessed to have known him! May the Lord's peace and comfort be with all of you!"

Following is a letter I found as I began packing Stuart's belongings. It is a letter that refers to his calling as an elders quorum president.

"Stuart,

"I just want you to know how much I have enjoyed working with you this year. You are the most amazing person—truly a Christlike leader! I am continually amazed at the things you are able to accomplish—your vision, faith, and example have been so inspiring to me personally and everyone in our ward. I know that the Lord has great things in store for you and that He is so pleased with your diligence in serving Him. You're the greatest, Stuart!"

The second letter was written to the *BYU Daily Universe* shortly before Stuart's death. There had been several very homophobic letters published in the newspaper, and Stuart responded to them. He wrote:

"Dear Editor:

"I am gay. I am also LDS. My first same-gender attraction occurred when I was seven, and over the ensuing twenty-five years, I have never been attracted to women. I realized the significance of my sexuality when I was around thirteen, and for the next two decades I traveled down a tortuous path of internalized homophobia, immense self-hatred, depression, and suicidal thoughts. Despite the calluses on my knees, frequent trips to the temple, fasts and devotion to my mission and Church callings such as elders quorum president, I have never been able to attenuate my homosexuality.

"Last year I told my bishop and my family about my challenge. After I did so, my bishop and my father each gave me a blessing inspired by the Spirit. In both I was told that I was indeed gay and that my challenge would remain. Thus, I read a recent letter to the editor with great pain. The author equated my gay friends and me to murderers, Satanists, prostitutes, pedophiles, and partakers of bestiality. Imagine having to live with this hateful rhetoric constantly being spewed at you.

"I implore the students at BYU to reassess their homophobic feelings. Seek to understand first before you make comments. We have the same needs as you. We are not a threat to you or your families. We are your sons, daughters, brothers, sisters, neighbors, co-workers, and friends, and most importantly, we are all children of God."

Chapter 9

The Love of the Brethren

Stuart took his life on the Friday morning before an area conference was held in San Jose, California. Elder Jeffrey R. Holland of the Quorum of the Twelve Apostles was, with others, assigned to that conference. Early that Friday morning, he was to have held a missionary meeting with the full-time missionaries in the Los Altos Stake Center.

Shortly before the meeting, Elder Holland received a phone call telling him not to go to the stake center because there had been a shooting incident there. The details were not clear. Elder Holland, however, felt some responsibility to know of any such incident on Church property or involving Church members, so he changed the location and the hour of the missionary meeting and then with President David Lowe, president of the Los Altos Stake, went to the stake center to investigate.

When Elder Holland reached the chapel, he saw Stuart's body lying at the entrance to the back door of the stake center. Police officers were on the scene, and the immediate area was being cordoned off with police tape. After a brief consultation and in response to the request of the officers, President Lowe and Elder Holland left the scene, having arranged to obtain further information from the police as they were able to provide it.

The following day, Saturday, Elder Holland told the priesthood leaders gathered at the area conference that although he did not know as yet the full circumstances of the incident, he did know the Lord and His love.

And he knew that the blessings of the Atonement covered the tragedy that had taken place at the Los Altos Stake Center the preceding day.

Stuart's bishop called to see if we would meet with Elder Holland. When we met in his office in Salt Lake City some time later, Elder Holland was tender and understanding. He once again affirmed that suicide is not the answer to life's problems, but he knew that the mercy of the Atonement covered Stuart's last desperate act. He told us that his being at our stake center in Los Altos and seeing Stuart's body was not an accident and that the Lord obviously intended that he be able to give comfort to us and to so many others who were affected by this event.

"God does not do anything by accident," he said. We told Elder Holland that Stuart had always been faithful to his temple covenants and had tried hard always to do what was right. We saw tears in his eyes when we told him that Stuart's knees were callused from the many prayers he had offered, including the prayers he offered in the temple, which he had faithfully attended ever since his mission. Elder Holland remarked, "We want so much to help everyone we can, with a special desire to help those who are striving so courageously to be faithful. We must find ever-better ways to help the Stuart Matises of the Church, who strive so hard to keep the commandments and their covenants while they 'fight the good fight' in the gender-attraction they face. I am only heartbroken that he felt that he could not keep on fighting." We have appreciated the chance to stay in touch with Elder Holland and the interest he has shown in our family.

We are grateful for the increased understanding and compassion we have seen exhibited towards those who have feelings of same-gender attraction. Since Stuart's death, we have seen some changes take place. Perhaps the most notable change was in the youth pamphlet, *"For the Strength of Youth."* The previous pamphlet read: "Homosexual and lesbian activities are sinful and an abomination to the Lord (see Romans 1:26–27, 31)."[1] The more recent pamphlet reads: "Homosexual activity is a serious sin. If you find yourself struggling with same-gender attraction, seek counsel from your parents and bishop. They will help you."[2] How grateful we are for the clarification.

In the October general conference of 2000, President Boyd K. Packer of the Quorum of the Twelve Apostles delivered a sermon in which he set the moral benchmark for all members of the Church. In his address, he spoke about those who struggle with same-gender attraction. He remarked, "That may be a struggle from which you will not be free in this life."[3] During the April 2002 general conference, Elder Russell M. Nelson of the Quorum of the Twelve Apostles commented, "Gender disorientation is poorly understood."[4] And in an address in November 2000, Elder Alexander Morrison of the Seventy stated: "The question invariably arises as to whether persons with same-gender attraction can ever change. While some assert—not on acceptable evidence—that same-gender attraction is immutable and unchangeable, there is good evidence that some individuals have indeed changed to a normal heterosexual lifestyle. . . . Others, however, despite valiant and prayerful effort, continue to struggle with the challenge of same-gender attraction. Their burdens are heavy, and their tears many. . . . They can, however, struggle on in faith, keeping the commandments of God, with the assurance He will strengthen and sustain them. It is not easy, but perhaps it is not intended to be so. Few of life's real challenges are easy to deal with."[5]

With Elder Morrison, we believe that although some individuals appear to have found comfort in a "normal lifestyle," others have not. It is also true that each individual (male or female) has his or her own level of attraction to one of the same gender. We have discovered that some individuals feel comfortable with the hope of someday having a relationship with a person of the opposite gender. Some, however, do not find comfort in such thoughts. Stuart, for example, dated for a short time after his mission. The girl he dated was very popular in his ward at Brigham Young University, and many young men commented to him on how lucky he was to be dating Susan (not her real name). Stuart said, "It felt so good to be like everyone else." And yet, after a couple of months of dating, he realized that he could not entertain any thought of marrying Susan. He said that the thought of having an intimate relationship with a woman made him feel physically ill.

Chapter 10

Submitting to God's Will

Less than two weeks before Stuart died, he received an e-mail from a distant cousin, Jared (not his real name). He wrote that when he had come home from school for Christmas vacation, his parents had told him that Stuart had feelings of same-gender attraction. Jared wrote, "I also have same-gender attraction, and I am getting ready to put my mission papers in. What do I do?" Stuart wrote back: "Tell your parents, send in your mission papers, go on your mission, and come home and take one day at a time."

Jared served an honorable mission. While he was on his mission, we wrote faithfully to each other. His letters were filled with stories of success because of obedience and hard work, great love for his mission, and humbling spiritual experiences. At the end of his mission, he returned to Brigham Young University. While there, he started to bring young men to our home to visit with Fred and me. These young men, all of whom struggled with feelings of same-gender attraction, were returned missionaries, active in the Church, and trying desperately to reconcile their feelings with their faith in the gospel they had grown to cherish.

We have been anxious to comfort and help these young men stay focused on the gospel. In many ways, the meetings have been spiritual experiences. When we have been asked by these young men and their families who come to our home seeking for understanding, we have suggested, "Let the Lord set the timetable for all events in your life."

Although we may wish for all challenges to be taken away on this side of the veil, the Lord may have other plans for us. We do try, however, to encourage each young man who visits us to stop focusing on trying to change his sexual orientation. We feel that if a person focuses only on changing from a homosexual orientation to a heterosexual orientation, he or she fails to see that same-gender attraction is only a very small part of who he or she really is.

My husband, Fred, illustrates the point of not focusing on change by asking each young man to hold a sheet of paper close to his nose. Fred asks, "What do you see?"

The young man answers, "The paper."

"Can you see anything else?"

"No."

This application illustrates what can happen if a person with same-gender attraction obsesses with the orientation challenge to the point that he or she fails to see anything in life beyond that challenge.

Then Fred asks the young man to hold the paper as far out in front of his face as he can reach. Fred asks, "Now what do you see?"

The answer is obvious. When the paper is held away from his face, the young man can then see far more than just the paper.

Fred and I try to help each young man realize that there is more to his life than having a challenge with same-gender attraction. In other words, *a person's challenge does not define who he or she is!*

We ask each young man who comes to our home for comfort and hope, "What *does* define you?" The answer should be obvious, and yet, the answer does not always come easily to these young men. The answer we are trying to help each young man to understand is this: "I am an active and worthy member of The Church of Jesus Christ of Latter-day Saints. I am a returned missionary. I am a valiant Melchizedek Priesthood holder. I am temple worthy. I am part of a loving family. I have good friends who respect me. I am getting a great college education. I have many wonderful gifts and talents that bless my life."

As Fred and I have continued to meet with these young men, we have come to the conclusion that it is unwise for them to refer to themselves as *being homosexual* or *being gay.* Fred and I feel that the terms *homosexual* and *gay* are negative labels that people use to *define them.* In addition, we feel it is important for the young men and women and their families to be cautious about the language they use to describe themselves or the nature of their attraction. Although much of the debate over which terms are most appropriate is simply semantic, we feel it is very important that the language individuals use to describe themselves or their attraction reflects their inspired understanding of their eternal identity as literal children of God with an eternal, divine potential.

We also urge each young man to focus with all his heart upon the Savior and his teachings. On January 17, 1989, Jeffrey R. Holland, then president of BYU, gave a devotional address to students and faculty entitled "The Will of the Father in All Things": "No amount of university education, or any other kind of desirable and civilizing experience in this world, will help us at the moment of our confrontation with Christ if we have not been able—and are not then able—to *yield, yield all that we are,* all that we have, and all that we ever hope to have to the Father and the Son. . . .

". . . Accomplishment of *any* kind is in vain if we cannot, in those crucial moments of pivotal personal history, submit ourselves to God *even when all our hopes and fears may tempt us otherwise.* We must be willing to place all that we have—not just our possessions (they may be the easiest things of all to give up), but also our ambition and pride and stubbornness and vanity—*we must place it all on the altar of God, kneel there in silent submission, and willingly walk away.*"[1]

Peace will come to those who suffer because of their same-gender attraction, as well as to their families, only when they have submitted to God's will. As President Holland said: "Let us all place our will upon the altar of God, kneel there in silent submission, and willingly walk away." We must let God be the author of our lives. We must leave to Him the decision about when change will occur—whether it is on this side of the veil or on the other side. Too frequently those who suffer try to force events to happen in their lives, and as they do so, they bring unhappiness into their own lives and also into the lives of others. As we are willing to submit to our Savior, He will bring events into our life at the time He feels is for our best good.

Chapter 11

Reaching Out in Christlike Love

As Fred and I meet with young men who have feelings of same-gender attraction, we encourage each one to tell his parents about his challenge. Unfortunately, not all of the parents and families are understanding. It is devastating when some families reject their son and refuse to allow him to be around family members. Some have actually stated, "If you come to family gatherings, we will leave!"

A few months after Jared began bringing young men to our home, we received a phone call from him late one night. He was crying and asked if we could come to Provo and take him to the hospital, because one of his friends had tried to take his life. The attempted suicide was exactly one week before the third anniversary of Stuart's death. All the feelings I experienced about Stuart's death came flooding back over me.

As we walked into the hospital room, Jared ran to his friend's bed, leaned down to hug him, and wept bitter tears. He quietly said over and over to his friend, "We promised each other! We promised each other! You promised me!" They had promised each other to reach out for help before either one attempted suicide.

As Fred and I drove home from the hospital, I asked, "When will the suicides stop? When will we, as members of Christ's Church, begin to realize the pain that so many young men and women experience because of the challenge of same-gender attraction? When will we begin to love and succor them in their time of need?"

When we arrived home, I said, "I know that Elder Holland is in

Chile, but I have to call his office to see if someone can help us." The next morning, I spoke with Elder Holland's secretary, Sister Randi Greene, who remembered us from our visit nearly three years before. As a result of my call, Elder Cecil Samuelson of the Seventy phoned us to set up an appointment. My husband and I had not met Elder Samuelson, and we knew very little about him. But by the time Fred and I left his office, we were overwhelmed at the great knowledge Elder Samuelson had on the subject of homosexuality. Not only was he knowledgeable but he was most kind and sympathetic.

In our meeting with Elder Samuelson, I told him of the stress I felt in trying to help these young men with same-gender attraction. I told him that it would be easier for me to stop trying to help them, but I kept doing it for Stuart. I expressed the sorrow I felt when the families of these young men were not always loving and supportive, and I wondered if we were really helping—or if we were actually adding to the pain these young men already had. Before we left, Elder Samuelson gave me a blessing. And so, we continue.

In the years since Stuart's death, we have realized how very important it is for those who struggle with same-gender attraction to tell their families. That is often extraordinarily difficult for them to do. Each young man who has come to our home has expressed the great fear he felt in revealing to his family the secret he has so carefully guarded for so many years. Each one has said that he doesn't want to disappoint his family. Some have said that there were other challenges in their families, and they didn't want to add to the already heavy burden of their parents.

Recently, Matthew (not his real name) shared his feelings and experience with us. The following is his story (told here with his permission):

"I was unsure exactly how to go about telling my father that I dealt with same-gender attraction. I had been counseled to do so by some friends who felt very strongly that it would be beneficial for me in my progress in dealing with the issue. I couldn't believe I was even considering taking such a step, because I had sworn many times before that I would never tell either of my parents. When it came right down to it, I was terrified and had no idea even how to start to tell them. What I did know was that if I were to tell either of them, it would need to be my dad. I felt he would be able to handle the news better than my mom, and then he could eventually help my mom to understand.

"I began to pray for my father. I began to pray that he would be spiritually prepared to hear what I now felt strongly that he needed to hear. I began to pray that he would be inspired to give patriarchal counsel. I prayed that his heart would not break when I told him something I despised about myself. At the same time I began to pray for myself. I prayed that I would be spiritually prepared to tell him something so personal. I prayed that I would know the right time to tell him. I prayed that I would have the courage and strength to get the words out of my mouth when the time came. I prayed that Heavenly Father would comfort me as I faced what I felt to be one of the hardest tasks I would ever face in my life. I wanted so badly not to hurt my parents, but I tried to maintain the faith that I would receive divine guidance throughout the experience.

"I thought about what a friend had told me as I traveled from Provo to my home in Oregon: 'Give your parents one bite of the pie at a time. Don't throw the whole thing in their face.' I had an appointment with a specialist to assess my need for a tonsillectomy. During the hours of the drive home, I was alone, and I prayed and made the decision that I would tell my father of my trial. Much to my confusion, however, as the weekend at home came and went and the opportunities to tell my father passed by, never once did I feel it was the appropriate time to tell him. I had spent hours in the car preparing and rehearsing, but for whatever reason, the time to tell him was not right.

"I did not give up in my determination to let my secret be known. It was a strange feeling. I did not want to tell my father or anyone else in my family, but I knew it was something I had to do. I could not understand what good it would do, but I had faith in what my friends had told me. My biggest fear, something I was sure of, was letting my parents down. I did not want to cause them any pain.

"When I returned to Oregon two weeks later for the operation, I promised the Lord I would tell my father if He would arrange a time that we could be alone with time to talk. I felt it was important for my dad to have an opportunity to ask me questions that potentially could arise.

"I was scheduled for a pre-op the day before the actual operation. The doctor wanted to visit with me and get some last-minute information. It was planned that I would make the one-hour trip to the neighboring town by myself, but on the morning of the pre-op, I woke up nauseated, too sick to drive. I informed my parents, and my dad willingly volunteered to be my chauffeur for the day. Just a short time after we left home and got on the freeway, the nausea I had been feeling all morning went away. It was then I realized what had happened. My prayers had been answered. There I was, in the car, alone with my dad, for at least two hours. The time had come to tell him, and I was more nervous than I had ever been for any other single moment in my life!

"I said, 'Dad, if I were struggling with something in my life, would you want to know about it?'

"He replied very calmly, 'Well, if it were something I thought I could help you with, of course I would want to know.'

"I began to explain to him. 'Well, there is a battle I have been fighting for as long as I can remember. I know that, as a bishop and under other circumstances, you have dealt with this situation to some degree. I have dealt with this issue since I was a little kid, and at times I have thought it just might drive me to insanity. It has caused me more pain and frustration than any other thing I have experienced. I feel like I need to tell someone, but it is something I have never told anyone except for my priesthood leaders.'

"Then I paused for a moment, and he was silent. By this time my eyes were filled with tears of frustration at not wanting to say the words. I wasn't sure what to say next, so I said one more brief prayer in my heart, swallowed what pride I had left, and quietly said, 'Dad, I deal with same-gender attraction.' Again he was silent. I could tell he was thinking. I was expecting him to begin asking me questions, such as, 'What have you done,' or, 'Do you have a boyfriend?' But the first words out of his mouth were, 'Well, that doesn't change how much I love you, and with whatever happens, I don't want you to forget that.'

"He couldn't have said anything more appropriate. There was nothing more I needed to hear. We just sat there for a moment and then began to discuss the issue. He asked me questions, and I answered. In my mind I couldn't believe it was over. I couldn't believe he had reacted so well, but then I realized how strong the Spirit was in the car, and I realized my dad had been prepared to hear what was so important for me to tell him.

"Since our first discussion, we have had many more. There have been moments of frustration as I try to understand where my dad is coming from and as he tries to understand where I am coming from, but I can feel his love and concern. I can feel the power of prayers from both my mom and my dad. In a new way they have begun to study the scriptures, listen to general conference, and understand things in a whole new light. They are always telling me little things that have been revealed to them that they think might help me.

"It was almost a year after telling my father that I realized the importance of having my parents be aware of my situation and my trials. I always thought it would do no good, because they had no idea where I was coming from. I was sure my friends who dealt with the same issues and who were not willing to give in to the adversary were a much better source of help. I have since learned that this is not so. Although they are a wonderful support to me, they are not entitled to receive revelation for me as my parents are. My parents are still learning, and although they do not understand everything about same-gender attraction, they have given me much counsel, which has blessed my life."

In addition, Matthew told us that as he thought about all his friends who struggle because of same-gender attraction, he quickly realized that the friends who seem to have the most peace in their lives are the friends who have told their parents about their challenge. We have encouraged the young men who have met with us to be as patient and as understanding with their parents as they want their parents to be with them. The parents will have to go through a learning curve, and, in most cases, the parents are trying very hard to understand their child's challenge.

Recently, one of our daughters asked me how old I thought a child should be before same-gender attraction is discussed. Because every young man and young woman receives the pamphlet *"For the Strength of Youth"* at age twelve when they enter the Church youth program and because the pamphlet discusses same-gender attraction, I responded, "Twelve is a good age." This would be an opportune time to talk to a young person about this sensitive topic by using the pamphlet to facilitate a discussion. In fact, all the topics in the pamphlet could be talked about so the teenager wouldn't feel targeted or awkward.

If, in a discussion, parents were to help their young teenagers under-stand the difference between same-gender orientation and the activity of that orientation, there would be more compassion and less judgment. It is vitally important to understand that one's orientation does not define who one is. Same-gender orientation is a challenge, not a character defect.

So many times my husband and I have asked ourselves, "If we had known about Stuart's challenge when he was much younger, and if he had known that we understood and accepted him, as he was, would that have changed the course of his life?" As a result of many lengthy conversations, we have felt the necessity for all families to be open in their discussion of same-gender attraction. How wonderful it would be if all children with the challenge knew that they were loved and accepted by their families! One of the greatest blessings that could come as a result of such family awareness is for children with a same-gender challenge to feel comfort-able sharing their "secret" with their parents and asking for their love and support. If all youth knew that they were loved and accepted, there would be fewer suicides and fewer children lost to the gospel of our Savior.

Each young man who has come to our home has had his own indi-vidual experiences, but each one has a great desire to stay focused on the Savior and His gospel. The level of spiritual maturity that has been shown by these young men is profound. One of them said to me, "If Abraham could put his only son on the altar as a sacrifice, then I can put my same-gender attraction on the altar as a sacrifice to my Savior."

Each time we meet with someone with same-gender attraction, we read a quotation from Elder Henry B. Eyring: "That realistic view of our limitations creates a humility which can lead to dependence on the Spirit and thus to power."[1]

As these young men and women realistically face their challenge and the limitations the challenge brings to their life, they will recognize the need to lean on the Spirit for guidance. And as they humbly do so, they will have the power to remain faithful and Christ-centered. It is to this end that Fred and I continue our journey with these choice and noble children of our Heavenly Father.

Part 2

A Young Adult's Search for Purpose and Peace

Chapter 1

Prologue

One Sunday morning while I was serving a full-time mission for the Church, my companion and I were handed two pieces of paper during a priesthood executive committee meeting. On them were the names of two men who had moved to the East Coast a few months earlier but who had not yet attended church meetings. Their records had been forwarded from a previous ward in Salt Lake City, and the bishop asked us to find the men and report on any potential needs they might have. As I studied their information, I saw that both had been born under the covenant, and both had served honorable full-time missions.

My companion and I gladly accepted the assignment and made several attempts to contact these two men before we were finally successful. The man who answered the door was clean-cut and extremely polite. But with a look of shock—and even a sense of nervousness—at seeing us on his doorstep, he invited us in. My eyes toured the lavishly renovated home as we were escorted into the living room. He offered us a seat, and we continued to talk and get acquainted. He told us about his family in Utah and spoke fondly of experiences he had had on his mission. Although he was one of the kindest and most hospitable men I had ever met, I had a feeling that my companion and I were about to learn more than we had anticipated.

After a few minutes of chatting, we mentioned our purpose in visiting him. At first he hesitated to open up to us, but after a while he decided to share a more personal part of his life story. His move to the

East Coast was more than a simple desire for a change of scenery. It was partly to escape from an environment where he was continually reminded of the past he felt he was no longer a part of—a past of active fellowship in the Church. He and the other man we had been sent to speak with were living in a homosexual relationship and had been together for nearly two decades. He continued to explain his history, and as I sat listening, I wasn't quite sure what to think or how to respond.

I was intrigued and intensely confused, for he was not what I had always understood homosexuals were like. He was a good, kind, and normal-looking man. I later learned that after these two men returned from their missions, they continued to be active in the Church and dated women until their feelings of homosexual attraction became so intense that each one decided it was time to "face reality"—and they gradually became inactive. This was my first experience speaking with someone who was living in such a relationship or who even experienced such attractions, as far as I knew. Our discussion that night was an experience upon which I have often reflected.

As we walked away, my companion and I talked about the experience. Not able to understand how someone could be attracted to others of the same gender, my companion expressed lack of comprehension of how anyone could sincerely believe he had been "born that way," born with feelings that were obviously not natural. While he expressed his confusion at the situation, I remained silent and ached. I wasn't sure how to respond, for I did understand—more than I thought I could ever admit, even to myself. And though at the time I didn't feel it was something I would ever share with others, I understood in a very real way the feelings and emotions that these men experienced. I had experienced similar attractions and emotions for as long as I could remember.

Chapter 2

Facing Reality

Raised as a member of The Church of Jesus Christ of Latter-day Saints, I grew up with an idealistic view of life and of the gospel. The formula was simple: Be good, and you'll be happy. As a child, I had faith in the teachings of my parents and of the Church. The future course of my life seemed already laid out for me: I would graduate from high school, go to college, serve an honorable mission, marry a beautiful and faithful daughter of God in the temple, graduate from college, get a good job, and live a life faithful to Christ and the Church, raising ten-plus kids along the way.

During junior high and high school, I was pretty involved with school and other extracurricular activities and had a really good group of friends. I rarely missed any of the dances or other school activities and served in student leadership throughout high school. I dated often and had a lot of great friends who were girls. Once a teacher, the ski club advisor in high school, bet me a hundred dollars that I would be married within six months after returning from my mission. I have never collected on that bet, but my reasons for not getting married were certainly not that I didn't need the money, because at the time it was a fairly attractive sum to a prospective young college student with little cash and a world to conquer.

I have heard it said that we don't see the world as *it* really is but rather as *we* really are. As we grow and change and learn and encounter life's many wonders, we experience paradigm shifts in the way we view our surroundings. As part of that growth, there come times in our life when our belief system conflicts with our experience—when aspects of what we have believed or have been taught are called into question by what we are, what we feel, and what we see around us. We have to ask ourselves why we believe the way we do. When that questioning occurs, something must change for that conflict to be resolved. Either our beliefs must change or we must reinterpret our feelings or our experiences in light of our belief system—or possibly a combination of both.

One of my first memorable experiences with this was on my mission. I had been raised in a predominantly Latter-day Saint community where anything outside Utah was referred to as "the field"—where the converts were ripe, thirsting for the restored gospel, and ready to be "harvested" (D&C 4:4). Being a member of the "only true and living Church" (D&C 1:30), I, in my naïveté, interpreted that to mean we had a monopoly on God and truth and goodness and that a world hungry for God and truth and goodness was just waiting for me to don that black name tag and lead the soon-to-be-translated cities to their eternal deliverance. In my idealistic eye, I could envision my companion and me joyously waving the Book of Mormon in the streets, and truth-seekers running from their homes to hear the true message of salvation with the same eagerness that we approached the ice cream truck that traversed the neighborhood in the summertime when we were kids.

Needless to say, that is not quite how things transpired. I was awakened all too quickly to the struggle, the rejection, the canceled appointments, the Book of Mormon in a plastic bag hanging from the knob on the front door, and the unmet baptismal dates that often came with missionary work. Being part of a Church trademarked for its focus on families, I was surprised to witness how many healthy, stable, and happy families thrived outside the Church, many of whom were highly religious and more knowledgeable of the Bible and seemingly more faithful to God than I was at the time. I was awed by how many had genuinely seemed to experience God outside of Christianity and Christ outside of Mormonism—many whose eyes bespoke sincere peace and faith. I also witnessed the many seemingly good and moral people who had no interest in God or religion in any degree, and my heart ached for them. These experiences caused me to reflect deeply upon what I had always understood to be true. I was forced to turn to God for the light and knowledge I needed to reconcile the incongruity between my preconceptions and my experience.

That is also how my experience with same-gender attraction has been. Most of the information—or, rather, misinformation—I have been taught about homosexuality from the media, and even from some members of the Church, included the ideas that homosexual men were all effeminate men; men who wore dresses; men who molested children; men who wore only leather; promiscuous men who had sex in parks, restrooms, and bathhouses; men who paraded themselves and their "diversity" annually through the streets of large cities; men who had no belief in God or who hated Him and had no moral values. I had occasionally heard homosexuals in general compared to or equated with murderers, Satanists, prostitutes, pedophiles, and partakers of bestiality. But I fit none of those descriptions, so I was certain I couldn't be one of "them." I was fearfully conscious of my attraction to other men, but in light of all the hateful rhetoric I had ever heard, I felt that if I were honest about my own feelings, I would simultaneously be admitting that I was at best a bad person and at worst a pervert, an abomination to God and all that is good, destined to be thrust into the fiery pits of an eternal hell.

As far as life is concerned, hindsight has a funny way of telling a different version of history than the one you thought you were experiencing. At least that is how it has been for me. From my earliest recollection I was attracted to guys. Looking back, I can see experiences and feelings that reflect that attraction, but though I was conscious of them, I never admitted them to myself and thought of every reason imaginable to rationalize them away. Looking back through my journals, I have found several entries where I deduced reasons why I was "now sure" I wasn't and couldn't be gay.

I've always had a fair number of male friends, but as we grew older I became increasingly aware of the disparity between my own attractions and those of my friends. While they were developing attractions toward girls, mine were toward other guys. There were plenty of girls, though, who were fun to be with and with whom I enjoyed spending time, and surely whatever attraction I had for men was a phase. So I dated often and had plenty to add when the topic of women came up in guy conversations. I also had plenty to say about homosexuals whenever that topic arose, but though vocal in my criticism, I always had an intense curiosity that never seemed to fade.

I was fully aware of what would likely result socially if anyone were ever to discover my attraction. In my early years of junior high school, I vividly remember, rumors were still floating about a young man from a couple years previous whose attraction to other men was embarrassingly evidenced one day while he was taking the mandatory shower after gym class. Any positive reputation he had was completely destroyed, and he became an outcast. Because of the things still being said about him, I determined at that point that no one would ever discover that about me. I wanted to be loved and accepted, and I knew that if anyone knew the "real" me, I would be deemed unworthy of all love and acceptance and that which I had would be lost forever. I refused to allow anyone to get too close to me for fear that person might discover my forbidden feelings. I resolved to remain quiet about my attraction—desperately quiet.

During this period, I maintained a strong belief in the Church and wanted it as a significant part of my life. I grew up in a religious home with good parents who, I knew, loved and supported me. My family was always active in the Church, but at that time I did not distinguish between spirituality and religiosity. During my senior year of high school, I began to realize my lack of spiritual understanding, despite having been raised in a religious environment. Because the time for choosing a college had come, I wanted to be in a positive, spiritually strengthening atmosphere where I could grow in the gospel. I applied to Brigham Young University and was accepted.

While attending school that first year, away from the watchful eye of parents and family, I began an intense process of self-discovery. In the dorm I quickly recognized that many other students had grown up in areas where they, as Latter-day Saints, were a minority—sometimes the only member of the Church in their high school—and I felt in them a sense of spirituality and commitment and conversion to the Church and to Christ I didn't recall seeing in anyone my own age and certainly didn't feel myself. As I watched some of them, I realized to an even greater degree that I was lacking something and decided to begin my own quest for conversion. I sensed an increasing need to seek my own personal testimony of the gospel and develop a deeper relationship with God.

With spiritual and personal study goals in place and religion classes registered for, my journey began. I sought quiet places where I could study the scriptures and immerse myself in prayer without interruption. Sometimes I would wake up early in the morning and study at my desk before my roommate arose. Other times I had to seek out someplace more secluded, and I soon discovered the basement music rooms. Often I would go there for hours to study the scriptures, ponder, pray, and record my feelings. I began to have experiences with the Spirit that opened up my mind and heart. I began to better understand my relationship to God and the truthfulness of the gospel I had always taken for granted. There was a feeling of conversion, of an internal change, taking place that I had not previously felt. In a real way, I no longer simply believed or accepted the truthfulness of the Church and its teachings about our relationship to the Father as an intellectual or even spiritual acknowledgment. I knew it in my heart and truly "felt to sing the song of redeeming love" (Alma 5:26).

A verse in the book of Mosiah reflects the way I feel about the things I learned in that basement music room and at the corner desk in my dorm room. After Alma was touched by Abinadi's words, he hid in the woods to escape Noah and his priests and began to teach others who dared venture to his retreat. The feelings expressed by those who were converted through Alma's preaching express the feelings I had as I began to experience my own conversion that year: "All this was done in

Mormon, yea, by the waters of Mormon, in the forest that was near the waters of Mormon; yea, the place of Mormon, the waters of Mormon, the forest of Mormon, how beautiful are they to the eyes of them who there came to the knowledge of their Redeemer; yea, and how blessed are they, for they shall sing to his praise forever" (Mosiah 18:30).

Those two private places will forever have a place in my heart because it was there that I came to the knowledge of my Redeemer, and I felt for the first time the desire to sing His praise. My perspective of reality began to change from that of the world's view of reality to that of God's reality. I learned by the Spirit to see things as I had never seen or understood them before. I began to learn how to receive personal revelation and to understand to a greater degree how the Lord communicates with me through His Spirit. That understanding has been the key to my spiritual growth since that time. I ceased to see the plan of salvation as circles on a chalkboard, and it began to vividly define the world surrounding me. I learned the significance of Jacob's statement that "the Spirit speaketh the truth and lieth not. Wherefore, it speaketh of things as they really are, and of things as they really will be" (Jacob 4:13).

During this time of spiritual growth, I still recognized my attraction to other men but was unwilling to acknowledge it for fear of what it might mean—and I believed those attractions would be extinguished by my growing conversion to the gospel and love for God. After all, these attractions were "against nature" (Romans 1:26) and an "abomination" to God (Leviticus 20:13), and one couldn't fully have the Spirit and still experience such feelings—or so I thought. Things didn't change, but I still had my whole mission ahead of me, so I continued with the expectation that these "unnatural" feelings would go away if I was patient and continued to serve God full time during the next two years.

I did serve an honorable mission, and as I strove to give my whole "heart, might, mind, and strength" (D&C 4:2) to the Lord's work, I grew immeasurably. The conversion to the gospel I felt during my freshman year of college intensified and increased. But even as my gospel understanding deepened, my feelings of attraction toward other men never diminished. I felt spiritual strength and focus while serving the Lord that decreased any inclination I had to act on those feelings, but the attractions themselves remained. I understood very well the feelings of the men I met on my mission who had moved to the East Coast from Salt Lake City. I could empathize with them; I ached for them. But because of my testimony and deep love for God and for truth, compromising a life in the Church I dearly loved and believed was His did not seem an option to me.

Upon returning home, I continued my university studies, and having been taught that marriage was naturally the next step in life, I engaged myself in the quest of finding an eternal companion. Although I was in no hurry to get married, I felt I had truly given my all to the Lord during the previous two years and experienced a genuine sense of fulfillment. The problem was that I couldn't seem to find it within me to feel any romantic attraction to women. I often dated different young women, all of whom were beautiful and the kind of truly incredible people I felt would be great companions, but as time went on, I could feel nothing more for them than deep friendship and admiration for their goodness. The thought of being physically intimate with any one of them seemed almost unbearable. Still hoping, though, that my attraction to other men was a passing phase, I tried to be patient and I dated diligently, hoping the "right one" would come along.

Shortly after returning from my mission, I began working as a teacher at the Missionary Training Center. With the gratitude I felt for all the Lord had taught me on my mission, I wanted to give something back by striving to kindle in the hearts of missionaries the kind of fire that had earlier been kindled in mine. I worked over a period of about three years, and my understanding of the gospel and my sensitivity to the Spirit both reached an all-time high.

But at one point during that period of employment, I was confronted for the first time with the reality that I had been wrong in assuming that living the gospel was a guaranteed formula for ridding me of my feelings of same-gender attraction. No matter what level of personal righteousness

I attained or how close I felt to God, the feelings weren't going away. To the contrary, they were increasing. It was a paradox! Was it truly possible to have an increased love for God and a deeper understanding of His gospel and simultaneously to have a greater desire for something that I had always been taught was an abomination? I wasn't sure if I should feel a greater sense of self-worth or greater self-condemnation. It was as if I were experiencing joy in Christ and tasting hell at the same time, and it didn't make any sense.

I felt real discouragement concerning this issue for the first time and decided I needed to disclose my forbidden feelings. The only person I could think of to turn to was my bishop, but revealing something so "dark" about myself was a step I thought I could never take. I was scared. The topic was something I had never heard discussed without derogation or discomfort. But finally I swallowed my inhibitions and took the largest step of faith I had ever taken. As I discussed my feelings with him, I felt a huge burden lifted. I was finally able to admit vocally something I had always silently tried to deny, even to myself. My bishop and I discussed some things he personally felt would help me, and I began a journey— or rather, a battle—that has been frightening, strengthening, and enlightening.

Through the tears and trauma and searing heat of the refiner's fire, I have slowly come to understand that—like any other trial, challenge, or experience in life—there is always good that can be learned and strength that can be gained, even in the furnace of affliction. In the years since that time, I've done a lot of learning and growing both spiritually and emotionally. What I believed and understood concerning the Church and the gospel of Jesus Christ was in conflict with the attraction I experienced, and my experience with same-gender attraction was different from what I had been taught about homosexuality. I've had to ask myself some deep, soul-searching questions. In this process of reconciliation, my perspective on life, the Church, the gospel, myself, and homosexuality in general have changed dramatically in many respects. Through discussing with others who also experience this attraction, reading much of what I could find on the subject, spending time in fasting and prayer so that I might be tutored by the Lord, and studying the scriptures and words of those I believe are prophets of God, I have finally largely reconciled my belief system with my attraction to other men and have discovered much of the peace and purpose I have been seeking for so long.

Though it was extremely difficult, I'm so grateful for that time when I was forced to confront my feelings. I'm grateful for all I've learned about the Atonement, faith, and love because of this challenge and in being honest about it with myself. I sincerely believe there is an enabling power through the Atonement that has comforted me and given me strength. I pray that it will continue to support me throughout my life as I experience these feelings of attraction. I long to stay faithful to Christ and to His Church, and as I do remain true, I feel that rather than suppressing my "true" self, I will be submitting to a higher self—the self that is eternal and the literal offspring of a divine Father in Heaven. As C. S. Lewis wrote: "Our real selves are all waiting for us in Him. The more I resist Him and try to live on my own, the more I become dominated by my own heredity and upbringing and natural desires . . . It is when I turn to Christ, when I give myself up to His personality, that I first begin to have a real personality of my own."[1]

A religion teacher once said that his desire for our class was for us to immerse ourselves in the Spirit so that we would be better prepared to go out and deal with the "real world." After he spoke these words, he stopped, pondered, and recalled his words, saying, "No, I want your experience here to be an opportunity to immerse yourselves in the *real* world so you will be better able to go out and function in the fallen, artificial one." Those words rang true and profound. The light of Christ within me has helped me to recognize a greater reality—or the *real* world—in "the great plan of the Eternal God" (Alma 34:9). I've finally come to "face reality"—the reality of God's eternal plan of redemption, as I have learned to understand it.

"Be Ready Always to Give Reason of the Hope That Is in You"

I thought my faith was strong before I started trying honestly to sort out my feelings, but my experience revealed to me significant chinks in my spiritual armor. There was a time in my journey of reconciliation between my experience with same-gender attraction and my belief system when I hit a wall in my faith and was no longer sure what I really wanted. One of the most difficult things for me during that time was that I firmly believed that the gospel of Christ as it is taught in the Church was true—I felt it in the deepest parts of my being—but I also desired so deeply a loving, romantic relationship that felt natural and good and that I had always been taught was such a significant source of happiness and joy.

Eventually, I lost hope that I could ever have such a relationship in the way I had always dreamed and expected. I felt this particularly after my mission, when dating began to take on more than mere social purposes, and I couldn't sense any genuine feelings of romantic love for women. In this temporal world that often speaks to the immediate physical and emotional desires, there has been a very real war going on between the natural man and the spiritual man deep within me. The two are completely at odds, and yet both have at times felt natural and real. The natural man would wonder—and my natural side has—why I should not simply "face reality" and satisfy the natural feelings and emotions that hunger within me, the ones that feel most instinctive to me. The path has been marked with highs and lows—the inner war between Jekyll and Hyde often feeling like the perfect analogy—but even when I felt distant from the Lord as the result of a loss of faith and resulting choices, I had never felt stronger at any point in my life that the Lord loved me, was with me, and would not forsake me.

The love I felt from Him carried me through a lot of dark times, times when I wondered if everything I had ever been taught, believed, and hoped was true was even a possibility. There was even a period when I no longer wanted the gospel truths I had been taught and grown to love to be true so the incongruities in my heart and mind would be less agonizing. Although during the most difficult period of my struggle to understand and reconcile my feelings I made choices that I deeply regret, I'm incredibly grateful for the supernal gift of the Atonement, for the mercy and grace of a forgiving Redeemer, whose "arm is lengthened out all the day long" (2 Nephi 28:32) and who willingly and lovingly receives all who will repent and come unto Him. For a while, the only thing that kept me from fully following through with my attraction and seeking a long-term homosexual relationship was not that I believed I couldn't find some level of genuine fulfillment or temporal happiness in such a relationship, if it were loving and committed. Rather, it was the simple truth that I knew my having a romantic relationship with a man could never be eternal, and I didn't want to give my whole heart and soul and life to a relationship that could not last beyond this mortal existence. One thing I've always held a firm conviction of—even in my moments of doubt and wavering faith—is the eternal nature of the family.

The prophet Jeremiah said something that epitomizes the way I have often felt. During a time of discouragement when Jeremiah wanted to abandon his faith and discipleship, he said, "I will not make mention of him, nor speak any more in his name. But his word was in mine heart as a burning fire shut up in my bones, and I was weary with forbearing, and I could not stay" (Jeremiah 20:9). I feel the word of God is in my heart as a burning fire shut up in my bones, and even though I sometimes long to submit to the passions of the flesh and pursue a life based on my attraction, I weary when I try to withhold my life from Him and I cannot "stay." He and the fulness of His gospel, which He restored through the Prophet Joseph Smith, mean too much to me.

After a period of real depression and hopelessness, I had to ask myself some deeper questions about God and worship and discipleship and the plan of salvation, and I had to seek the mind and will of God on the matter. I had to understand more deeply the relationship between the feelings of attraction I experience and the gospel I love if I was to move forward in faith and discipleship. Elder B. H. Roberts wrote: "'Mormonism' . . . calls for thoughtful disciples who will not be content with merely repeating some of its truths, but will develop its truths. . . . The disciples of 'Mormonism' . . . will yet take profounder and broader views of the great doctrines committed to the Church; and . . . will cast them in new formulas; co-operating in the works of the Spirit, until 'they help to give to the truth received a more forceful expression, and carry it beyond the earlier and cruder stages of its development.'"[2]

As I sought further inspiration from the Lord, I began to understand more deeply and profoundly the power of hope. I had always had hope, I thought, but I began to realize more fully the power and importance of understanding the hope we truly can have because of Christ. I had to rediscover the meaning of hope and the significance of its relation to His atoning sacrifice. Sharing the truths of the gospel has given me new hope. I believe that even with an experience of same-gender attraction—which in a mortal, fallen world a minority of people may come to feel, for a myriad of reasons—individuals can find real peace with what we have been taught through the Lord's prophets concerning the importance of marriage and family. Despite the challenge of same-gender attraction, they can reconcile their challenge with a life completely faithful to Christ and to His Church, The Church of Jesus Christ of Latter-day Saints.

Years ago I read two statements—one by President Joseph F. Smith and the other by Elder John A. Widtsoe—that had a profound effect upon the way I approached the gospel and my study of it. President Smith said: "The greatest achievement mankind can make in this world is to familiarize themselves with divine truth, so thoroughly, so perfectly, that the example or conduct of no creature living in the world can ever turn them away from the knowledge that they have obtained. . . . From my boyhood I have desired to learn the principles of the gospel in such a way and to such an extent that it would matter not to me who might fall from the truth, who might make a mistake, who might fail to continue to follow the example of the Master, my foundation would be sure."[3]

Elder Widtsoe expanded upon the same idea, declaring: "An effort must be put forth to learn the gospel, to understand it, to comprehend the relationship of its principles. The gospel must be studied; otherwise no test of its truth may sanely be applied to it . . . It is a paradox that men will gladly devote time every day for many years to learn a science or an art; yet will expect to win a knowledge of the gospel, which comprehends all sciences and arts, through perfunctory glances at books or occasional listening to sermons. The gospel should be studied more intensively than any school or college subject. They who pass opinion on the gospel without having given it intimate and careful study are not lovers of truth, and their opinions are worthless."[4]

With as much as there is to learn about scriptures and doctrine, the history of Christ's Church in the latter days, and the delicate revelatory workings of the Spirit, I am by no means an expert on any one of those things. There have been times in my life when all I could say was, "I know that he loveth his children; nevertheless, I do not know the meaning of all things" (1 Nephi 11:17). But these words of President Smith and Elder Widtsoe affected me, and they have guided my search for truth since I first read them. I have tried to learn and understand the gospel of my God on both a spiritual and an intellectual level so that I might be able to heed the counsel of the ancient apostle Peter when he said, "Sanctify the Lord God in your hearts: and be ready always to give an answer to every man that asketh you a reason of the hope that is in you with meekness and fear" (Peter 3:15).

Even though the challenge of this experience has often felt unbearable, I do now feel hope—the kind of hope that comes with eternal perspective and faith in God. And I now feel peace, a kind of peace I have felt only through the Spirit of the Lord when I have diligently strived to follow His word given through ancient and modern prophets. Someone once said that many Latter-day Saints seem to know the gospel just well enough to feel guilt for their sins and imperfections but not well enough to feel the peace, joy, and hope that faith in the redemption of Christ can bring—to hear the voice of the Lord and to feel His grace and love and mercy. I have tried to learn and live the gospel well enough to feel the peace that faith in the redemption of Christ can bring.

As I have read about and studied homosexuality, I've wearied of the varying and conflicting perspectives concerning possibilities and impossibilities and the shoulds and shouldn'ts of "change." I've wearied of the biology, psychology, and sociology of both the "cause" and the "cure" for the "problem of homosexuality." Reading these conflicting philosophies didn't help me. The eternal part of me tired of science and of the philosophies of men with their limited capacity and understanding.

Although science—biological, psychological, and sociological—can help us to understand more about the nature of same-gender attraction and may be a means through which God brings us greater light and knowledge, I think the following words by Hugh Nibley are quite profound: "The words of the prophets cannot be held to the tentative and defective tests that men have devised for them. Science, philosophy, and common sense all have a right to their day in court. But the last word does not lie with them. Every time men in their wisdom have come forth with the last word, other words have promptly followed. The last word is a testimony of the gospel that comes only by direct revelation. Our Father in heaven speaks it, and if it were in perfect agreement with the science of today, it would surely be out of line with the science of tomorrow. Let us not, therefore, seek to hold God to the learned opinions of the moment when he speaks the language of eternity."[5]

Often, when I have felt overwhelmed by this attraction and challenge, the only place I have been able to find peace and solace is in the scriptures as I have strived to immerse myself in the Spirit—in the arms of the Comforter. I longed to hear the language of eternity. I needed peace and comfort in dealing with an attraction I did not choose. It is when the Spirit has spoken to and nourished my eternal self—my covenant self—that I have received strength. Then the desire to remain faithful to God and to seek the power of my personal Redeemer has been renewed.

"True Doctrine, Understood, Changes Attitudes and Behavior"

My study of the gospel and my understanding of it have given me the sense of peace and perspective I now have. I believe that understanding

70

the doctrines of the gospel in their beauty, purity, and poignancy inspires discipleship. As President Boyd K. Packer has said: "True doctrine, understood, changes attitudes and behavior.

"The study of the doctrines of the gospel will improve behavior quicker than a study of behavior will improve behavior. . . . That is why we stress so forcefully the study of the doctrines of the gospel."[6]

I write from the perspective of a committed Latter-day Saint who subscribes fully to the doctrines of The Church of Jesus Christ of Latter-day Saints—one who sustains the leaders of the Church as prophets, seers, and revelators; who believes in the divinity and historicity of the Book of Mormon, the Bible, and other Latter-day Saint scripture; who believes in the reality of the restoration of the fulness of the gospel of Jesus Christ and in the special destiny of Christ's Church; and, ultimately, who believes in both the redeeming and the enabling power of the atoning sacrifice of the Lord Jesus Christ.

Not everyone considers homosexual attraction to be only a mortal challenge or temptation that can be overcome or faithfully endured through mortality, and not everyone considers homosexual behavior to be contrary to the Father's eternal purposes for His children. These chapters are not an attempt to defend the Church's position on homosexual behavior; they are an attempt to help those who believe in the doctrines and teachings of the Church of Jesus Christ—or who at least "desire to believe" (Alma 32:27)—and who are trying to understand how the unsolicited challenge or experience of same-gender attraction could possibly fit into the context of a plan of salvation that is so focused on marriage and family. They are an attempt to provide the peace that comes with perspective and vision. They are a call to embrace the hope provided within the outstretched arms of the Lord's undying love and mercy. Indeed, they are a call to worship our Father and our God.

These chapters are written to those who long to stay faithful to Christ and to His Church and who want to find safety and peace within the walls of the kingdom but who either find it difficult to reconcile their attraction with their beliefs or struggle to stay faithful within a community that doesn't understand their battle and therefore often exhibits some prejudice. Last of all, these chapters are also for the families, friends, and leaders of those who struggle, and who want to understand so they can better reach out and provide greater love and support and hope for their loved ones during their time of trial.

I do not approach the subject of same-gender attraction through the eyes of scientific research, cognitive therapy, or mere observation of family or friends who experience it. I approach it as one who has lived with it for as long as he can remember. I approach it as one who has felt the feelings of being torn between an ideal belief system and the reality of experiencing longings that make the thought of conforming to that belief system almost unbearable at times. I approach it as one who has felt the agonizing pain of wondering if he is an abomination to God simply because of an attraction that most certainly was not chosen. I approach it as one who has spent hours on his knees and in tears pleading for the Lord to take away this challenge so he could be "normal" and live the life faithful to Christ and His Church that was his ultimate desire. I approach it as one who has felt the pangs of the derogatory and hateful rhetoric echoing through society. I approach it as one who understands the feelings of confusion that come when hearing sermons about the "natural" longing God has bestowed upon His sons and daughters to draw them together and wonders why these "natural" feelings have felt so "unnatural" to him.

Factors involved in the development of same-gender attraction—whether biological, psychological, familial, or cultural—will be only minimally addressed in the following chapters, though continuing research in that area serves a purpose and may be of help to some individuals. My primary concern is not how I came to have feelings of same-gender attraction but rather what I'm going to do about that attraction when it comes to my faith and commitment to Christ and His gospel, as it is taught in His Church.

These chapters are an attempt to look at the challenge of same-gender attraction from an eternal perspective. The understanding of gospel doctrines that I have gained by the power of the Spirit has given me peace and provided purpose to the pain I have at times felt. It is difficult to convey in words the things I've been taught by the Lord, but I have tried within these pages to do so. My feelings may be like those of Oliver Cowdery, who wrote, "I know much may be conveyed to the understanding in writing, and many marvelous truths set forth with the pen, but after all it is but a shadow, compared to an open vision of seeing, hearing and realizing eternal things."[7]

In truth, these chapters are much more about the gospel through the eyes of one individual who experiences same-gender attraction than they are about same-gender attraction itself. To be certain, these chapters are about "change," and they are about "overcoming" but not in the same way usually referred to in discussion on homosexuality. I don't mean by "change" or "overcoming" that same-gender attraction must or will completely be eradicated in this life for everyone. These chapters are about a "change" of heart (Helaman 15:7) and of "overcoming" the world (John 16:33) through faith in Jesus Christ. I believe that with His love and guiding Spirit, and through His atoning sacrifice and enabling grace, we can live faithfully through whatever tragedies, trials, challenges, temptations, or tendencies may be part of our mortal experience. We live in fallen, mortal bodies in a fallen society in a fallen world and should expect a host of tragedies, trials, challenges, attractions, tendencies, temptations, weaknesses, sicknesses, hardships, and other problems to plague us until the world is fully redeemed through the Only Begotten Son of God.

A friend asked me why I, with my past struggle and doubting, felt qualified to write on this subject from this perspective. It was a question I reflected upon for days afterward. I acknowledge that within the vast array of gospel knowledge—and considering the wide range of different individuals' experience with same-gender attraction—my own understanding is minimal. What could I, in my limited knowledge and experience, possibly share that would be of benefit to others who share this attraction? What qualifications do I have to give insight to those seeking to learn more and understand this issue with greater perspective? The more questions I asked, the more clearly I realized the simple answer: I'm not qualified. I'm not a Church leader or a doctrinal or scriptural scholar. I'm not a psychologist, psychiatrist, psychotherapist, sociologist, or biologist. I understand only a fraction of the debate concerning the potential mixture of biological, social, and psychological factors influencing an individual's experience with same-gender attraction.

But what I do have to offer is a growing love for the Lord and an increasing understanding of the importance of His infinite atonement, a desire to build His kingdom, and a will to share some of the insights I've gained through study of the scriptures and the words of the living prophets, through fasting and prayer, and through the Lord's Spirit as He has schooled me through various life experiences. Though I'm no expert on homosexuality, I have researched the subject extensively. I offer some of the insights I've gained through study and discussions with others on the issue of same-gender attraction and, ultimately, my own personal experience with it. And I write in the hope that the Lord will qualify me by guiding my words with His Spirit and by confirming the truth of these principles by the Spirit to the reader.

As has already been evidenced, I have used primarily the term "same-gender attraction"—rather than "gay" or "homosexual." To be honest, when I first heard the term "same-gender attraction," I didn't like it. It sounded empty, sterile, and clinical, void of the depth of the feelings and emotions that accompany it for me and for many other individuals. But the more I've studied and pondered the subject—and my own experience with it specifically—the more comfortable I have felt with the term and the more appropriate it seems in conjunction with the approach toward homosexuality taken in this book. This phrase gets to the root of what homosexuality really is, and it is used with the hope of eliminating many of the stereotypes and as much of the baggage associated with the other terms as possible. The purpose is to get sex out of it, because for many it isn't simply about sex; it's about attraction. Granted, for many it does become sexual, but for most, sexual activity is not the sole root of this attraction any more than it is the sole root of heterosexual attraction. For many, there are emotional, psychological, social, and even spiritual components as well. And it is necessary to get the stereotypes out of the way, because to generically say someone is "gay," "homosexual," or "experiences same-gender attraction" is not accurate. It isn't that black and white. There is a spectrum. The degree to which someone experiences same-gender attraction, the factors that influenced it, and the direction in which that individual chooses to go with it are different for each person. In addition, to refer to a gay or homosexual "lifestyle"—as if there were only one—is also inaccurate. There is a spectrum there as well, ranging from committed, monogamous relationships to promiscuity and complete lack of commitment.

Finally, most of the ideas expressed in the following chapters are not new. They are principles that have been taught by prophets of the Lord for millennia and have been taught and expounded upon again in this last dispensation by living prophets and gospel scholars. Usually, however, they have not been taught in the specific context of same-gender attraction. But since my experience with same-gender attraction has framed the lenses through which I view the world and the gospel, those are the lenses through which I will present those doctrines and principles here, even though they are universal and could apply to anyone.

The thoughts that follow reflect an idea expressed by Elder Bruce R. McConkie in his final conference address: "In speaking of these wondrous things I shall use my own words, though you may think they are the words of scripture, words spoken by other Apostles and prophets.

"True it is they were first proclaimed by others, but they are now mine, for the Holy Spirit of God has borne witness to me that they are true, and it is now as though the Lord had revealed them to me in the first instance. I have thereby heard his voice and know his word."[8]

Contained in this book are the principles and doctrines that the Lord through His mercy has helped me to understand and that have given me perspective and peace and the desire to live faithful to Him. Though they are often the words of others, they are now mine, for the "Holy Spirit of God has borne witness to me that they are true."

Chapter 3

A God of Miracles

For years I pleaded in tears with the Lord that he would take away my feelings of same-gender attraction so I could have a family, serve in the Church, and live for Him the way I always desired to do. But nothing changed, and I wondered why He wouldn't grant what I felt was the most righteous of desires. I believed it would require a miracle, but I believed the Lord's word to Nephi when He declared, "Behold, I am God; and I am a God of miracles" (2 Nephi 27:23), and I believed Moroni when he questioningly pleaded, "Has the day of miracles ceased? . . . for it is by faith that miracles are wrought . . . wherefore, if these things have ceased wo be unto the children of men, for it is because of unbelief" (Moroni 7:35, 37). I believed in Him, and I wanted to have the faith that if Jesus could give the blind eyes to see and the deaf ears to hear, that if He could give to the cripple legs to walk upon, and raise the dead to life, that if He could miraculously deliver Israel from Egypt by parting the Red Sea, then surely He could and would also grant me my own miracle. Surely He—if the attractions I felt were an "abomination" and "against nature"—would conquer my "enemies" as He did the Egyptians.

My perspective began to change when years ago I heard Elder Dallin H. Oaks teach: "The greatest miracle is not in such things as restoring sight to the blind, healing an illness, or even raising the dead, since all of these restorations will happen, in any event, in the Resurrection. Changing bodies or protecting temples are miracles, but an even greater miracle is a mighty change of heart by a son or daughter of

God (see Mosiah 5:2). A change of heart, including new attitudes, priorities, and desires, is greater and more important than any miracle involving the body. I repeat, the body will be resurrected in any event, but a
change affecting what the scripture calls the 'heart' of a spirit son or
daughter of God is a change whose effect is eternal. If of the right kind,
this change opens the door to the process of repentance that cleanses us to
dwell in the presence of God. It introduces the perspective and priorities
that lead us to make the choices that qualify us for eternal life, 'the greatest of all the gifts of God' (D&C 14:7)."[1]

When I heard these words I realized I had been praying for the wrong
miracle. The miracles that Jesus performed were merely types of the
greater miracles he desired to perform in the hearts of the children of
God—and more importantly, in my heart—giving the spiritually blind
eyes to see, the spiritually deaf ears to hear, the spiritually crippled legs to
walk upon in faith, and the spiritually dead rebirth and spiritual life in
Christ. Although at the time I had never acted on my feelings of same-
gender attraction and tried diligently to follow the teachings of the
Church, I was still blind to some aspects of the gospel, and the Lord had
yet to teach me some profound lessons that would help me to have "a new
heart and a new spirit" (Ezekiel 18:31).

One of my biggest concerns when I first started confronting my feelings was in regard to the nature of our spirits and what we take with us
when we die. Amulek taught the poor among the Zoramites: "That same
spirit which possesses your bodies at the time that ye go out of this life,
that same spirit will have power to possess your body in that eternal
world" (Alma 34:34). Without studying these words in their full context
to understand what Amulek was really saying, I feared that if I wasn't
"cured" or didn't overcome my attraction to other men here in this
mortal probation, it would be harder to overcome it in the spirit world
without a body. I would become discouraged and depressed when my
increasing spiritual growth and attempts to "change" my feelings of attraction didn't change anything.

Then I read the verses in their full context and came to understand their meaning to a greater degree. It had seemed to me that those verses were entirely about repentance and had little or nothing to do with challenges or trials or temptations. Immediately before Amulek speaks of the spirit that will possess our body in the hereafter, he exhorts us to "not procrastinate the day of [our] repentance until the end." He then tells us what will happen if we do procrastinate: "Ye cannot say, when ye are brought to that awful crisis, that I will repent, that I will return to my God. Nay, ye cannot say this; for that same spirit which doth possess your bodies at the time that ye go out of this life, that same spirit will have power to possess your body in that eternal world" (Alma 34:34).

As I read this verse with new eyes, I understood that it is not actually talking about our own spirit—or our temptations, attractions, or tendencies—as I had once thought. If we think we have to be fully rid of every attraction or inclination to do wrong in order to move on to the next life, we are setting a standard that we simply cannot reach. Amulek shortly thereafter clarifies what "spirit" he is talking about: "For behold, if ye have procrastinated the day of your repentance even until death, behold, ye have become subjected to the spirit of the devil, and he doth seal you his; therefore, the Spirit of the Lord hath withdrawn from you, and hath no place in you, and the devil hath all power over you; and this is the final state of the wicked" (Alma 34:35).

If we allow Satan to have power to possess our bodies in this world by avoiding repentance, that same spirit of lacking in faith and repentance will continue to have power over us in the next world. But if we have a constant attitude of repentance and thirst for righteousness here, the Spirit of the Lord will have power to possess our bodies there. Our challenges may not necessarily go with us, but our hearts will—what we have become as a result of our challenges. That is what I understood Amulek to be referring to. Same-gender attraction may or may not always be a part of my mortal experience. If the Lord takes it away, I'll praise Him all the more. But it is our spirit of repentance—or our hearts and our faith in Christ—that is essential to our receiving salvation.

"The Greatest of All the Gifts"

The deliverance of Israel out of Egypt and through the Red Sea, as well as the signs from God through Moses that preceded it, were divine and wondrous. They were miracles and manifestations of the Almighty in every way, but I have come to feel that the most awe-inspiring miracle was not in getting Israel out of Egypt—it was in getting Egypt out of Israel. The greater miracles occurred in the forty years of wandering when hearts were changed, when the worldliness, doubt, fear, pride, and unbelief were replaced by hearts turned to God, hearts that learned over time to rely "wholly upon the merits of him who is mighty to save" (2 Nephi 31:19).

As Israel had been in bondage, so I too had felt for the longest time that I was in bondage to an attraction, an attraction I desperately wanted to be released from. I don't know exactly what factors in my life influenced the attraction, but regardless of the specific cause, it has come as the result of living in a fallen world. I felt the Spirit many times testify of the truthfulness of the gospel, and I believed that by following my Deliverer—as Israel followed Moses—I would soon be freed, and I continued forward, clinging tightly to that hope.

Then there came a point in my journey when I recognized the painful reality that I might always experience this attraction in mortality, a point when for the first time I wondered if I was doing the right thing by following the commandments of God as I had been taught them. I questioned again if it was all really true and if I really wanted eternal life—if the promised land would really be worth the journey through the wilderness. I wondered if I really would or even *could* marry a woman if I continued to follow the path I had been taught to follow. I doubted that I could find in that wilderness the kind of romantic love I had always hoped and dreamed and lived for. I hit a wall, and I wasn't sure if I wanted to go forward anymore. For the first time I met individuals who shared my challenge and who made surrender to the attraction seem more enticing than traversing the desert alone, despite the "land flowing with milk and honey" promised at the final destination (Exodus 3:8). For a time I no longer believed I could stay with the Church. The glimmer of hope I had for a family faded as I continued to date incredible young women, only to be confronted again and again with the reminder that I felt no romantic attraction to them.

I understood in a personal way the feelings I believe the children of Israel must have felt as they faced the wall of water that caused them to fear and doubt their course as they watched the pursuing Egyptians. As I sometimes have, they forgot the earlier miracles and their earlier illumination. "When Pharaoh drew nigh, the children of Israel lifted up their eyes, and, behold, the Egyptians marched after them; and they were sore afraid" (Exodus 14:10). Elder Jeffrey R. Holland commented on those verses: "Some . . . said words to this effect: 'Let's go back. This isn't worth it. We must have been wrong. That probably wasn't the right spirit telling us to leave Egypt.'"[2]

What the Israelites said to Moses was: "Wherefore hast thou dealt thus with us, to carry us forth out of Egypt? . . . It had been better for us to serve the Egyptians, than that we should die in the wilderness" (Exodus 14:11–12). Though I have always maintained to some degree the hope that I would marry in this life, I have also known that if I were not to marry and still continue faithful to Christ and His laws of chastity and morality, that would mean living a life of celibacy. And when I could feel no romantic attraction toward women I dated, it was intensely daunting to think of an existence that, in my mind, seemed barren of life and romantic love, seemingly the essence of joy in our often difficult and lonely mortal sojourn. Even the Lord Himself declared, "It is not good that the man should be alone" (Genesis 2:18). The more I thought of the potential reality of what faith in God meant, the more I feared, despite my belief in Christ as my Deliverer and in His redeeming and enabling atonement. With my back to the sea—and the Lord seemingly nowhere in sight—I longed at least for the romantic companionship I thought I could have here and now.

As if in response, though, Elder Holland said: "And I have to say,

'What about that which has already happened? What about the miracles that got you here? What about the frogs and the lice? What about the rod and the serpent, the river and the blood? What about the hail, the locusts, the fire, the firstborn sons?' How soon we forget. It would not have been better to stay and serve the Egyptians, and it is not better to remain outside the Church . . . Of course our faith will be tested as we fight through these self-doubts and second thoughts. Some days we will be miraculously led out of Egypt—seemingly free, seemingly on our way—only to come to yet another confrontation, like all that water lying before us. At those times we must resist the temptation to panic and give up. At those times fear will be the strongest of the adversary's weapons against us."[3]

What happened next seems to be a type of the way the Lord has worked in my life as well. "And Moses said unto the people, Fear ye not, stand still, and see the salvation of the Lord. . . . The Lord shall fight for you" (Exodus 14:13–14). In confirmation, the great Jehovah said to Moses, "Speak unto the children of Israel, that they go forward" (Exodus 14:15). Despite the seeming impossibility of a forward journey posed by the barrier of the Red Sea, the waters were parted—and Israel escaped the Egyptians.

And so it has been for me. When my back was against the sea and my feet were pointing toward Egypt, I have felt the delivering power of my Redeemer—I have seen "the salvation of the Lord" through sacred personal experiences. During the period of my greatest struggle, all I knew to do was continue doing that which I knew how to do: to study His word and pray for understanding. As I have left my heart open—even in my times of doubt and fear—to potentially feeling the comfort and instruction of the Spirit, He has helped me, through personal spiritual experiences, to internalize for the first time in my life certain principles I had always believed or already "known." As I felt the power and grace of Christ actively working in me, I felt the glimmer of hope and the fire of faith begin again to grow brighter in my heart. My barriers of doubt and faithlessness were being parted, and I was given the strength and desire to continue forward once again.

Elder Holland's final comment on Israel's exodus was that "the . . . lesson from . . . the miracle of crossing the Red Sea is that along with the illuminating revelation that points us toward a righteous purpose or duty, God will also provide the means and power to achieve that purpose. Trust in that eternal truth. If God has told you something is right, if something is indeed true for you, He will provide the way for you to accomplish it . . . The Lord would [later] tell Joseph [Smith] again and again that just as in days of old the children of Israel would be 'led out of bondage by power, and with a stretched-out arm . . . Therefore, let not your hearts faint . . . Mine angels shall go up before you, and also my presence, and in time ye shall possess the goodly land' (D&C 103:17, 19–20)."[4]

I often used to read the Old Testament and wonder with amazement at the stubbornness and unbelief of Israel as they wandered through the wilderness—especially after they had witnessed the profound signs of the Lord's delivering power and mercy. But I have since come to realize my own stubbornness and unbelief, and I wonder with amazement at how often I have doubted the power of my Savior.

Even with the miracles God has shown me, and the truths I have learned, I have at times continued to doubt and in my blindness and unbelief sometimes longed for that which cannot be—I've longed to return to Egypt (Exodus 16:3). I ache at how often I have "set at naught his counsels, and [would] not that he should be [my] guide" (Helaman 12:6). But I'm also humbled at how often He has shown me mercy and let me know of His undying love for me. I'm humbled at His patience as I have slowly learned to rely upon Him. As I look toward that desert, I am grateful for the promise of the Comforter that has taught me that He will be my manna in the wilderness and in Him I "shall find pasture" (1 Nephi 22:25). He will be my Bread of Life and my Living Water.

People have often said that unless I was true to my "real" self and found a male companion to share my life with, I could never be truly happy. My response to that is this: I have. I have found Christ, my God and my King. And it is His blessing and the companionship of His Holy Spirit that mean more to me than any mortal companionship. It is in

Him that I find joy and happiness, and it is in His name and in the "good news" of His life and atoning sacrifice that I glory. And though I do hope that with His help and strength, marriage is still a possibility for me in mortality—though it may not be for some—I'm also deeply grateful for the understanding I am gaining of the importance of making Him and His righteousness the prime focus of my life. I am slowly learning to rely wholly upon Him for the love, support, and strength I will need to make it through the scorching desert of mortality—married or not—and to the promised land of eternal life, "the greatest of all the gifts of God."

"A New Heart and a New Spirit"

When Alma the Younger was contending with Zeezrom about God's mysteries, he said: "It is given unto many to know the mysteries of God; nevertheless they are laid under a strict command that they shall not impart only according to the portion of his word which he doth grant unto the children of men, according to the heed and diligence which they give unto him. And therefore, he that will harden his heart, the same receiveth the lesser portion of the word; and he that will not harden his heart, to him is given the greater portion of the word, until it is given unto him to know the mysteries of God until he know them in full. And they that will harden their hearts, to them is given the lesser portion of the word until they know nothing concerning his mysteries; and then they are taken captive by the devil, and led by his will down to destruction. Now this is what is meant by the chains of hell" (Alma 12:9–12).

The greatest miracle—and our greatest deliverance—comes not in deliverance from our trials, challenges, temptations, or tendencies, but rather in deliverance from our unbelief, our faithlessness, independence, vanity, and pride. As we give "heed and diligence" to Him (Mosiah 1:16), the Lord gives us "a new heart and a new Spirit" (Ezekiel 18:31) that can understand His mysteries—His mercy, His grace, His love, and His redeeming and enabling power being among the greatest of them.

When Alma and his brethren were captured by Amulon and the other priests of Noah as they fled the city of Nephi, they covenanted with the Lord and pleaded for freedom from the bondage they were in. Even though they were a willing and faithful people who had first heeded the word of Abinadi and then of Alma, they were still subject to some spiritual blindness, and there were lessons the Lord wanted to teach them before their physical deliverance. They needed to learn greater patience and faith and humility.

As "they did pour out their hearts" unto God, He poured out His Spirit in return, consoling them in the midst of the time of their greatest need, saying, "Lift up your heads and be of good comfort, for I know of the covenant which ye have made unto me; and I will covenant with my people and deliver them out of bondage. And I will also ease the burdens which are put upon your shoulders, that even you cannot feel them upon your backs, even while you are in bondage; and this will I do that ye may stand as witnesses for me hereafter, and that ye may know of a surety that I, the Lord God, do visit my people in their afflictions" (Mosiah 24:12–13).

With the word of their Master in their heart, "the burdens which were laid upon Alma and his brethren were made light; yea, the Lord did strengthen them that they could bear up their burdens with ease, and they did submit cheerfully and with patience to all the will of the Lord" (Mosiah 24:15). This cheerful submission and patience—their new heart and spirit—were something they needed to learn before they could truly be free, even in the absence of their captors. The patience, humility, and willingness to "wait upon the Lord" that came as the result of faith and prayer are something that each of us can hope and pray and live for (Isaiah 40:31).

Another powerful type for eternal deliverance can be found in the circumstances of Israel leading up to the coming of the Messiah. It had long been prophesied that Christ would come into the world to redeem His covenant people. Since the beginning of Roman rule, the Jews had looked forward to His coming, thinking that Christ would save them from their physical bondage and set them free. But the long-awaited Christ came in a manner entirely unexpected to most. He came as a child, a seemingly insignificant babe in a manger, who had no intention of freeing the Jews from their Roman captivity—at least, not their physical captivity. He knew that it was much more important to free them from their spiritual captivity.

So instead of trying to destroy those whom the Jews viewed as their enemies, which would have done nothing for the eternal salvation of His people, Jesus Christ made it so anything the enemy did to those who accepted Him would be eternally ineffectual. It is most tragic that when Jesus did not deliver His people in the way they hoped or expected, many were blinded to the eternal deliverance that He did offer them. They turned their backs and hardened their hearts. Likewise, most of us will die without ever witnessing complete physical deliverance from our enemies, whatever form of trial, challenge, or temptation that may be. But that is secondary to the spiritual deliverance of a mighty change of heart, increased faith in Christ, and affections toward righteousness, despite the wickedness and temptation beating upon us incessantly in this fallen world.

The physical deliverance is promised, but that deliverance may not happen when we want or expect it. Even in the "bondage" of same-gender attraction, I am grateful that the Lord has put into me "a new heart"— that He comforts me and strengthens me as I strive to learn to more fully "submit cheerfully and with patience" (Mosiah 24:15). While I was once in bondage to a lack of understanding of God's purposes, I feel I am now in the process of being delivered through the faith and understanding that God has a purpose in allowing me to experience my particular trials.

I cannot say that I do not have the hope that the physical deliverance—deliverance from the nature of my attractions—will come at some point in mortality, but that may not be the miracle I receive. My salvation does not depend upon that happening in this second estate. The miracle here may be a continual increase of faith, a change of heart, and deeper love for the Savior—faith and affections strong enough to see me through further storms, tempests, and temptations. I don't believe I can righteously expect more than that, though I can hope and pray and live for it. All I can do is open up my heart and my life and be prepared for whatever miracles He may continue to see fit to perform in me.

The Miracle of God

One miracle I experienced came at a time when I needed it most. I was feeling desperate and discouraged: I had reached a point where I was ready to give up in my fight. I turned to the scriptures—and to the Lord in prayer as I studied—in a final effort to find renewed hope and a reason to continue faithful. I read an account in the scriptures and felt a powerful spiritual witness that helped me to regain perspective and the hope I was longing for. It's an event in the life of Jesus that has come to epitomize the way I feel about my life and my relationship with Him. It's the miracle of Peter walking on the water toward Jesus.

The disciples were commanded by the Lord to "go before him unto the other side" while he remained to disperse the multitudes and to pray. By evening the ship was "in the midst of the sea, tossed with waves: for the wind was contrary." Later, "Jesus went unto them, walking on the sea. And when the disciples saw him walking on the sea, they were troubled, saying, It is a spirit; and they cried out for fear.

"But straightway Jesus spake unto them, saying, Be of good cheer; it is I; be not afraid.

"And Peter answered him and said, Lord, if it be thou, bid me come unto thee on the water.

"And he said, Come.

"And when Peter was come down out of the ship, he walked on the water, to go to Jesus. But when he saw the wind boisterous, he was afraid; and beginning to sink, he cried, saying, Lord, save me.

"And immediately Jesus stretched forth his hand, and caught him, and said unto him, O thou of little faith, wherefore didst thou doubt?

"And when they were come into the ship, the wind ceased. Then they that were in the ship came and worshipped him, saying, Of a truth thou art the Son of God" (Matthew 14:22–33).

As Peter walked toward the Savior, he "saw the wind boisterous" and feared and began to sink. The Spirit impressed upon me with great power when I read these verses that the wind was "boisterous" before Peter began to walk on the water, but when Peter's eyes were fixed on the Savior, he didn't notice—he seemed completely unaware—and he walked on water. Not until he took his eyes off the Son of God did Peter notice the storm, fear, and begin to sink. I too at times have shifted my gaze from the Savior and toward the storms, tempests, and temptations of mortality. As I have allowed myself to do that, I have feared, and my faith has wavered. As I have focused on divorce statistics, broken homes, and broken covenants in the lives of others who also experience same-gender attraction, I have begun to sink in faith and in desire for righteous goals. The storms are blowing today, and Satan is raging. I hear the voice and feel the influence of the adversary beating upon me incessantly.

But one of the most beautiful parts of the story is that as soon as Peter turned his focus back to the Savior, crying, "Lord, save me," Jesus "immediately . . . stretched forth his hand, and caught him." As surely as He was there for Peter, when I have cried out, "Lord, save me," I have felt Him reach forth His hand, catch me, and lift me up. When my eyes and focus have returned to my Redeemer, I have resumed walking upon the waters. I have lived a miracle.

Could I really live the rest of my life faithful to Christ if I were never to marry, which means living without romantic love and companionship and the accompanying family we naturally yearn for? Just as the natural man would tell me no, so would natural law require Peter to sink as he tried to walk on the water. Yet I believe in a power and a law much greater than that of the natural world. Thus, the only fair and truthful answer is related to Peter and his experience with the Savior: Peter walked on water as long as he was focused on Christ. I believe I will be able to live faithful to Him only as long as I am doing the things that will help me to keep my focus on Him. To do so will require a miracle. But the Lord has said, "I am a God of miracles" (2 Nephi 27:23), and I must believe Him. I have to believe that our Father in Heaven, as a literal Parent, loves me personally, is interested in my life and progress, and is willing to bestow upon me whatever blessing I truly need and am open to receive. President Brigham Young said poignantly, "If you do not believe it, cease to call him Father; and when you pray, pray to some other character."[5]

I believe that Jesus can perform miracles just as readily today as when He walked the streets of Jerusalem. I've witnessed and experienced them. Working with individuals on my mission and with youth in the Church and in the Missionary Training Center, I've seen hearts change as they have felt the power of the Spirit of the Lord. I have friends whose parents and family members once lived not only with misunderstanding but with prejudice and phobia toward those who experience same-gender attraction. I have witnessed the softening of their hearts, and they have embraced their children and me not just in spite of our attraction but *with* it. To me, such a change of heart and increase in charity and understanding is a miracle. Even if I do experience same-gender attraction for the rest of my life, I believe I can have peace with the challenge and live completely faithful to the gospel of Christ. To me, that is likewise a miracle.

People have come to Christ in the past and partaken of the fruit of His love only to turn away for one reason or another toward the "great and spacious" building (1 Nephi 8:26). Alma once asked of the backsliding Nephites: "If ye have experienced a change of heart, and if ye have felt to sing the song of redeeming love, I would ask, can ye feel so now?" (Alma 5:26). Israel had their doubts, and Lot's wife looked back at Gomorrah.

The greatest miracle is in the continued change of heart—the ability through the enabling grace of Christ to turn to Him without looking back, despite our trials and challenges, not in the absence of them. There is also the superlative miracle of forgiveness provided by the infinite and redeeming atonement of the Savior for those who have turned away after partaking of the fruit and who yearn to return to Him whose "arm is lengthened out all the day long" (2 Nephi 28:32).

Referring to those who were converted through the preaching of the sons of Mosiah on their mission to the Lamanites, the record of Alma reads, "As many as believed, or as many as were brought to the knowledge of the truth . . . according to the spirit of revelation and of prophecy, and the power of God working miracles in them—yea, I say unto you . . . as many of the Lamanites as believed . . . and were converted unto the Lord, never did fall away" (Alma 23:6). Many of the real miracles of God today that have impressed me most are those I know who experience same-gender attraction and who quietly choose every day to follow their Father in Heaven, who daily strive to turn their hearts to the Lord because of their faith in the Christ and in His delivering power.

I feel as though I am living a miracle as I continue forward in my faith. The miracles I pray for now, though, are much different. Now I plead for the miracle of an ever-continuing change of heart. I pray for the change of heart that will lead me to continue to walk to Him across the waters of mortality. I pray for miracles and then choose to live for them. As I give up my life—my natural life—so that He might live in and through me, I am a miracle of God. Yes, I do believe He is "a God of miracles" (2 Nephi 27:23).

Chapter 4

"That I May Prove Them"

In the premortal councils, a loving Father made known a plan that would allow each of His children to have all that He has and become all that He is. If His life—eternal life—truly is the life of joy and goodness that He has revealed it to be, His very nature of selfless love and righteousness requires Him to want the same for us. The Lord declared to the mortal Moses, "This is my work and my glory—to bring to pass the immortality and eternal life of man" (Moses 1:39). But eternal life is not simply living forever. God is eternal, and eternal life is God's life—it is the kind of life He lives (see D&C 18:4–12). And if He is married in the heavens, as He has revealed through modern prophets, then eternal marriage is essential for us—if we want not just to be *with* Him in the celestial kingdom but also to be *like* Him in the highest glory or degree within that kingdom. Marriage is the institution of the highest of all heavenly realms. It is the highest order of the Gods.

These wondrous doctrines restored in the last days through the Prophet Joseph Smith provide a theological foundation for the latter-day Church, now noted for its emphasis on marriage and family. But those same doctrines are bittersweet to those who believe them—or who at least "desire to believe" them (Alma 32:27)—and are pained to understand how the unsolicited challenge of same-gender attraction could possibly fit into the theological framework of God's "great plan of happiness" spoken of in the scriptures (Alma 42:8).

Marriage has always been something I looked forward to. Though I knew for the longest time that I was attracted to other men, I also knew that marriage was something in the fairly distant future that I didn't have to worry about then, so I didn't need to confront my feelings yet. But after returning from my mission and facing the now pressing need to find an eternal companion, I was forced to recognize that for me, any natural attraction to women was all but absent.

Still, never doubting that marriage was a realistic option for me, I took a religion class on marriage and family that seemed appropriate for learning how to better fulfill my future role as a husband and father. On many occasions in those classes, the Spirit impressed upon me a feeling for the sanctity of marriage and the importance of the role of the family in the eternities. The fire and desire within me to have an eternal family intensified. I remember leaving class on a few occasions with great hope that I would someday have the kind of family that idealistically I saw as not being too far from reality. But I was rarely far from the classroom door when I was confronted with a much more present reality—a different fire, a fire kindled by my attraction to the men I saw, which contrasted harshly with my desire for that ideal family.

The war within me gradually became more intense, and discouragement plagued me as I continued to suppress my feelings. Once while I was skiing, I saw a man who was incredibly attractive. I stopped for a second to watch what he was doing, and then my heart ached and the internal conflict raged again. I watched him patiently and encouragingly wait for his four-year-old son to ski up to him, after which he tutored the eager young disciple. In that moment, the two different fires were contrasted more sharply than I had ever felt them, and I cried at the increasing loss of hope that I might never have in mortality that which I most wanted. I slowly continued down the slope, longing for the possibility that I might someday have my own family and my own sons to teach how to ski.

After I finally hit the point of despair that led me to confess my suppressed attractions to my bishop, I went on a trip to Nauvoo, Illinois. While there, I left the group one night to wander the historic city. I needed time to think and be alone as the newness of my confrontation with my very real challenge continued to consume my mind. At one point I found myself at the Memorial to Women garden outside the LDS Visitors' Center. I wandered through the garden until I came to a statue of young parents teaching a child to walk. As my gazed fixed upon this touching scene, an almost audible voice spoke directly to the immortal part of me: "Behold, the plan of God." I felt I was standing on sacred ground as the power that accompanied those words encompassed me. The Spirit impressed upon me the significance and importance of the family in the eternities, and the hope and desire to strive for that kind of family was rekindled within me.

While pondering that simple statue in a new, powerful light, I received an additional insight. The Spirit impressed upon me the importance of understanding that as a literal father, God is trying to teach me something here in mortality, in my spiritually infant state. Just as important—or more so—as striving to achieve an eternal companionship is understanding that during my experience here in this second estate, He is teaching me how to walk by faith, how to follow the example of His Son, and how to become like Him. I felt that though I would stumble and fall many times in the process, I am His child, and because He is actively involved in my life, He would lovingly encourage me to get back up and continue striving forward so that I would learn the spiritual lessons necessary for exaltation. I would be chastened, tried, and sent through a refining fire—He would allow me to suffer whatever challenges were necessary so that I would be purified. That night I learned something more about the ultimate purpose of mortality.

"Thine Only Son Whom Thou Lovest"

As I have continued to ponder the primary purpose of this mortal existence, the life and experiences of Abraham have often come to my mind. After the Father had presented His plan of salvation in those premortal councils, the foreordained Savior stood before the premortal Abraham and other noble spirit children of God and said, "We will make an earth whereon these may dwell; and we will prove them herewith, *to see if they will do all things whatsoever the Lord their God shall command them*" (Abraham 3:24–25; italics added). Even though the Eternal Father wants us to be like Him, we first have to go through a period of probation and testing to see if we will faithfully put Him first in our lives.

During his mortal sojourn, that same Abraham was later known as "father of the faithful" (D&C 138:14). He exemplified one who honestly and earnestly seeks for truth. "He believed in the Lord; and he counted it to him for righteousness" (Genesis 15:6). But even in his righteousness he had to learn just how heartrending the Lord's premortal declaration would be. When the childless Abraham was in his old age, the Lord visited him, covenanted with him, and offered him profound blessings concerning his seed (Genesis 17:1–9). Mighty blessings concerning his mortal posterity and eternal life and eternal increase were promised, but these blessings were not unconditional. The Lord had confidence in Abraham, but he would still have to prove himself and keep his part of the covenant to "keep the way of the Lord, to do justice and judgment; that the Lord may bring upon Abraham that which he hath spoken of him" (Genesis 18:19). Before the blessings could be bestowed, God tested Abraham to see if he would follow that premortal call to obey Him in *all* things (Abraham 3:24–25).

Years later, Sarah finally conceived in her old age and bore the miraculous birthright child of promise—the fulfillment of the Lord's earlier blessing. In that belated birth, Abraham knew the Lord's promises were sure and that He was powerful "unto the fulfilling of all his words" (1 Nephi 9:6). Several more years later, the Lord's purifying process was driven into the very heart of Abraham. The Great Jehovah commanded him: "Take now thy son, thine only son Isaac, whom thou lovest, and get thee into the land of Moriah; and offer him there for a burnt offering" (Genesis 22:2).

The story of Abraham taking a willing Isaac to the top of Mount Moriah is a touching and inspiring type of the future offering of the Only Begotten for all mankind, but it is also more. It was essential that Abraham place that which represented his very heart and soul—his son, whom he loved—on the altar to prove his faith in, commitment to, and fear of God so his exaltation could be realized (Genesis 22:1–14). Abraham must have been at a loss to know how the Lord would fulfill His promises concerning his seed if He was commanding him to sacrifice that very seed. Despite the mind-boggling contradictions of the situation, however, Abraham had undoubting faith; though the experience was heartrending, he had full confidence that somehow God could and would fulfill all His promises.

The apostle Paul later bore witness of Abraham's profound faith: "By faith Abraham, when he was tried, offered up Isaac: and he that had received the promises offered up his only begotten son, Of whom it was said, That in Isaac shall thy seed be called: accounting that God was able to raise him up, even from the dead; from whence also he received him in a figure" (Hebrews 11:17–19). With all the seeming incongruities and inconsistencies between the former blessings promised to Abraham and the current commandment from the Lord, for some reason Abraham had to be tried as he was. It was excruciatingly painful for Abraham, but the Lord sometimes commands us to give up that which we love most to teach us to love Him even more. The Prophet Joseph Smith taught, "If God had known any other way whereby he could have touched Abraham's feelings more acutely and more keenly he would have done so."[1] And because of the faith Abraham exercised in the Lord, he has "received all things . . . and hath entered into his exaltation and sitteth upon his throne" (D&C 132:29).

"Even As Abraham"

The same kind of proving that qualified Abraham for his exaltation is also necessary for every one of God's children. Joseph Smith, in speaking to the Twelve Apostles in Nauvoo, said: "You will have all kinds of trials to pass through. And it is quite as necessary for you to be tried as it was for Abraham and other men of God . . . God will feel after you, and he will take hold of you and wrench your very heart strings, and if you cannot stand it you will not be fit for an inheritance in the Celestial

Kingdom of God."[2] The Prophet Joseph Smith also taught that before any individual can be exalted, or have his calling and election made sure, he must learn to live "by every word of God" and be "thoroughly proved" until the Lord "finds that the man is determined to serve Him at all hazards."[3] Professor Larry Dahl of Brigham Young University commented, "'All hazards' may at times mean there will be no ram in the thicket, no angel to stop the knife, as there were with Abraham."[4]

Unlike Job who, though he was severely tried, received back all he had lost while he was still in mortality, the apostle Paul faced the reality that his recompense might be delayed until immortality. In a verse that I have often looked to for peace and purpose, Paul said, "And lest I should be exalted above measure through the abundance of the revelations, there was given to me a thorn in the flesh, the messenger of Satan to buffet me, lest I should be exalted above measure. For this thing I besought the Lord thrice, that it might depart from me. And he said unto me, My grace is sufficient for thee" (2 Corinthians 12:7–9).

Robert L. Millet, also of Brigham Young University, once said, "No one really knows what his 'thorn in the flesh' was. . . . I rather think that when Paul states that he 'besought the Lord thrice' for the removal of the thorn that he is not describing merely three prayers but instead three seasons of prayer, extended periods of wrestling and laboring in the Spirit for a specific blessing that never came."[5]

Larry Dahl commented: "Not only Paul but many of us may suffer from a thorn in the flesh or a weakness that is painful but purposeful, and which God may see fit not to remove. . . . Neither prayers nor tears nor blessings nor medicine relieves the condition. All that is left is to endure patiently. Truly, that wrenches the heartstrings."[6] Like Paul, I, too, have wrestled with the Lord for years that my thorn might be removed from me, but He has not yet seen fit to do so. And although it doesn't make the challenge easier, it does give meaning and purpose to my trial to know that the Lord is primarily concerned not in the nature of my attractions or challenges but rather in the nature of my heart and commitment to follow Him.

Like Abraham, who was tried by the Lord in a way that seemed inconsistent with previous promises, Latter-day Saints who belong to a Church that holds marriage and family among its most central and sacred of all eternal doctrines may wonder at the seeming inconsistency of an attraction that is so contrary to all they have been taught to value. But to receive the blessings of Abraham, Latter-day Saints who experience same-gender attraction must learn to exercise the faith of Abraham that somehow God can and will fulfill all His promises at some point in our eternal journey toward Godhood, whether those blessings are realized in this life or not.

With all the seeming incongruities and inconsistencies between the Lord's focus on marriage and the sacredness of sexual expression between eternal partners in creation, and the romantic or sexual attraction of some of His children toward their same gender, we must have faith that there is a reason we are being tried as we are. It may be at times painful or lonely, but we—even as Abraham—may be asked by the Lord to give up that which we love and think we want most in order to teach us to love Him and what He wants for us, even more. Such is the nature of this mortal probationary experience.

Elder Neal A. Maxwell observed: "In time each person will receive a 'customized challenge' to determine his dedication to God."[7] For some of the early Saints in the Church, the practice of plural marriage was a proving ground of faithfulness. Brigham Young, for example, said when first introduced to the idea: "I was not desirous of shrinking from any duty, nor of failing in the least to do as I was commanded, but it was the first time in my life that I had desired the grave, and I could hardly get over it for a long time. And when I saw a funeral, I felt to envy the corpse its situation, and to regret that I was not in the coffin, knowing the toil and labor that my body would have to undergo; and I have had to examine myself, from that day to this, and watch my faith, and carefully meditate, lest I should be found desiring the grave more than I ought to do."[8]

Since that time, the Saints of God have had their varying and individual tests and challenges to prove them in precisely the same fashion.

The Lord has specified that the faithful were to be tried, even unto death (D&C 98:12). To be sure, some needed to be tried even as Abraham in consequence of their righteousness. Some are prone to believe the false notion that goodness and righteousness exempt them from testing, trial, and tragedy; often it is quite to the contrary.

C. S. Lewis observed: "When a man turns to Christ and seems to be getting on pretty well (in the sense that some of his bad habits are now corrected), he often feels that it would now be natural if things went fairly smoothly. When troubles come along—illnesses, money troubles, new kinds of temptation—he is disappointed. These things, he feels, might have been necessary to rouse him and make him repent in his bad old days; but why now? Because God is forcing him on up, to a higher level: putting him into situations where he will have to be very much braver, or more patient, or more loving, than he ever dreamed of before. It seems to us all unnecessary: but that is because we have not yet not the slightest notion of the tremendous thing He means to make of us."[9]

A Fallen World

In speaking about Abrahamic tests, Professor Dahl cautioned: "We should remember that not all the difficulties that try the souls of men are specially designed Abrahamic tests from God. Most, in fact, are the inevitable consequences of living in a mortal, fallen world, where natural law and agency, for the most part, are allowed full sway. . . . Everyone experiences bumps in the road of life, which expose weaknesses and strengths, giving opportunity for self-understanding, growth, and refinement. We are not wise enough to sort out all the factors that contribute to our challenges in this life. The critical issue is not the source of the challenges, anyway. The critical issue is how we respond to them. We can lose our focus and our progress if we constantly examine every bump in the road to determine whose fault it is."[10]

When it comes to tests, trials, challenges, tragedies, and disappointments, it is important that we distinguish between what the Almighty *causes* to take place and what an all-powerful and all-loving God *allows* to take place. President Spencer W. Kimball once observed: "Did the Lord cause the man to suffer a heart attack? Was the death of the missionary untimely? Answer, if you can. I cannot, for though I know God has a major role in our lives, I do not know how much he causes to happen and how much he merely permits. . . . Could the Lord have prevented these tragedies? The answer is, Yes. The Lord is omnipotent, with all power to control our lives, save us pain, prevent all accidents, drive all planes and cars, feed us, protect us, save us from labor, effort, sickness, even from death, if he will. But he will not. . . . The basic gospel law is . . . agency and eternal development. To force us to be careful or righteous would be to nullify that fundamental law and make growth impossible."[11]

I have often wondered if the challenge of same-gender attraction is, for me, simply the fruit of living in this fallen world. Has the Lord simply allowed this trial to remain with me, knowing the good that could come from it, or has He caused or designed this challenge for me with a specific purpose in mind? In the end, though, the answer doesn't really matter, as long as I do live so that I learn whatever the Lord would have me learn. Many of the conditions we experience here on earth are simply consequences of the Fall, and we are frequently brought face to face with the truth that for this temporal time and season not all well-laid plans or cultural expectations will come to fruition.

Professor Millet taught, "It seems to me that there is a mindset characteristic of our day, that opens us to despair. That mindset is one in which we assume, given all the pleasures and luxuries of our day and age, that all should be well with us, that we should be perpetually happy. Many of us imbibed the jargon and the philosophy of our pop psychology world. The fact is, life can be tough. We are not guaranteed a stress free existence, nor did the Lord promise us a mortal life void of challenge and difficulty . . . It is especially challenging for persons who view God solely as a dispenser of good gifts and happy times to fathom how and in what manner he is related, if at all, to earthly trauma. Having been brought up on a constant diet of 'God is love' or 'God is good,' they inevitably equate such goodness with kindness."[12]

C. S. Lewis said: "By the goodness of God we mean nowadays almost exclusively His lovingness; and in this we may be right. And by Love, in this context, most of us mean kindness—the desire to see others than the self happy; not happy in this way or in that, but just happy. What would really satisfy us would be a God who said of anything we happened to like doing, 'What does it matter so long as they are contented?' We want, in fact, not so much a Father in Heaven as a grandfather in heaven—a senile benevolence who, as they say, 'liked to see young people enjoying themselves,' and whose plan for the universe was simply that it might be truly said at the end of each day, 'a good time was had by all.'"[13]

Or, as another Christian scholar has observed: "Theism does not affirm that God is always 'nice' or pleasant or kindly. God's goodness is absolute purity, as much like the purity of a blast furnace . . . as it is like the indulgence of a sweet grandmother. God always does the right thing; God always wills what is best; God always thinks without error, incompleteness, or prejudice. Such a God may not always be likable, nor always comfortable. But such a God may well be worthy of worship."[14]

Elder Neal A. Maxwell reminded us: "When we tear ourselves free from the entanglements of the world, are we promised a religion of repose or an Eden of ease? No! We are promised tears and trials and toil! But we are also promised final triumph, the mere contemplation of which tingles the soul."[15]

Just as Abraham knew in our first estate that he would have to enter a mortal probation where his obedience and faithfulness would be proved, we also were very much aware that challenges and tests would lie ahead, and we were aware to some degree of what life would be like here. But still we shouted for joy in that premortal day (Job 38:4, 7) because we knew that there were lessons and principles to be learned on earth, relationships to be developed, feelings to be felt, and tests to be passed—things we could neither grasp nor experience in our first estate.

Every one of us will, at one time or another, face adversity, whether in the form of personal tragedy, challenges such as same-gender attraction, or simply profound disappointment from any number of causes. We must not yield to discouragement. Rather, we must put our trust in a perfect Father who has perfect love and perfect vision. "Where is God when it hurts?" Robert Millet asked. "He is in his heavens. He is aware. He knows. In ways that we cannot even comprehend, he knows. And he blesses and lifts and liberates and lightens the burdens of his children whenever he can. But he cannot remove us from the toils and tragedies and contradictions of life without robbing us of mortal experience. These things come with the turf. They are part of the test. So much depends upon how we choose to look upon what most consider to be the unfairness and the senseless nature of temporal trauma. So much depends upon what we understand about God our Father, about his plan of salvation, and about how vital it is for us to move ahead, even when our burdens or the burdens of others seem unbearable."[16]

One thing that has been deeply impressed upon me in trying to understand the seeming inconsistency between the nature of a challenge such as same-gender attraction and the central role of the family in the gospel—especially when the attraction feels so innate and much more than physical or sexual—is that there is so much we simply do not know about influencing factors and the degree to which we may have understood in the premortal existence the challenges or tests we individually would experience here in our second estate. President Boyd K. Packer made an analogy that has helped me to feel much more comfortable about the many things that I don't understand or that the Lord has chosen not to reveal to his children at this time. President Packer said: "There are three parts to the plan. You are in the second or the middle part, the one in which you will be tested by temptation, by trials, perhaps by tragedy. Understand that, and you will be better able to make sense of life and to resist the disease of doubt and despair and depression. . . .

"In mortality, we are like one who enters a theater just as the curtain goes up on the second act. We have missed Act I. The production has many plots and sub-plots that interweave, making it difficult to figure out who relates to whom and what relates to what, who are the heros and who are the villains. It is further complicated because you are not just a spectator; you are a member of the cast, on stage, in the middle of it all!

"As part of the eternal plan, the memory of our premortal life, Act I, is covered with a veil. Since you enter mortality at the beginning of Act II with no recollection of Act I, it is little wonder that it is difficult to understand what is going on. That loss of memory gives us a clean start. It is ideal for the test; it secures our individual agency, and leaves us free to make choices. Many of them must be made on faith alone. Even so, we carry with us some whispered knowledge of our pre-mortal life and our status as offspring of immortal parents . . .

"If you expect to find only ease and peace and bliss during Act II, you surely will be frustrated. You will understand little of what is going on and why [things are] permitted to be as they are. Remember this! The line 'And they all lived happily ever after' is never written into the second act. That line belongs in the third act when the mysteries are solved and everything is put right . . .

"Until you have a broad perspective of the eternal nature of this great drama, you won't make much sense out of the inequities in life. Some are born with so little and others with so much, some in poverty, with handicaps, with pain, with suffering, premature death even of innocent children. There are the brutal, unforgiving forces of nature and the brutality of man to man . . . Do not suppose that God willfully causes that, which for His own purposes, he permits. When you know the plan and purpose of it all, even these things will manifest a loving Father in Heaven."[17]

The wonderful part of the plan of salvation—one in which we who live in the fulness of times and who know of the restored gospel can be especially grateful for—is that the Lord has not left us alone in trying to figure things out for ourselves. Although we have been given limited insight into the premortal existence through the scriptures, it is not sufficient to eliminate all confusion about why things are the way they are. Perhaps it was intended to be that way. Our Father in Heaven has called prophets today to lead and guide us as to how we should live and respond to the various challenges, trials, and temptations mortality presents us with. Those who insist on making life's most crucial and defining decisions based solely on what they can see and understand in this fallen state and in their immediate environment—independent of the men whom the Lord has called to sit as "watchmen on the tower"—will surely be frustrated.

The Potential to Purify

James Allen suggested that "circumstance does not make the man; it reveals him to himself."[18] There is a purifying work of pain, a divine work that can transform the soul of the distressed individual, if he or she approaches the difficulty with the proper attitude. The response of the Nephites at the end of the series of wars recorded in the book of Alma demonstrated that trials, challenges, and chastening can make us bitter or they can make us better. Mormon writes, "Because of the exceedingly great length of the war between the Nephites and the Lamanites many had become hardened, because of the exceedingly great length of the war; and many were softened because of their afflictions, insomuch that they did humble themselves before God, even in the depth of humility" (Alma 62:41).

Our challenges or other tragedies can bring us strength but only if we allow them to. Spiritual strength and faith in Jesus Christ is not just something that happens to us. It is Christ and His atonement—not the trial itself—that strengthens and purifies us, but He can do so only if we consciously turn to Him. Most of these Nephites were members of the ancient Church. Both those whose hearts were hardened and those who were humbled through their challenges likely heard the same sermons and Sunday School lessons and had much of the same knowledge, but their hearts were obviously different. They most likely knew the teachings of the prophets, but many didn't apply that knowledge.

Agency is an essential gift when it comes to practicing and applying the Lord's word and choosing either our circumstances or our attitude within a set of circumstances, should aspects of our lives fall victim to others' unrighteous use of agency. In describing the attitude of some

Holocaust victims, one survivor has written: "We who lived in concentration camps can remember the men who walked through the huts comforting others, giving away their last piece of bread. They may have been few in number, but they offer sufficient proof that everything can be taken from a man but one thing: the last of . . . human freedoms—to choose one's attitude in any given set of circumstances, [and] to choose one's own way [of life]."[19]

A most poignant scriptural example in which circumstance revealed character and either purified or caused dissention—and which, to me, demonstrates parallel attitudes on both sides to what I have seen in individuals who experience same-gender attraction—is that of Nephi and his brothers in the wilderness. Lehi, a prophet, did not hesitate when he was commanded to take his family into the wilderness. It did not seem to his family to be an ideal opportunity, but the Lord commanded, and Lehi trusted that the Lord would take care of them. He simply "was obedient unto the word of the Lord, wherefore he did as the Lord commanded him" (1 Nephi 2:3). Although it seems from the record that Nephi had not yet received his own spiritual witness at the time of what the Lord was requiring them to do, he believed his father and followed him. It was later, while in the wilderness, that he received his own confirmation.

Nephi, who had "great desires to know the mysteries of God," cried unto the Lord. He sought diligently a personal witness from the Lord, and the Lord visited him through the power of the Holy Ghost and softened his heart, so that Nephi "did believe all the words which had been spoken by [his] father" (1 Nephi 2:16). That personal communion with the Lord gave him the knowledge, faith, courage, power, and strength to continue on in the wilderness in the way the Lord would have him go. Because of his willingness to go to the Lord, the Lord purified him through a trial Nephi didn't immediately understand the significance of.

Laman and Lemuel, on the other hand, murmured at being asked to leave all their worldly possessions—"their inheritance, and their gold, and their silver, and their precious things"—and the life that was most natural and comfortable to them, only to "perish in the wilderness." And they murmured, according to Nephi, because they did not understand "the dealings of that God who had created them" (1 Nephi 2:11–12). When the commandment came for them to go back to Jerusalem, Laman and Lemuel again murmured; Nephi, on the contrary, declared: "I will go and do the things which the Lord hath commanded, for I know that the Lord giveth no commandments unto the children of men, save he shall prepare a way for them that they may accomplish the thing which he commandeth them" (1 Nephi 3:7).

I really believe that dealing in a healthy way with same-gender attraction and staying true to the faith can be compared to traveling in the wilderness. Being led into the wilderness away from that which is natural and comfortable to those who face this challenge is not necessarily an enticing prospect, but if we—individuals who experience same-gender attraction—keep the commandments of God, He will nourish us and strengthen us and purify us in the process, providing means whereby we can accomplish the thing that He has commanded us to do. We can stay true to His word and His commandments during this struggle, and we can have faith that our life will not be barren if He is in it. When we understand more fully the dealings of God, we are much less likely to murmur because of our trials and challenges. This challenge has been terribly difficult for me, and I have done a lot of murmuring myself, but as the Lord has helped me to see more fully His dealings with me and the rest of His children, I have felt much less inclined to murmur and more inclined to faithfully submit.

One other thing that really struck me as similar to the response of many who experience same-gender attraction is Lehi's telling Nephi of the commandment to go back to Jerusalem to get the plates. "Behold thy brothers murmur, saying it is a hard thing I have required of them; but behold I have not required it of them, but it is a commandment of the Lord" (1 Nephi 3:5). Individuals who experience same-gender attraction are asked, along with all other members of the Lord's Church, to live a life of complete chastity, which means seeking a marital relationship with someone of the opposite gender when we are ready for that step, or, if there is no opportunity for marriage in this life, to live celibate.

When that doctrine is taught, many question the authority of the Church to make such a requirement, but in reality it is the Lord requiring it. Such questioners utter nearly the exact words of Laman and Lemuel: "Thou hast declared unto us hard things, more than we are able to bear." Nephi's stinging rebuke is especially potent: "If ye were righteous and were willing . . ." (1 Nephi 16:1, 3). Those who murmur are those who have not developed personal communion with the Lord and sought His will on the matter with a sufficiently willing heart. Those who have testimonies of the Lord's chosen servants need not question that what they have been taught about chastity and morality is directly from the Lord Himself. They are entitled to a spiritual witness, but Nephi's witness came after he already believed in the commandments of the Lord to his father and acted on that belief—and not before. We must have the faith to put our lives completely in His hands and trust that he will not leave us to die in the wilderness. We must believe that He will sustain us and that we can have happiness and peace even in the most seemingly unlikely of circumstances.

A parallel attitude is found in the way Laman and Lemuel felt about the commandment to build a ship. They murmured against Nephi, saying they didn't feel he could build a ship that could cross the great waters. It was a monumental task, and they "were desirous that they might not labor" (1 Nephi 17:18). First of all, the required effort was tremendous. Second, "they did not believe" Nephi could build a ship (1 Nephi 17:18). They did not believe it was either possible or necessary to do such a thing. Many individuals who experience same-gender attraction have a similar attitude. They do not believe that it's possible—or desirable or necessary—to cross the waters of mortality in the way the Lord has commanded.

The contrast of attitudes between Nephi and his brothers is significant to me. I've been so inspired by individuals who have sought the attitude of Nephi and approached their circumstances with faith, believing that because the Lord has commanded, He will prepare a way. As the children of God, we are "gods in embryo,"[20] and the Lord has indicated that being chastened and tried is a prerequisite to being sanctified (D&C 101:4–5). C. S. Lewis taught, "We are, not metaphorically but in very truth, a Divine work of art, something that God is making, and therefore something with which He will not be satisfied until it has a certain character." Thus it is perfectly "natural for us to wish that God had designed for us a less glorious and less arduous destiny; but then we are wishing not for more love but for less."[21]

The Eternal Eye

One of the lessons I think the Lord is trying to teach me, and which I am only beginning to learn, is that there is a lot more equality to all the trials, challenges, and tests of mortality than I would like to think. He knows and loves every one of us equally as His children. He knows our weaknesses and our strengths, and He tailors our experience to fit our needs—what we individually need to learn and experience to help us to become more like Him and to gain the "mind of Christ," as Paul termed it (1 Corinthians 2:16). President Boyd K. Packer stated:

"Our lives are made up of thousands of everyday choices. Over the years these little choices will be bundled together and show clearly what we value.

"The crucial test of life, I repeat, does not center in the choice between fame and obscurity, nor between wealth and poverty. The greatest decision of life is between good and evil.

"We may foolishly bring unhappiness and trouble, even suffering, upon ourselves. These are not always to be regarded as penalties imposed by a displeased Creator. They are part of the lessons of life, part of the test.

"Some are tested by poor health, some by a body that is deformed or homely. Others are tested by handsome and healthy bodies; some by the passion of youth; others by the erosions of age.

"Some suffer disappointment in marriage, family problems; others live in poverty and obscurity. Some (perhaps this is the hardest test) find ease and luxury.

"All are part of the test, and there is more equality in this testing than sometimes we suspect.

"It is possible to be both rich and famous and at the same time succeed spiritually. But the Lord warned of the difficulty of it when He talked of camels and needles (see Matt. 19:24)."[22]

It has been difficult for me—as one who experiences same-gender attraction, a challenge that often seems impossible to bear and remain faithful—to recognize the possibility that my cross is not more unbearable than those that others may be called to carry; to be sure, it is different, but it is not unequal or more unbearable. For the way we see our own trials or the trials of others depends upon the lenses through which we view them—through social, mortal eyes or through spiritual, eternal eyes. When viewed through the latter, almost all challenges, attractions, temptations, or tendencies can try our commitment to God and full worship of Him. The poor can be just as wicked as the rich, the young as the old, and those with heterosexual attractions as those with homosexual attractions.

Francis Webster, a member of the Martin handcart company, said, "We suffered beyond anything you can imagine and many died of exposure and starvation, but . . . every one of us came through with the absolute knowledge that God lives for we became acquainted with him in our extremities."[23] On more than one occasion I have wished I could have suffered with the worst conditions the handcart companies endured rather than experience this challenge. But in reality, my own challenges have equal capacity to draw me to my knees. Once, while I was visiting with a counselor, he wisely stated, "Well, if you're going to remain faithful, you are going to need to stay close to the Savior. With a challenge like this there is certainly no room for spiritual apathy." Those words rang true to me when he first said them, and I have since come to understand to an even greater degree how profound they are.

We see the great differences between the types of challenges we experience when we view those challenges through social eyes. According to Elder Packer's statement, some would feel it much less of a trial to have an extremely beautiful and healthy body—there is little social condemnation for that—than to have an ugly, malformed, or unhealthy body. Concerning attraction and sexuality, some may prefer the trial of an unhealthy or overzealous heterosexual appetite, because popular culture as a whole is much more accepting of a hyper-heterosexual drive and often promiscuous indulgence of that drive than it is of even minimal homosexual attraction.

When we view challenges from an eternal perspective, however, we realize there is more equality in the trials than we would sometimes like to admit. The principles of salvation are not always in accord with political correctness or social acceptability or justice. It takes a true sense of eternal vision or eternal eyes to see it, but it is there, and "where there is no vision, the people perish" (Proverbs 29:18).

It is true that heterosexuals who fail to keep their thoughts clean and master the flesh will find their passions just as damning as will those who experience homosexual attractions and succumb to them. I read a statement a while ago that was tough to hear, but the Spirit testified to my heart it was true. Elder Vaughn J. Featherstone said: "President J. Reuben Clark gave me great light many years ago on a great tremendous subject. He said (and these are my words, not his) that the sex urge does not have to be satisfied. That is Satan's old lie that it *does* have to be satisfied."[24]

The eternal standard of chastity in thought and in action is the same, whether one experiences homosexual or heterosexual attraction. Those who experience same-gender attraction may think the real test is to become heterosexual, but that is false. It's not about getting married, having "x" number of children, or reaching an ideal level of heterosexual attraction. The real test is in mastering the flesh and placing our hearts and wills on the altar of God. The real test is not in our attractions or tendencies but rather in turning our hearts to the Savior. The point is, all of us have tests that must bring us to submission before the Master of our souls.

While recognizing that on a spiritual plane there is more equality in the testing than we may at first think, some compare the plight of those who experience same-gender attraction with the challenge of other single individuals who are unable to marry for whatever reason. Because God's work and glory are the eternal life of His children—and eternal life includes eternal marriage—our ultimate work and glory should be the same, which means preparing for or seeking an eternal relationship with someone of the opposite gender. All of God's children are asked to live His law of chastity in thought and action, but that requirement of spiritual and moral fidelity manifests different social challenges for different individuals, depending on the nature and degree of their mortal attractions. Single, heterosexual adults are urged to date, to seek romance, and to marry a member of the opposite sex for whom they feel a natural attraction. They are asked to temper their attractions until they are able to find someone with whom they can naturally share their heart and life and most intimate unifying passions. But if they are faithful to the gospel of Christ and yet, for whatever reason, are unable to marry and find love, emotional intimacy, and fulfillment in this life, they are reminded that no matter how difficult the emotional and physical loneliness may be, it is only temporary—all their loneliness and trials will be stripped away in the next life, and they will find peace. They are painstakingly given something of immeasurable value in the struggle to stay faithful and true—hope.

On the other hand, those who have feelings of same-gender attraction and who desire to remain true to the gospel of Christ and His law of chastity experience different social challenges. Same-gender attraction brings with it a stigma, misunderstanding, and taboo. Most who experience this attraction grow up feeling that they or their attractions are inherently evil and, therefore, they learn quickly how to hide or suppress their feelings in order to be accepted by those they love and to fulfill the social and religious roles expected of them. If those who feel such attractions are unable to change their attraction, despite persistent efforts, they are often—whether intentionally or not—caused to feel guilt and shame for it. Because same-gender romantic relationships cannot be eternal, if persons with same-gender attraction want to remain faithful to the gospel of Christ, they cannot date, seek romance, and fall in love with one to whom they feel naturally attracted. The reminder of eternal hope—unqualified by the condition of "change"—is often withheld or too slowly extended. And something that is often a greater challenge than the feelings of same-gender attraction themselves is the fear of rejection by parents or siblings—a fear that is, sadly, sometimes a reality—and the fear that others may not allow them associate with their children lest those children become infected or recruited, as if same-gender attraction were a disease or something that is always taught.

Whether one is heterosexual or homosexual, however, the call to "believe in Christ, and view his death, and suffer his cross and bear the shame of the world" (Jacob 1:8) and come unto Christ is the call of every true Christian. It is important to recognize that though we may perceive similarities and differences in our trials, we must be careful in comparison, for the mortal suffering we experience cannot be quantified. Regardless of the nature of the cause, pain is still pain, and deprivation is still deprivation—but to every one of us is extended the promise of hope and peace that if we have willing and humble hearts, our individual challenges or tests will bring us to Christ and help us to learn the eternal lessons He would have us learn in this mortal, probationary state. Each one of us has the promise that the Savior of the world will dry our tears, heal our wounds, and bind our broken hearts. We can know that He is watchful, careful, and ever mindful and loving. He knows the needs of each one of his children and is aware of our individual passions, fears, trials, and challenges.

"The Will of the Father in All Things"

Joseph Smith taught that "a religion that does not require the sacrifice of all things never has power sufficient to produce the faith necessary unto life and salvation."[25] It is through the challenge of same-gender attraction more than any other that I have had to learn to put my life completely in the Lord's hands—to try to develop the kind of faith that the Prophet is speaking of here. I'm grateful that the Lord has given me—or allowed to remain with me—whatever experience He felt was necessary to teach me this lesson on faith and sacrifice and the many other lessons that will accompany it.

While serving a full-time mission for the Church, I thought I was beginning to understand what it means to sacrifice—what it means to "offer your whole souls as an offering unto him" (Omni 1:26). Since then, as I have had to confront my feelings of attraction, I think I am just now beginning to understand the principle of sacrifice. What I understood before was minimal compared to what the Lord has been teaching me through this experience. I've had to learn to trust as I have never before trusted. There are times when I wonder if I really have the faith to refrain from submitting to my attraction for the rest of my life, but I'm willing to do what is asked of me so that I can develop that level of perfect faith. There are times even now when, if I look too far ahead, I get discouraged. All I can do at those times is choose to follow Him that day—choose to place my will on the altar for that short time. I'm quickly learning that as we take care of the hours and the days, the weeks, months, and years take care of themselves.

Giving our full heart to the Lord is a process rather than an event, so we must remember not to allow discouragement to plague us if the idea seems overwhelming. As the saying goes, one can only eat an elephant one bite at a time. Even the most able and willing person who tries to swallow too much at a time is going to choke. The road to perfect faith begins with the desire to have faith. We sing, "Savior, may I learn to love thee, walk the paths that thou has shown."[26] I continually pray that I might learn to love Him more, to love Him enough to offer Him more of my whole soul.

As I discussed this principle with a friend—one who feels similarly about the importance of sacrificing and being faithful to the Lord and His Church—he shared some of his feelings and experiences that, for me, put a "seal of living reality," as Elder McConkie called it, on this principle.[27] It has been so difficult for me to try to express just how personal and real and heart-wrenching this challenge can be, and as he shared with me his own feelings, I felt as though some of his words could have been my very own. He wrote:

"I think I understand exactly how you feel, even to the point that I met a guy who I was attracted to in every way. It was so new and unusual that I was shocked. I finally understood how it felt to want to write and sing those cheesy love songs, and even what it was like to naturally want to kiss someone. Whenever I dated a girl (my longest relationship topped out at 2 1/2 months) I would always think, 'I think I'm supposed to kiss her now'—but I never wanted to at all (and consequently, never did). I thought that I was just more focused on more important parts of the relationship, but that wasn't it. The drive to keep the relationship going was never there. 'Homosexuality' is such a misnomer. It is about so much more than sexual attraction.

"So when I met this guy, and longed to just be with him all the time, it really threw me off. It felt so good and natural. I was so torn, because we both had a conviction that we wanted to stay true to our covenants, and that any relationship beyond friends just wouldn't be in any way consistent with what we know to be true. But that was so hard for me. Finally I had the feelings for someone that I had waited my whole life to feel, filling an ever-increasing void and longing for emotional intimacy—and I couldn't have it. The thought crossed my mind that I might never have these feelings for a woman, or anyone else, for the rest of my life, because I, too, had prayed and fasted countless times that they would go away, to no avail.

"Well, in the end, I am at peace with my decision. I know that the gospel path is the path that will fulfill me in the deepest and most meaningful way.

"You know, part of me really does still question why I have to go through this, what I did to deserve it, and whether I really can get through it at all. But deep down I am so sure of what is right and what is required of me that I know what I have to do. I know that I can do it too.

It really all depends on what I want more in the end. Can I give up satisfying my deepest desire to have the love and romantic companionship that feels so natural to me right now for blessings of eternal life that seem so distant? All the talks and lessons on faith and sacrifice I've heard have always seemed to make sense and feel good when they come from the manual, but they really don't mean anything until you are truly tested and what was once only on paper has now become a wrenching part of your heart and life.

"This is definitely the hardest test of faith I have ever experienced! After finally feeling for the first time what romantic love was really like, knowing what it is like to kiss someone and have it race through your mind for the rest of the day, to meet someone that you connect with emotionally, socially, physically, spiritually, who seems to complete you in every way, to miss him so much when he isn't around, to have him fill a void that you didn't even know was there, to actually feel truly loved and to truly love in return, to know what it's like to want to spend your entire life with someone, and for everything logically and emotionally telling you that this is good and right and natural and that you should embrace it, and then to willingly give it up because something deeper—something more eternal—tells you it's not right and that it's not God's will, that for me is the essence of sacrifice—that is the only thing that I know of that I could give up to truly show God how much I love Him and how much I want to serve Him and be with Him someday."

"I heard Elder Henry B. Eyring say once that to have the blessings of Abraham, Isaac, and Jacob, we need to face and pass comparable tests. The greater the test, the greater the compliment from a loving Heavenly Father. I know that when Abraham was told to sacrifice his only son, after waiting so long for him to fulfill the promise of posterity, when everything logically and emotionally must have been telling him that this was not right, still, he was willing to obey because he knew God required it. He trusted that God would provide a way."

The eighteenth-century British clergyman William Law said, "If you have not chosen the Kingdom of God first, it will in the end make no difference what you have chosen instead."[28] Regardless of whether the tests, trials, challenges, or tragedies in our lives are the result of God's intentional proving or simply the by-product of living in fallen bodies in a fallen world, it is nevertheless essential that we put God first and choose to serve Him at all costs. King Benjamin said in his classic sermon: "The natural man is an enemy to God, and has been from the fall of Adam, and will be, forever and ever, unless he yields to the enticings of the Holy Spirit, and putteth off the natural man and becometh a saint through the atonement of Christ the Lord, and becometh as a child, submissive, meek, humble, patient, full of love, *willing to submit to all things which the Lord seeth fit to inflict upon him,* even as a child doth submit to his father" (Mosiah 3:19; italics added).

When we make covenants at baptism and again in the temple, we covenant to live lives of chastity and of consecration. We, in essence, covenant to hand over our entire will and being to the Man of Holiness who has promised He can make more out of us than we can make out of ourselves. Elder M. Russell Ballard stated: "Sometimes we are tempted to let our lives be governed more by convenience than by covenant. It is not always convenient to live gospel standards and stand up for truth and testify of the Restoration. It usually is not convenient to share the gospel with others. It isn't always convenient to respond to a calling in the church, especially one that stretches our abilities. Opportunities to serve others in meaningful ways, as we have covenanted to do, rarely come at convenient times. But there is no spiritual power in living by convenience."[29] And it is certainly not convenient to place a life of willing submission to the law of chastity and other covenants on the altar—to take attractions that often seem so natural and powerful into Moriah (see Genesis 22:2).

Elder Neal A. Maxwell eloquently taught: "The submission of one's will is placing on God's altar the only uniquely personal thing one has to place there. The many other things we 'give' are actually the things He has already given or loaned to us. However, when we finally submit ourselves by letting our individual wills be swallowed up in God's will, we will really be giving something to Him! It is the only possession which is truly ours to give. Consecration thus constitutes the only unconditional surrender which is also a total victory."[30] He later observed: "Alas, even when you and I do place something on the altar, we sometimes hang around as if waiting for a receipt."[31]

God lives, and the fulness of the gospel of Jesus Christ as restored through the Prophet Joseph Smith is eternal truth. And there will come a time when all must recognize it for what it is—when "every knee shall bow, and every tongue confess before him" (Mosiah 27:31). President Spencer W. Kimball prophetically declared, "The time will come when there will be a surrender of every person who has ever lived on this earth, who is now living, or who ever will live on this earth; and it will be an unforced surrender, an unconditional surrender. When will it be for you? Today? In twenty years? Two hundred years? Two thousand or a million? When? Again . . . it is not if you will capitulate to the great truth; it is when, for I know that you cannot indefinitely resist the power and pressure of truth. Why not now? Much time has been lost. The years ahead can be far more glorious for you than any years in the past."[32]

The world would have us believe that if same-gender attraction is inborn—an idea that in some respects should not be entirely discounted—then to fully be free and true to ourselves, we must surrender to it. The idea that we must surrender instead to God, in spite of challenges that may be very natural, is not a popular one and receives great criticism. But God's way has been and always will be unpopular, until Christ comes to rule and reign as "Lord of lords, and King of kings" (Revelation 17:14). The Prophet Joseph Smith stated: "To get salvation we must not only do some things, but everything which God has commanded . . . The object with me is to obey and teach others to obey God in just what He tells us to do. It mattereth not whether the principle is popular or unpopular, I will always maintain a true principle, even if I stand alone in it."[33]

Once we have covenanted with Christ, we are no longer our own being. I don't know if there is anything that I could give to the Lord that is more fiercely a part of who I am than one of my strongest attractions. King Lamoni's father, in humble prayer declared, "Make thyself known unto me, and I will give away all my sins to know thee . . . that I may . . . be saved at the last day" (Alma 22:18). To give away our sins to come to know God doesn't mean that same-gender attraction must or will be overcome in mortality, but it is the willingness to place our hearts and any behavior associated with those attractions on the altar of God. Again, we must remember that the attraction itself is a challenge, not a sin.

When the Savior first appeared to His flock in the New World, in a voice that penetrated the soul, He declared: "Behold, I am Jesus Christ, whom the prophets testified shall come into the world." His next words represented the essence of His life and mission: "And behold, I am the light and the life of the world; . . . I have drunk out of that bitter cup which the Father hath given me, and have glorified the Father in taking upon me the sins of the world, . . . I have suffered the will of the Father in all things from the beginning." It was after these few simple but powerful words that "the whole multitude fell to the earth" (3 Nephi 11:10–12).

Elder Jeffrey R. Holland commented on these profound verses: "I cannot think it either accident or mere whimsy that the Good Shepherd in his newly exalted state, appearing to a most significant segment of his flock, chooses first to speak of his obedience, his deference, his loyalty, and loving submission to his father . . . [This is] the first and most important thing he wishes us to know about himself.

"Frankly, . . . this is the first and most important thing he may want to know about us when we meet him one day in similar fashion. Did we obey, even if it was painful? Did we submit, even if the cup was bitter indeed? Did we yield to a vision higher and holier than our own, even when we may have seen no vision in it at all? . . .

"No amount of university education, or any other kind of desirable and civilizing experience in this world, will help us at the moment of our confrontation with Christ if we have not been able—and are not then able—to yield, yield all that we are, all that we have, and all that we ever hope to have to the Father and the Son.

"The path to a complete Christian education passes through the Garden of Gethsemane, and we will learn there if we haven't learned it before that our Father will have no other gods before him—even (or especially) if that would-be god is our self . . . It will be required of each of us to kneel when we may not want to kneel, to bow when we may not want to bow, to confess when we may not want to confess—perhaps a confession born of painful experience that God's thoughts are not our thoughts, neither are his ways our ways, saith the Lord (see Isaiah 55:8) . . .

"Accomplishment of any kind is vain if we cannot, in those crucial moments of pivotal personal history, submit ourselves to God even when all our hopes and fears may tempt us otherwise. We must be willing to place all that we have—not just our possessions (they may be the easiest things of all to give up), but also our ambition and pride and stubbornness and vanity—we must place it all on the altar of God, kneel there in silent submission, and willingly walk away."[34]

Chapter 5

Hope through the Atonement

Shortly after I first confided in my bishop, I began seeing a counselor upon his recommendation. I was having a particularly difficult time one day, and as I left my counselor's office, I silently pleaded, "Why?" Why did this have to be so hard? Why, when I wanted only to serve God and have a family and build the kingdom, did I have to have such a strong attraction that was inconsistent with everything I ever wanted in relation to the gospel? As I silently pleaded for answers to these questions, I received a powerful impression. The words of Alma concerning the suffering of Christ came to my mind: "And he shall go forth, suffering pains and afflictions and temptations of every kind; and this that the word might be fulfilled which saith he will take upon him the pains and the sicknesses of his people. And he will take upon him death, that he may loose the bands of death which bind his people; and he will take upon him their infirmities, that his bowels may be filled with mercy, according to the flesh, that he may know according to the flesh how to succor his people according to their infirmities" (Alma 7:12).

As I felt the power of those words upon my mind, several simultaneous impressions concerning these words came over me. First, I knew the Savior understood my pain and my afflictions. I felt it. I didn't understand how, but I knew that He did. To truly be able to succor and comfort me, He had to have somehow felt the pain and heartache that I was experiencing. He suffered as He did so that He could have perfect empathy for each of us in our individual pain. Second, as an extension of that same principle, I felt impressed that we too must suffer and be tempted so that we can relate to others and succor them more effectively. By doing so, we may help to turn them to the Savior—and in this way we may become, in a way, saviors of men.

I remembered hearing Elder Jeffrey R. Holland in a devotional address at the Missionary Training Center. The context was missionary work, but as the Spirit brought the words to my remembrance, I felt they applied to me in the context of same-gender attraction. Elder Holland said: "Anyone who does any kind of missionary work will have occasion to ask, Why is this so hard? Why doesn't it go better? . . .

"You will have occasion to ask those questions. I have thought about this a great deal. I offer this as my personal feeling. I am convinced that missionary work is not easy because salvation is not a cheap experience. Salvation never was easy. We are the Church of Jesus Christ, this is the truth, and He is our Great Eternal Head. How could we believe it would be easy for us when it was never, ever easy for Him? It seems to me that missionaries and mission leaders have to spend at least a few moments in Gethsemane. Missionaries and mission leaders have to take at least a step or two toward the summit of Calvary . . .

"I believe that missionaries and investigators, to come to the truth, to come to salvation, to know something of this price that has been paid, will have to pay a token of that same price.

"If He could come forward in the night, kneel down, fall on His face, bleed from every pore, and cry, 'Abba, Father (Papa), if this cup can pass, let it pass,' then little wonder that salvation is not a whimsical or easy thing for us. If you wonder if there isn't an easier way, you should remember you are not the first one to ask that. Someone a lot greater and a lot grander asked a long time ago if there wasn't an easier way . . . The only way to salvation is through Gethsemane and on to Calvary. The only way to eternity is through Him—the Way, the Truth, and the Life."[1]

These words pricked my heart with an intensity of the Spirit I have rarely felt. I felt strongly that part of why Christ had to suffer as He did was so that He could understand my pain, so his bowels could be filled with mercy, and so he could know how to succor me in my affliction. In addition, I had the strong feeling that I needed to experience this trial partly because it would help me better understand to some small degree His suffering and commitment and love of God. I'm just beginning to understand what it means to be a true Christian. It is necessary for me to bear this cross and to resist the temptation to succumb to my attraction in order to better understand both the Savior and the power of His Atonement.

Elder Holland cautioned: "Now, please don't misunderstand. I'm not talking about anything anywhere near what Christ experienced. That would be presumptuous and sacrilegious. But . . . [the] reason I don't believe missionary work has ever been easy, nor that conversion is, nor that retention is, nor that continued faithfulness is, I believe it is supposed to require some effort, something from the depths of our soul."[2]

C. S. Lewis made a powerful observation: "No man knows how bad he is till he has tried very hard to be good. A silly idea is current that good people do not know what temptation means. This is an obvious lie. Only those who try to resist temptation know how strong it is. After all, you find out the strength of the German army by fighting against it, not by giving in. You find out the strength of a wind by trying to walk against it, not by lying down . . . That is why bad people, in one sense, know very little about badness. They have always lived a sheltered life by always giving in. We never find out the strength of the evil impulse inside us until we try to fight it; and Christ, because He was the only man who never yielded to temptation, is also the only man who knows to the full what temptation really means—the only complete realist."[3]

To know God and to better understand our Savior's redeeming and enabling atonement, we must learn to live more as He lived, serve more as He served, love more as He loved, and, at least to some tiny degree, suffer more as He suffered. Each of us, saint and sinner alike, becomes acquainted with the Suffering Servant through our suffering. Persecution and pain are the lot of the Saints of God in every dispensation. As the apostle Peter counseled, "Beloved, think it not strange concerning the fiery trial which is to try you, as though some strange thing happened unto you: but rejoice, inasmuch as ye are partakers of Christ's sufferings; that, when his glory shall be revealed, ye may be glad also with exceeding joy" (Peter 4:12–13).

"A Perfect Brightness of Hope"

Of all the doctrines and principles of the gospel, the atonement of Christ is by far the most difficult for me to share my feelings about. I've written and rewritten my ideas, fasted and prayed, and studied and pondered. And still, I am at a loss for words to express that which I feel. That difficulty has two principal causes. First, there is still so much I don't understand about the Atonement, and I feel Him continually teaching me and tutoring me through my life's experiences. Second, concerning the things that I do understand somewhat, how can I really express in a limited, finite vocabulary something that is so universal and infinite as the atoning sacrifice of the Only Begotten of the Father—something so boundlessly eternal and yet so intimately personal? How do I help others to feel something that has so deeply transformed my heart and life and that can only be understood by a humble, willing heart and by the power of the Holy Spirit?

Just as Fred and Marilyn Matis shared their feelings about how their experience with their son Stuart helped them to really internalize and understand the power of the Atonement for the first time in their life, so has my experience with same-gender attraction forced me to my knees to seek power and understanding and mercy from the Most High. Certain things will never be understood only through listening to discourses or reading the written word, for they are but a shadow of what must be felt and experienced through the outpouring of heaven by every individual who seeks salvation. I know the power of the Atonement and redeeming power of Christ is real, because I have felt it.

The regenerating effects of the Atonement that come through an individual's faith are not something that can be experienced vicariously through priesthood leaders or parents or spouse or children. Those effects

must be lived and gained through the smelter of adversity and the whis-
perings of the Spirit. And the most powerful feeling that has come to me
as a result of what the Lord has taught me through my experiences is
hope.

There was a time when I had lost this invaluable feeling. I had a difficult time reconciling things that I had felt and experienced regarding
the spiritual truths of the gospel and my experience with same-gender
attraction. There were times when I felt completely alone and lost as I
considered possible alternative courses my future life could take. With the
testimony I had of the gospel of Christ, I didn't feel I could be completely
at peace with myself living in a homosexual relationship, even one that
was fully committed and loving—though I did believe I could find a
measure of happiness and fulfillment. On the other hand, when I tried
to think about the gospel objectively, I didn't know how I could ever be
truly whole and at peace living the standards of the gospel when I would
be "suppressing" something that seemed to be such a natural part of me.

It is impossible for me to adequately relate the experiences that
helped me to finally find peace in living completely faithful to gospel
standards while still experiencing this challenge, but as I reached the point
where I was able to fully and humbly open myself up to understanding
from the Lord, the Spirit spoke to my understanding, and I again felt
hope for the first time in a long time.

"O the wisdom of God, his mercy and grace!" (2 Nephi 9:8). These
words have been forever immortalized in my heart. No other words can
describe how I feel about Christ and the power of His atonement. There
is really no adequate way to express my gratitude for the understanding
of the Atonement I have and the hope I feel in consequence of that
understanding.

Though the experience of my attraction is still extremely challenging
and difficult at times, my faith and hope in Christ no longer wavers. Even
when I do get discouraged, that hope keeps me moving forward in faith.
Elder Neal A. Maxwell taught: "No wonder Apostles and prophets have
told us not to be moved away from the hope of the gospel, for hope is 'an

anchor of the soul' to 'make them sure and steadfast, always abounding in good works.' (Eth. 12:4; see also Col. 1:23). . . .

"The very way in which . . . illuminated individuals 'take up [the] cross daily' is a sermon in itself. They lead lives not of quiet desperation but of quiet inspiration, constituting what Paul would call their 'defence and confirmation of the gospel.'

"Theirs represents a tinier and quieter history within the larger and noisier human history, a joyful and reassuring drama within the more despairing drama being played out on this planet."[4]

I believe that those who truly understand and have internalized the eternal vision of the plan of salvation and its essential doctrines would never view submission to Christ and their eternal potential as "suppression." And I do not believe that those who understand the glory and majesty of the love of Christ and His infinite atonement would feel "desperate" in their discipleship. As Elder Maxwell pointed out, their hope in Christ transforms their feelings of desperation to inspiration and suppression to submission. In their faith and understanding of the gospel, they maintain a "perfect brightness of hope" for a "better world" (2 Nephi 31:20; Ether 12:4).

Robert Millet has said: "I know that the day is coming when all the wrongs, the awful wrongs of this life, will be righted, when the God of justice will attend to all evil. Those things that are beyond our power to control will be corrected, either here or hereafter. Many of us may come to enjoy the lifting, liberating powers of the Atonement in this life and all our losses will be made up before we pass from this sphere of existence. Perhaps some of us will wrestle all our days with our traumas and our trials, for He who orchestrates the events of our lives will surely fix the time of our release. I have a conviction that when a person passes through the veil of death, all those impediments and challenges and crosses that were beyond his or her power to control—abuse, neglect, immoral environment, weighty traditions, etc.—will be torn away like a film and perfect peace will prevail in our hearts."[5]

The Peace of Perspective

Much of the attitude with which we approach our challenges depends upon the degree of eternal perspective we have. Elder Richard G. Scott pointed out: "When you face adversity, you can be led to ask many questions. Some serve a useful purpose; others do not. To ask, Why does this have to happen to me? Why do I have to suffer this now? What have I done to cause this? will lead you into blind alleys . . . Rather ask, What am I to do? What am I to learn from this experience? What am I to change? Whom am I to help? How can I remember my many blessings in times of trial?"[6]

I feel that in addition to the Lord's comforting Spirit, vision and perspective are key to feeling the lasting peace and hope that keep us firm in the gospel of Christ and away from following after the spiritually destructive philosophies of men. Challenges, regardless of their form, give us the opportunity to develop strength and understanding. Through them our hearts may be opened and softened so the Lord can teach us the characteristics of godliness. With a proper perspective on the purpose of our trials—believing that this experience can actually be good for us—we can approach our attraction in a whole new light and with a whole new attitude.

There have been many others whose severe afflictions have molded them into what God wanted them to become. Out of the fiery furnace of Liberty Jail, the Prophet Joseph Smith emerged more powerful in his preaching and firm in his discipleship than ever before. I have thought often about the exchange between him and the Lord when the Prophet cried out in frustration:

"O God, where art thou? And where is the pavilion that covereth thy hiding place?

"How long shall thy hand be stayed? . . ."

"My son, peace be unto thy soul; thine adversity and thine afflictions shall be but a small moment;

"And then, if thou endure it well, God shall exalt thee on high; thou shalt triumph over all thy foes. . . .

"Thou art not yet as Job" (D&C 121:1–2, 7–8, 10).

"If thou shouldst be cast into the pit, or into the hands of murderers, and the sentence of death passed upon thee; if thou be cast into the deep; if the billowing surge conspire against thee; if fierce winds become thine enemy; if the heavens gather blackness, and all the elements combine to hedge up the way; and above all, if the very jaws of hell shall gape open the mouth wide after thee, know thou, my son, that all these things shall give thee experience, and shall be for thy good.

"The Son of Man hath descended below them all. Art thou greater than he?

"Therefore, hold on thy way. . . . Thy days are known, and thy years shall not be numbered less; . . . God shall be with you forever and ever" (D&C 122:7–9).

Many times as I have read these passages I have felt overwhelmingly humbled and embarrassed because of my complaints over comparatively petty trials. I have too often felt "overcome because of my afflictions" and considered with Nephi that "mine afflictions were great above all" (1 Nephi 15:5). The Son of Man truly did suffer incomparably more than I suffer—how could I consider that I was greater than He? How could I consider that what I was going through could compare in any way to what He suffered? And yet, even as we experience our trials and in our eyes the jaws of hell seem to open up after us, the Lord and His angels are round about us to bear us up, and the eternal experience gained from such adversity is immeasurable to our mortal minds.

I believe strongly that we are not alone in our fight to live faithfully the standards of the gospel we have been entrusted with. I have been deeply impressed with the words of Elisha: "Fear not: for they that be with us are more than they that be with them." Israel was being attacked by Syria, and the servant of Elisha said to him in great concern, "Alas, my master! how shall we do? And he answered, Fear not: for they that be with us are more than they that be with them. And Elisha prayed, and said,

Lord, I pray thee, open his eyes, that he may see. And the Lord opened the eyes of the young man; and he saw: and, behold, the mountain was full of horses and chariots of fire round about Elisha" (2 Kings 6:15–17).

We are born with royal blood and a royal destiny. Sometimes mortality may seem like a dismal experience, and in a way that is rightfully so. This isn't our home. We are celestial beings in a telestial world trying desperately to make sense of celestial principles. Many times when I have thought what my future would hold if I were to seek a homosexual relationship, I stop and think, "No, I was made for so much more than that." Though I do believe that a measure of happiness and fulfillment could be found in such a relationship, as I contemplate the glorious doctrines of the Restoration, I know that I do not want to settle for anything less than living true to my eternal self and the eternal joy promised to those who endure in Christ.

A powerful principle taught by Elder Neal A. Maxwell gave me some perspective once when I was feeling desperate and praying that the Lord would take away my challenge. Elder Maxwell said: "We may at times, if we are not careful, try to pray away pain or what seems like an impending tragedy, but which is, in reality, an opportunity. We must do as Jesus did in that respect—also preface our prayers by saying, 'If it be possible,' let the trial pass from us—by saying, 'Nevertheless, not as I will, but as thou wilt,' and bowing in a sense of serenity to our Father in Heaven's wisdom, because at times God will not be able to let us pass by a trial or a challenge. If we were allowed to bypass certain trials, everything that had gone on up to that moment in our lives would be wiped out. It is because he loves us that at times he will not intercede as we may wish him to. That, too, we learn from Gethsemane and from Calvary."[7]

Paul's response to his particular "thorn in the flesh" (2 Corinthians 12:7) is reminiscent of the more general principle spoken by the Lord to Moroni: "And if men come unto me I will show unto them their weakness. I give unto men weakness that they may be humble; and my grace is sufficient for all men that humble themselves before me; for if they humble themselves before me, and have faith in me, then will I make weak things become strong unto them" (Ether 12:27).

The Lord said to Paul: "My grace is sufficient for thee: for my strength is made perfect in weakness." Paul, with an increased vision and sense of purpose, proclaimed: "Most gladly therefore will I rather glory in my infirmities, that the power of Christ may rest upon me. Therefore I take pleasure in infirmities, in reproaches, in necessities, in persecutions, in distresses for Christ's sake: for when I am weak, then am I strong" (2 Corinthians 12:9–10).

Some do refer to same-gender attraction as their "weakness," as if it were some kind of spiritual illness, often quoting the words of Moroni about the Lord giving "men weakness that they may be humble" (Ether 12:27). But to refer to same-gender attraction as a "weakness" can be misguided. Our challenges and our temptations are not what should be considered "weak," for it is through challenge and opposition that we are made strong—if we will turn to Christ and to the power and grace He offers through His atoning sacrifice. Our challenges simply reveal unto us our true weaknesses or spiritual illnesses—the doubt and fear of putting our lives completely in the Lord's hands—and the weakness of faith in God that would allow us to submit to whatever challenges or temptations beset us. Christ was tempted, and He had challenges, but He was never weak.

The "weakness" that Moroni was speaking about is, in part, the natural limitations in strength, knowledge, and power imposed upon us by the Fall. But as we acknowledge these limitations in view of God's infinite wisdom and power, we will then depend more upon the power of God than on the "arm of flesh" (2 Nephi 4:34). Challenge and hardship are often given to us or allowed by God, for it is through them that we can learn the eternal principles of faith and strive to put the Lord first in all things. The natural weaknesses in our strength, knowledge, and power that we must deal with because of the Fall are made strong through our coming to Christ in humility. His grace and the blood of His atonement transform our souls, buoy up our spirits, and strengthen and spiritually enlarge us beyond our natural abilities.

It seems likewise misguided to refer to same-gender attraction as a "problem." The biggest problem is not in our attractions or challenges or temptations themselves but rather in how we respond to them. The "problem" associated with same-gender attraction is in the misunderstanding, cynicism, bigotry, fear, prejudice, and hatred often associated with it. And homophobia is not limited to those who do not experience this attraction. Many of those who experience the attraction are scared to death of it or what it may imply for them in their life, and they often hate both the attraction and themselves for having it. The problem associated with same-gender attraction—or any other challenge we face here in mortality—comes when we allow ourselves to forget that we are the literal children of a literal Father in Heaven who sent us to earth for a purpose, when we forget that there is divine purpose to our trials and that God loves us, has promised eternal victory, and sent His Only Begotten Son so that we may be redeemed and regenerated through faith in His holy name.

An example of misunderstanding that is often associated with our challenges is the biblical story of the blind man, of whom Jesus spoke to his disciples. In His day, blindness was thought to be caused by sin. So, when Jesus passed by a blind man who had been blind since birth, His disciples asked Christ, "Master, who did sin, this man, or his parents, that he was born blind?" (John 9:1–2).

Wondering why same-gender attraction exists is like wondering why the blind man in the New Testament had to be blind. Christ told them that "neither hath this man sinned, nor his parents: but that the works of God should be made manifest in him" (John 9:3). What greater way for works of God to be manifest than through the healing and strength He can provide? Whether or not that blindness—or our attraction—is healed in mortality is of little importance, but allowing our challenges to turn us to Christ so that our spiritual blindness and misunderstanding can be healed is imperative. The strength gained through Him then gives purpose to our pain and empowers us to further the cause of Christ—to contribute to the "body of Christ," His Church and kingdom.

My understanding that mortality was meant to be a proving ground gives purpose to my experience, but it doesn't necessarily make the experience any less challenging, and it certainly does not take away the pain or loneliness that often comes with it. Elder Maxwell taught: "Knowing that one is in the midst of a testing time does not make the test any less real . . . The difference is that those who are (or who will become) Saints reach breaking points without breaking."[8]

I used to hate the fact that I experience this attraction. I hated the feeling of not being "normal." I hated playing a social role that didn't feel natural and living in continual fear that others would suspect and begin to see through my façade. I often still become frustrated and sometimes discouraged with this challenge, but I have learned not to hate it. So much good has come into my life because of it. Nothing in my life has ever driven me so quickly to my knees and into the scriptures to seek the knowledge and will and love of the Lord. I attribute the depth of my commitment to the Lord and my will to seek His will to this challenge. I attribute my understanding of the Savior's atoning sacrifice to the tears that have driven me to seek His mind and Spirit.

It is a challenge, but I strive to say with Caleb, "Give me this mountain!" When Israel was first commanded to possess the promised land and to overcome formidable obstacles to do so, most of the party that went with Caleb found that the land "made the heart of the people melt," because they faithlessly focused on the seemingly overwhelming odds (Joshua 14:8). They gave Moses and the people "an evil report of the land," saying, "We be not able to go up against the people; for they are stronger than we. The land . . . is a land that eateth up the inhabitants thereof; and all the people that we saw in it are men of great stature" (Numbers 13:31–32).

Then Caleb humbly and courageously stepped forward. With what the Lord called "another spirit," he gave an account of the journey and their challenges that was quite different from that of his fellow Israelites.

"Let us go up at once," he bravely declared, "and possess it; for we are well able to overcome it. . . . The land, which we passed through to search it, is an exceeding good land. If the Lord delights in us, then he will bring us into this land, and give it us; a land which floweth with milk and honey. Only rebel not ye against the Lord, neither fear ye the people of the land; for . . . the Lord is with us: fear them not" (Numbers 13:30; 14:8–9).

Some forty-five years later, Caleb had become an eighty-five-year-old man and Israel was again brought to the borders of the promised land and commanded to possess it. What had changed was that a new, faithful generation was now led by Joshua. The challenges ahead were as daunting as ever before—the people of Anak still possessed the land and were as large and numberless as they had previously been—but Caleb, even in his old age, was as courageous and faithful as he had been years earlier. He was willing to fearlessly confront all that the Lord would ask. Caleb said, "As yet I am as strong this day as I was in the day that Moses sent me: as my strength was then, even so is my strength now." Then came the valiant declaration by this humble disciple of the Lord that has over the years been deeply impressed upon my heart and which I have tried to remember as I have been coming to terms with this challenge in my life—"Give me this mountain!" (Joshua 14:11–12).

President Spencer W. Kimball commented: "From Caleb's example we learn a very important lesson. Just as Caleb had to struggle and remain true and faithful to gain his inheritance, so we must remember that, while the Lord has promised us a place in His kingdom, we must ever strive constantly and faithfully so as to be worthy to receive the reward."[9]

Serving for two years as a missionary for the Church, I daily taught people the importance of faith and commitment and eternal vision. Now the Lord is giving me an opportunity to put my life where my mouth was. He is allowing me to experience something that is forcing me to internalize principles to which I gave only lip service for much of my life. Once when Elder Neal A. Maxwell was pondering his leukemia, "the soul voice of the Spirit came into his mind to whisper, 'I have given you leukemia that you might teach my people with authenticity.'"[10] How could we teach the principle of faith if our own faith was never tried and exercised? How could we teach someone about the importance and power of resisting temptation if we have always given in? How could we teach the blessings of living the law of tithing or the law of chastity with power of the Spirit if we are not currently living them? In the words of Paul, "Thou therefore which teachest another, teachest thou not thyself? Thou that preachest a man should not steal, dost thou steal?" (Romans 2:21).

Because I no longer hate my attraction, I can now view it for what it is: a tremendous challenge—and an opportunity. It does not determine my destiny. Latter-day Saints, more than any other people, have reason to rejoice because we have the peace and assurance that our adversity and afflictions "shall be but a small moment" and that eternal glory and joy with our Father in Heaven are awaiting those who endure in hope and faith (D&C 121:7). The peace we can have here in this fallen world is *His* peace, promised through the Comforter. He told His apostles: "Peace I leave with you, my peace I give unto you: not as the world giveth, give I unto you. Let not your heart be troubled, neither let it be afraid" (John 14:26–27).

The familiar words ring, "Be still, and know that I am God" (Psalm 46:10; D&C 101:16). In the New World, Samuel the Lamanite prophesied that a sign would accompany the Savior's birth: "There shall be one day and a night and a day, as if it were one day and there were no night. . . . Ye shall know of the rising of the sun and also of its setting; therefore they shall know of a surety that there shall be two days and a night; nevertheless the night shall not be darkened" (Helaman 14:4).

Such is also the sign of the coming of God into the individual life of each one of His children. There will be times when the natural laws and the voice of the world declare that the pain of trials, challenges, or tragedy should be accompanied by darkness, but the promise of the gospel of Christ—the "good news"—is that when we allow the Savior and His peace and perspective and Spirit into our lives, the sun will go down but it will be "as if . . . there were no night" (Helaman 14:4). Again, our

Redeemer emphasizes, "My peace I give . . . not as the world giveth" (Helaman 14:4).

"Victory through Our Lord Jesus Christ"

Life is hard, and our challenges may often seem unbearable, but I'm grateful for the testimony that the adversity and affliction we experience here on earth is only temporary. I am grateful for the hope that I will then "with great mercies" (Isaiah 54:7) be gathered into the embrace of a loving Father and Savior who will say, "Well done, thou good and faithful servant: thou hast been faithful over a few things, I will make thee ruler over many things: enter thou into the joy of thy lord" (Matthew 25:21). As the apostle Paul declared, "Thanks be to God, [who] giveth us the victory through our Lord Jesus Christ" (1 Corinthians 15:57).

A professor at Brigham Young University told a story that illustrates the power and peace that come of knowing that eternal victory is assured through Jesus Christ. "A few years ago," he said, "before the time that all BYU games were televised live, I landed at the Salt Lake airport just as a BYU 'away' game was concluding. I rushed around the terminal until I finally found someone who could assure me that we had won, although by a very close score. That evening, after returning to Provo, I went downstairs to watch the replay of the game on KBYU. My demeanor was amazingly serene. When we fumbled or had a pass intercepted, I hardly reacted. My wife could even let our children get around me. Usually I feel obligated to help my brethren in striped shirts by pointing out their errors in judgment. Because my seats are on row 25, such correction often requires a rather high decibel level. This loudness has carried over to watching football on television. But on that day I remained absolutely calm, even when I had the benefit of instant replay to verify my claim that their defensive back clearly arrived early and that the ground had obviously caused our running back to lose the ball. I was a veritable model of football decorum, never becoming unduly upset or ill behaved.

"The cause of my improved behavior was obvious: I already knew the outcome of the game—BYU would win. It is amazing how that knowledge changes things: cornerbacks can get beat, running backs can fumble, linebackers can miss tackles, offensive guards can blow blocking assignments, and other things can go wrong. But when we know the final score, such things can be endured and sometimes even ignored.

"We also know the final score for the history of this world and for the life of the righteous. The Lord and his people will triumph. It is true that the sorrows of this world and the strength of Satan's forces will win a number of the skirmishes. Satan and his followers, as well as the natural circumstances of mortal life, will inflict many bruises and win many battles. But God, who knows the end from the beginning, has promised that those who serve him will receive the fullness of his blessings. When we realize that righteous living puts us on the winning side, we can learn to trust him during trying times."[11]

The game is fixed! But while we know Who will conquer in the end, we are still individually responsible to decide what color jersey we will be wearing. The Lord has indeed promised victory and that His people will be preserved (Moses 7:61), but He has never promised that the faithful will be spared pain or suffering. What He has done, however, is to give us vision and perspective that would give purpose to the pain, glory to the grief, and joy to the sorrow.

Concerning the perplexing cohabitation of both sorrow and joy in our lives, I am intrigued by the words of Jacob as he closed his record. With the sense of sorrow he had experienced in his life readily apparent, he reflected, "Our lives passed away like as it were unto us a dream, we being a lonesome and a solemn people, wanderers, cast out from Jerusalem, born in tribulation, in a wilderness, and hated of our brethren, which caused wars and contentions; wherefore, we did mourn out our days" (Jacob 7:26). It is most intriguing that even though Jacob had suffered much throughout his life, when his son, Enos, was having struggles of his own, all Enos recalled were "the words which [he] had often heard [his] father speak concerning eternal life, and the joy of the saints," and they "sunk deep into [his] heart" (Enos 1:3).

Because of the victory we are promised through Christ's atonement, some of the things we may see as obstacles to happiness here in mortality may be seen through eternal eyes that offer hope and perspective. For some, it is crucial to maintain vision and perspective concerning the principle of eternal marriage. Because of the Atonement, the plan of salvation provides a place for those who do not have the opportunity for marriage, regardless of their circumstances. Isaiah proclaimed: "Neither let the eunuch say, Behold, I am a dry tree. For thus saith the Lord unto the eunuchs that keep my sabbaths, and choose the things that please me, and take hold of my covenant; even unto them will I give in mine house and within my walls a place and a name better than of sons and of daughters: I will give them an everlasting name, that shall not be cut off. . . . Even them will I bring to my holy mountain, and make them joyful in my house of prayer: their burnt offerings and their sacrifices shall be accepted upon mine altar; for mine house shall be called an house of prayer for all people" (Isaiah 56:3–5, 7).

A eunuch is an emasculated man who is, consequently, unable to father children. Isaiah uses the eunuch as a symbol of anyone—male or female—who for one reason or another is not able to marry in the covenant and is "dry" in mortality. Keeping the Sabbath day holy is symbolic of keeping the whole law of the covenant, so if such persons are faithful and "take hold of [His] covenant" (Isaiah 56:4)—referring to the same covenant made with Abraham—they are entitled to every blessing promised to the faithful in the eternities, as symbolized by the eunuch entering the temple. The Lord promises "a place and a name" (Isaiah 56:5)—important parts of the temple covenants—to all those who come into his house and offer themselves as an offering before the Lord.

"He Is Able"

Even though we must experience a small portion of the burden He felt in order to better understand the power of Christ and His atonement, He has also promised that He will bear our burden with us. I know that there is an enabling power in Christ to help us to do that which we of our own strength cannot. I know that is true because I've felt it—I've experienced it. I have felt that enabling power most distinctly when I have been the most worthy of the guiding companionship of His Holy Spirit.

I suspect from my own experience with the gospel that many of us are more familiar with the redeeming power of the Atonement than we are with its enabling power. It is one thing to know that Jesus Christ came to earth to die for us. It is quite another thing to know that the Lord desires, through His atonement and by the power of the Holy Ghost, to live in us—not only to cleanse and to direct us but also to empower us. The Savior has paid the price and made it possible for us to be made clean from sin through His redeeming power. We know the Atonement is for sinners, but we may not fully understand that the Atonement is also for saints—for good men and women who, despite challenges, temptations, or attractions, continue striving to be obedient and worthy and to serve more faithfully.

The trial I experience has helped me to know myself better because I've had to search more deeply to discover what I truly believe. President Hugh B. Brown, in answering the question of why Abraham was asked to "offer as a sacrifice his only hope for the promised posterity," said: "Abraham needed to learn something about Abraham."[12] Knowledge about ourselves and our personal commitment to Deity gained through trials puts our relationship with Him on a higher plane, and our "confidence" begins to "wax strong in the presence of God" (D&C 121:45). That type of confidence is gained only when we have learned to exercise complete faith and trust in Christ and we have proven what the deepest yearnings of our hearts and souls really are.

Job had such confidence when he had been tried and had his heartstrings wrenched, and he withstood those who accused him of unrighteousness. "Hold your peace," he declared, "let me alone, that I may speak, and let come on me what will. . . . Though he slay me, yet will I trust in him. . . . He also shall be my salvation: for an hypocrite shall not come before him. Hear diligently my speech, and my declaration with your ears. Behold now, I have ordered my cause; I know that I shall be justified" (Job 13:13–18). He confirmed, "He knoweth the way that I take; when he hath tried me, I shall come forth as gold" (Job 23:10). Through his trials Job learned to trust in the Lord regardless of the trials he experienced. Through personal tragedy he learned the power of the Lord's atonement and gained the will to submit.

Concerning those lonely moments when the future seems bleak and we feel ready to collapse in spiritual fatigue, Elder Neal A. Maxwell consoled us: "We can be comforted to know that God, who knows our capacity perfectly, placed us here to succeed. No one was foreordained to fail or to be wicked. When we have been weighed and found wanting, let us remember that we were measured before and we were found equal to our tasks; and, therefore, let us continue, but with a more determined discipleship. When we feel overwhelmed, let us recall the assurance that God will not over-program us; he will not press upon us more than we can bear."[13] Christ has promised that His enabling power will give us strength to conquer whatever Goliaths may try to overpower us.

In a similar vein, Elder Howard W. Hunter reminded us that "whatever Jesus lays his hands upon lives. If Jesus lays his hands upon a marriage, it lives. If he is allowed to lay his hands on the family, it lives."[14] The hand of the Master empowers and gives life to all it is allowed to touch. I believe that to more deeply understand the Atonement, we must, as Elder Packer stated, go "to the edge of the light and step into the darkness to discover that the way is lighted ahead for just a footstep or two."[15] We can never understand the power of redemption until we allow Christ to be our Savior and have the faith to do His will. And we must recognize that we cannot do it alone, nor should we try to do it alone.

Knowing that Christ is my Redeemer, that He understands my pain and has allowed me to have the trials I have for a reason, has inspired me to turn to Him—to know Him better. I've felt the enabling power of his atonement when I have humbly sought His grace and feasted in His light. I am realizing how important it is for me to remember that—like everyone else—I'm a fallen being who cannot do it by myself as much as I may try or wish I could. To the degree that I try to do it alone, I will fail and fall again and again. The gospel—the "good news"—is that "I can do all things through Christ which strengtheneth me" (Philippians 4:13).

"O the Wisdom of God, His Mercy and Grace!"

The experience with same-gender attraction is different for everyone. Some live quietly with confidence in the Lord as they submit faithfully to His will and carry their individual crosses. Others, perhaps with less confidence or understanding, have tried to "white-knuckle" it, never allowing those feelings to have expression. And still others have either experimented or given in completely to their attraction and have chosen to live life accordingly. The range of experience is wide, and the pain of the required repentance often deep, but the Good Shepherd calls, and for those willing to heed, there is power through the Atonement both to enable repentance and to forgive. Elder Jeffrey R. Holland said, "Considering the incomprehensible cost of the crucifixion, Christ is not going to turn His back on us now."[16]

Even for those whose lives have become enmeshed in homosexual activity, the Lord's mercy is boundless when there is repentance. Elder Boyd K. Packer taught: "The deceiver preys upon some passion or tendency or weakness. He convinces them that the condition cannot be changed and recruits them for activities for which they never would volunteer. But sooner or later that spark of divinity in each of them will ignite. They can assert their agency as sons and daughters created in the image of God and renounce the destroyer. That which they had been led to believe could not be changed, will be changed, and they will feel the power of the redemption of Christ. Their burden will be lifted and the pain healed up. That is what the Atonement of Christ is all about. They can claim their inheritance as children of heavenly parents and, despite the tortured, agonizing test of mortal life, know that they are not lost."[17]

The Lord Himself pleaded, "I will be merciful unto them . . . if they will repent and come unto me; for mine arm is lengthened out all the day long, saith the Lord God of Hosts" (2 Nephi 28:32).

Isaiah uttered prophetic words that would find fulfillment in the mortal ministry of Jesus: "The Spirit of the Lord God is upon me; because the Lord hath anointed me to preach good tidings unto the meek; he hath sent me to bind up the brokenhearted, to proclaim liberty to the captives, and the opening of the prison to them that are bound; to proclaim the acceptable year of the Lord, . . . to comfort all that mourn. To appoint unto them that mourn in Zion, to give unto them beauty for ashes, the oil of joy for mourning, the garment of praise for the spirit of heaviness" (Isaiah 61:1–3; compare Luke 4:18–19).

"Jesus Christ came to bring beauty for ashes," Professor Millet said, "to replace distress with comfort, worry with peace, turmoil with rest. The Good Shepherd came . . . to right all the terrible wrongs of this life, to fix the unfixable, to repair the irreparable. He came to heal us by his tender touch, to still the storms of our startled hearts. Again, he came to replace ashes with beauty . . . Each one of us needs to know—needs the conviction, deep down in our souls—that our Master is not an absentee Landlord, not a distant Deity. He is 'touched with the feeling of our infirmities' (Hebrews 4:15), knows from firsthand experience all about our pains, our afflictions, our temptations (Alma 7:11–12), and thereby understands 'the weakness of man and how to succor them who are tempted' (D&C 62:1). He has not, as the deists proposed centuries ago, wound up the world clock and left it to run on its own. Rather, he is intimately involved in saving and succoring—literally, running to help—those who call upon him and learn to trust in his mighty arm. Indeed, our God's infinity does not preclude either his immediacy or his intimacy. As Enoch the seer learned, when we need God, when we reach out to him, he is there, his bosom is there; he is just and merciful and kind forever (Moses 7:30)."[18]

There have often been times when I have wanted to cry along with Nephi, "O wretched man that I am! Yea, my heart sorroweth because of my flesh; my soul grieveth because of mine iniquities" (2 Nephi 4:17). But God in His mercy has guided me and helped me to understand more fully the mysteries of His love and grace. I've felt His grace and the forgiving influence of His love when justice should have had its claim. He is changing my heart and giving me the desire to become something more than I am. He is giving me strength to continue progressing toward eternal life with Him. And He alone knows where I would be without the "good news" of His Son guiding my life and choices.

My eyes fill with tears when I ponder the mercy and love Christ has shown me, despite some of my rebellious choices. His atonement has made it possible for me to be redeemed, and if I continue faithful, it will enable me to remain strong no matter what challenges lie ahead. He works with us as we seek to be guided by Him. He knows us better than we know ourselves. His righteousness is our righteousness; His strength is our strength; His grace is our grace. We are not our own, and we are not on our own. Eventually, as he continually and patiently works with us, our faith and spiritual growth will be such that we can be "perfect even as [He], or [our] Father who is in heaven is perfect" (3 Nephi 12:48).

In the meantime, all He asks is our heart and our desire. We can obtain perfection in mortality only in His perfection as we strive to remain worthy of His Spirit. As He told the Nephites, "Blessed are they who hunger and thirst after righteousness, for they shall be filled with the Holy Ghost." He did not say, "Blessed are the perfect" or "Blessed are those who desire to become 'good people' . . ." or "Blessed are the married" or "Blessed are they who have reached the ideal level of heterosexual attraction . . ." As long as we are hungering and thirsting—and to the degree that we are hungering and thirsting—after Christ and His righteousness, we will be filled with His Spirit, and our salvation in His righteousness is secure.

Stephen E. Robinson, a Brigham Young University professor, shared a touching story of what the love and mercy and patient workings of the Lord can do with even the roughest of His children who are humble and who hunger and thirst after His righteousness. Initially "one of the roughest people" he had ever known, a woman he knew had been "abused as a child. She had run away from home and had lived on the streets for years. As a young woman, she traveled around the country with a motorcycle gang. In late middle age, her beauty gone, she spent most of her time in a pub, where some missionaries met her when they went in to get change for a pay phone outside. When she was baptized, many of the members worried that her conversion wouldn't last, and there were good reasons to suspect it might not.

"For a long time after her baptism, this sister still swore like a trooper, even in church, and never quite lived the Word of Wisdom one hundred percent. On one occasion during her first year in the Church, she lost her temper during a Relief Society meeting and punched out one of the other sisters. Her ex-husband is an alcoholic, and her children have all spent time in jail.

"Now the question before us is whether someone like this can seriously expect to be saved. What hope does a person like this, with all her faults and weaknesses, really have? With her background and problems, why bother coming to church at all?

"'Though your sins be as scarlet, they shall be as white as snow; though they be red like crimson, they shall be as wool.' God does not lie. Whoever will come, may come. All are invited; none is excluded. Though this sister had further to travel than most, the same covenant was offered to her: 'Do all you can. I will do the rest while you learn how.' And she was as faithful as she could be under her circumstances. She never said, 'No, I won't,' or 'Get off my back,' or 'Why talk to me? Talk to him, he started it.' She always said, 'I know; I'm sorry. I'll try to do better.' Then she would try to do better. Often she would fail, but little by little over the years, she improved a great deal. First she gave up coffee, tea, and alcohol. Then she stopped swearing. Later she overcame smoking and got her temper somewhat under control. Finally, after she'd been in the Church many years, she was ready to go to the temple. Can such a person really expect to inherit the kingdom of God? Of course.

"But now the harder question. At what point did this sister become a candidate for the kingdom? Was it when she finally gave up cigarettes, or when she got her language and temper under control? Or was it when she finally qualified for a temple recommend? No. It was none of these, though they were all important landmarks in her progress. She was justified through her faith in Jesus Christ on the day that she repented of her sins, was baptized, and received the gift of the Holy Ghost, for she entered into that covenant in good faith and in all sincerity. She believed in Christ, and she believed Christ. Like the widow with her mite, she gave all she had and held nothing back. It may not have been much, but it was everything.

"Every week she took the sacrament, having repented of her mistakes and resolving again to eliminate them. Some things took years to overcome. Other things perhaps haven't been overcome yet, but she still tries, and she won't give up. And as long as she won't give up but endures to the end in the gospel harness, pulling toward the Kingdom, her reward is sure. God knows our circumstances, and he judges us accordingly. He knows who is standing in a hole and who is standing on a chair, and he does not just measure height—he measures growth."[19]

Because of the forgiveness and enabling power promised through the Atonement of our God and King, life and hope can be ours again, and the pain, the struggle, the toil and the tears will be turned to us for our eternal good: he can make us holy and pure. "And one of the elders answered, saying unto me, What are these [people who] are arrayed in white robes? and whence came they? And I said unto him, Sir, thou knowest. And he said to me, These are they which came out of great tribulation, and have washed their robes, and made them white in the blood of the Lamb. Therefore are they before the throne of God, and serve him day and night in his temple: and he that sitteth on the throne shall dwell among them. They shall hunger no more, neither thirst any more; neither shall the sun light on them, nor any heat. For the Lamb which is in the midst of the throne shall feed them, and shall lead them unto living fountains of waters: and God shall wipe away all tears from their eyes" (Revelation 7:13–17).

Chapter 6

Son of Man or Son of God?

When he was "caught up into an exceedingly high mount," Moses saw God "face to face." The Lord appeared and "the glory of God was upon Moses; therefore Moses could endure his presence." The Lord called him by name and showed him visions of eternity. When he heard the Lord say to him, "I am the Lord God . . . [and] *thou art my son,*" Moses saw his relationship to the Almighty with new understanding (Moses 1:1–4; italics added; see also Exodus 33:11). He gained an eternal vision that washed away his previous mortal myopia. Then when the "presence of God withdrew from Moses, that his glory was not upon Moses," Moses was "left unto himself . . . [and] he fell unto the earth. And it came to pass that it was for the space of many hours before Moses did again receive his natural strength like unto man; and he said unto himself: Now, for this cause I know that man is nothing, which thing I never had supposed" (Moses 1:9–10).

This newfound understanding of his eternal relationship to God, along with feeling of His power, must have been a profound realization for a man who had been raised amongst the empty, heathen gods of Egypt. We know he was affected deeply, for when Satan appeared soon afterward, saying, "Moses, son of man, worship me," Moses' reply was simply, "Who art thou? For behold, I am a son of God. . . . Where is thy glory, that I should worship thee? For behold, I could not look upon God, except his glory should come upon me, and I were transfigured before him. But I can look upon thee in the natural man. . . . Get thee hence, Satan; deceive me not" (Moses 1:12–14, 16). Understanding both the power of God and the nature of his relationship with Him inspired within Moses the desire and determination to worship the Father, the faith to follow His Only Begotten Son, and the strength to withstand the enticements of the adversary.

The Spirit of Worship

As I have slowly gained my own testimony of the gospel and become converted to truths learned through the Spirit, I have started paying closer attention to individuals in the scriptures whom I admire for their dedication as disciples of God and whom I honor for their depth of worship—men such as Nephi, son of Helaman, who "with unwearyingness declared the word" and who did not seek his own life, men whose faith in the Lord was so strong that they would "not ask that which is contrary to [his] will" (Helaman 10:4–5). At least two common threads link valiant disciples such as Nephi. Even those who did not speak of them directly evidenced their understanding of them in their reverence for God and their worship of Him. The first is their understanding of the glory, the power, and the goodness of God, just as Moses had felt. The second is the naturally resulting understanding of their own nothingness in comparison to Him—as Moses had also felt—that led them to their reverence for God and their steadfastly obedient worship of Him.

When the brother of Jared knelt before the Lord in prayer, he humbly acknowledged, "We know that thou art holy and dwellest in the heavens, and that we are unworthy before thee; because of the fall our natures have become evil continually; nevertheless, O Lord, thou hast given us a commandment that we must call upon thee, that from thee we may receive according to our desires" (Ether 3:2).

Generations later, King Benjamin taught his people: "As ye have come to the knowledge of the glory of God, or if ye have known of his goodness and have tasted of his love, and have received a remission of your sins, which causeth such exceedingly great joy in your souls, even so I would that ye should remember, and always retain in remembrance, the greatness of God, and your own nothingness, and his goodness and long-suffering towards you, unworthy creatures, and humble yourselves even in the depths of humility, calling on the name of the Lord daily, and standing steadfastly in the faith of that which is to come" (Mosiah 4:11).

Their understanding of the glory, power, and goodness of God and the naturally resulting understanding of their own nothingness in comparison to Him—which came as a result of their humility and their calling upon Him daily—led them to their reverence for God and their steadfastly obedient worship of Him. This was the foundation of their discipleship. Interestingly, understanding of these two principles almost always comes in that order. It is important to understand the great distinction between acknowledging our nothingness before the omnipotent, omniscient Almighty God and feeling worthless. It was not a lack of confidence in themselves, low self-esteem, or feelings of worthlessness—for "the worth of souls is great in the sight of God" (D&C 18:10)—that led them finally to submit to His will. Rather, it was their perceiving His goodness and power, and recognizing their own fallen nature in comparison, that led them to worship as they did.

The tiny acorn is nothing compared to the great oak, but within that acorn is the DNA to become just like its parent, if it is given the proper nourishment and atmosphere in which to grow. Even though we may only have begun to understand the power of God and our potential as His offspring, we are still "gods in embryo" with "unlimited potential for progress and attainment."[1] Small as my own understanding may be, it has given me hope and a sense of worth. It has given me strength and the desire to choose discipleship of Christ over submission to my attractions. I have since come to understand that on some level gospel understanding, righteousness, and having the Spirit do not necessarily change the nature of attraction for those with homosexual attractions any more than it does for those with heterosexual attractions. Although my feelings of attraction have not diminished with increased understanding of the power and glory and goodness of God and my own comparative nothingness, this new understanding has changed the way I view and manage those attractions, and it has fueled the passion with which I worship my Father in Heaven and seek His righteousness.

"The Glory of God"

While teaching at the Missionary Training Center I had an experience that helped me to better understand how Moses might have felt before the Lord on the mount. I was teaching a group of elders who were a bit slothful and apathetic. They had good hearts, but they didn't sense the power and the urgency of the work they were engaged in. It showed in their conduct. When we prayed at the end of class, one of them refused to kneel but rather half sat in his chair. Others in one way or another prostrated themselves upon the ground but with an air of indolence rather than an attitude of reverence and submission. I poured out my heart in prayer that they would feel the Spirit of God to a greater degree and gain an appreciation for the magnitude of their calling.

One evening during class we had a very powerful spiritual experience. There was a feeling in the classroom I had rarely experienced before. A feeling of awe toward God and a greater understanding of His magnificence and goodness was manifested to each of the elders. When we prayed at the end of class to express our gratitude for the experience we had, the prayer was much more intense and sincere than anything I had ever heard escape the lips of any of these missionaries. Every elder's posture during prayer represented the feeling of worship and awe we felt that evening. These elders knew they were sons of God. Though this experience was different from that of Moses, I felt as though I had been in the presence of the Lord. I felt of my nothingness in comparison to His goodness and glory.

Afterward, I returned to my apartment with the memory of that experience still potent. Several of my roommates were watching a TV sitcom that I had thought pretty funny, so I sat down to watch it with them. Within moments I noticed its humor was tainted with lewdness and otherwise inappropriate innuendoes. I had never noticed it so distinctly before, but it was in sharp contrast to the experience I had just had at the

MTC. I was keenly aware that what I was watching was offensive to God. At that moment I felt a very clear and distinct impression from the Spirit: "One of us will have to leave. Will it be you or me?" In the spirit of awe and love I felt for God, and with the increased understanding of His goodness and glory I felt at the time, I had no desire to continue watching. I slipped out of the room and went to my bedroom. In making the decision that would allow me to bask in that feeling of the Spirit a little longer, I felt closer to God, and I was grateful for His love and guiding Spirit.

Through this and other similar experiences, I have glimpsed to a small degree the power of God and my relationship to Him. The one thing I have come to know for certain is that "for this cause I know that man is nothing, which thing I never had supposed" (Moses 1:10). The world and popular culture often present themselves as glamorous and enticing. The natural eye may seem to see a glory and attractiveness to it. But on that occasion I saw the glory of the world in a way that may have been somewhat similar to the perspective of Moses as he looked upon Satan, recognized his counterfeit grandeur for what it was, and cast him out.

After having felt so powerfully the Spirit of the Almighty and His power, the contrast between God and the adversary was undeniably distinct. I don't know that I had ever seen the emptiness and illusive glory of the world until I felt the glory of God to the degree I felt it that evening. The minute understanding of the character of God I have gained from such experiences has been a great comfort. It has often given me the strength and desire to do what Moses did—to look at the many faces and temptations of the adversary in the world today and declare with power, "Who art thou, for I am a son of God . . . Get thee hence, Satan; deceive me not."

In all honesty, though, having felt in a very real way something of the power of God and understanding my unique relationship to Him as His son have been at times a frustration as well as a comfort in my struggle with same-gender attraction. Sometimes the reality of those spiritual experiences has become merely a memory, and I have forgotten to some degree the power I felt. There have been times when part of me wanted so badly to give up completely, but at the same time, I didn't feel I could forget or rationalize away those spiritual feelings enough to be truly happy in surrendering to my attractions.

Despite that understanding, I have scars from the battle. There have been times I've forgotten the power of God and the feeling of reverence I had for Him. There have been times before I felt the Spirit to the magnitude I did with those elders when the adversary stood before me saying, "Son of man, worship me," and, hesitating, I thought "Why not?" I have at times allowed Satan to convince me that I am a son of man and not of God. I have at times allowed him to mislead me into seeing others as sons of men and not sons of God. But as the Lord in His mercy has helped me to remember those spiritual feelings when I have turned more fully to Him, I have come to understand more fully the power of President Spencer W. Kimball's statement: "When you look in the dictionary for the most important word, do you know what it is? It could be remember. Because all of you have made covenants—you know what to do and you know how to do it—our greatest need is to remember. . . . *Remember* is the word. *Remember* is the program."[2]

"The Fall of Our Natures"

Just as it is important to acknowledge and feel the power and glory of God, it is likewise essential that we all recognize and feel our own nothingness and our unholiness and our unworthiness in order for our worship of the Lord and, hence, our salvation ever to be complete. President Ezra Taft Benson taught why individual acknowledgement of this doctrine is so important. He said, "Just as a man does not really desire food until he is hungry, so he does not desire the salvation of Christ until he knows why he needs Christ. No one adequately and properly knows why he needs Christ until he understands and accepts the doctrine of the Fall and its effect upon all mankind."[3]

The Fall was necessary, and our understanding of it is foundational to at least two things. First, it is essential to our acceptance of Jesus Christ as our Savior and Redeemer. To lessen the importance of understanding the Fall is to lessen the importance of understanding the Atonement. If we do not understand the Fall, then we cannot understand the Atonement. "The Fall and the Atonement are a package deal," Robert Millet taught. "One brings the other into existence, and I am not aware of any discussion of the Atonement in the Book of Mormon that is not accompanied, either directly or by implication, with a discussion of the Fall. We do not appreciate and treasure the medicine until we appreciate the seriousness of the malady. One cannot look earnestly and longingly to the Redeemer if he or she does not sense the need for redemption. Jesus came to earth to do more than offer sage advice. He is not merely a benevolent consultant. He is our Savior. He came to save us."[4]

Second, our understanding of the effects of the Fall is essential to our understanding of why some individuals experience same-gender attraction—something that to many seems so contrary to all God has taught us through His prophets concerning the divine role of marriage and family in the eternities. And, as I'll explain in more depth further on, it is important to know that even though the Fall was foreordained as part of the Father's plan of salvation, God did not create fallen man. Doctrinally, especially in connection with many arguments concerning homosexuality, it is important to know that the Fall was a choice made by man, even though it was planned as part of our eternal progression toward godhood. And as Stephen Robinson has suggested, the Fall affects us physically, spiritually, mentally, emotionally, and morally, and every one of these things could affect to some degree an individual's experience with same-gender attraction.[5]

From the time we are in Primary, we learn from the Articles of Faith. The second reads: "We believe that men will be punished for their own sins, and not for Adam's transgression." We do not believe in original sin nor do we believe that mortal, fallen man is inherently evil. Even though an individual may experience same-gender attraction, he or she is not inherently evil. To the contrary, all of God's children are inherently good and noble. In the dawn of history God spoke concerning the effects of the Fall upon us: "Inasmuch as thy children are conceived in sin, even so when they begin to grow up, sin conceiveth in their hearts, and they taste the bitter, that they may know to prize the good" (Moses 6:55).

Elder Jeffrey R. Holland explained the difference between being inherently evil and being brought into a world where the seeds of the natural man have been sown in our flesh (see Moses 6:55) and—despite our divine spiritual heritage—where some of our most natural desires will be contrary to the will and plan of our Father and His Only Begotten Son:

"Because this doctrine is so basic to the plan of salvation and also because it is so susceptible to misunderstanding, we must note that these references to 'natural' evil emphatically do not mean that men and women are 'inherently' evil. There is a crucial difference. As spiritual sons and daughters of God, all mortal men and women are divine in origin and divine in their potential destiny. As Doctrine and Covenants 93:38–39 teaches, the spirit of every man, woman, and child 'was innocent in the beginning.' But it is also true that as a result of the Fall they are now in a 'natural' (fallen) world where the devil 'taketh away light' and where some elements of nature—including temporal human nature—need discipline, restraint, and refinement. . . .

"Natural man, with all of his new and wonderful but as yet unbridled and unregenerated potential, must be made 'submissive' to the Holy Spirit, a spirit that still entices and lifts us upward. . . . Our deepest desires, our pre-mortal yearnings, are still divine in their origins, and they are still deep in our souls. The echoes of our earlier innocence still reverberate, and the light that forsakes the evil one still shines. Our hearts can—and in their purity, do—desire that which is spiritual and holy rather than that which is 'carnal, sensual, and devilish.'"[6]

Elder Holland also taught: "Nevertheless, we (through Adam and Eve) made the conscious choice to live in and endure this mortal sphere of opposition in all things, for only through such an experience was godly progress possible. Adam and Eve—and we—knowingly and lovingly absolved God of the responsibility for the 'thorns and thistles' of a fallen world that was personally chosen by us, not capriciously imposed by him."[7]

In light of the doctrine of the Fall, it is important to realize that the experience of same-gender attraction—and the behavior it may lead to for many, behavior that Paul referred to as being "against nature" (Romans 1:26)—can feel very natural for some, for the natural man is fallen man, and our natural state is a fallen state, and what often feels natural in our fallen state is not natural to God or godliness. Even men as faithful and stalwart as Nephi, who exclaimed, "My soul delighteth in the things of the Lord; and my heart pondereth continually upon the things which I have seen and heard," have also wrestled with their fallen nature. Nephi immediately afterward lamented, "O wretched man that I am! Yea, my heart sorroweth because of my flesh; my soul grieveth because of mine iniquities. I am encompassed about, because of the temptations and the sins which do so easily beset me. And when I desire to rejoice, my heart groaneth because of my sins" (2 Nephi 4:16–19).

President Brigham Young observed: "There are no persons without evil passions to embitter their lives. Mankind are revengeful, passionate, hateful, and devilish in their dispositions. This we inherit through the fall, and the grace of God is designed to enable us to overcome it."[8] And probably to the comfort of those who, regardless of how hard they try, cannot seem to get rid of the inclination within them to do evil, President Young also said: "Will sin be perfectly destroyed? No, it will not, for it is not so designed in the economy of Heaven. . . . Do not suppose that we shall ever in the flesh be free from temptations to sin. Some suppose that they can in the flesh be sanctified body and spirit and become so pure that they will never again feel the effects of the power of the adversary of truth. Were it possible for a person to attain to this degree of perfection in the flesh, he could not die neither remain in a world where sin predominates. . . . I think we more or less feel the effects of sin so long as we live, and finally have to pass the ordeals of death."[9]

In the context of same-gender attraction, this truth is especially important for those who—whether single, married, or divorced—feel hopelessness and frustration because they cannot seem to get rid of the unwanted temptation to act on their feelings, despite the love they feel for God, His gospel, and possibly even a spouse and children. Though we must strive to live so that the Spirit of God can sanctify our hearts and our desires, we must also recognize that we may always feel temptation in some degree to act on our attractions while we are still in this mortal, probationary state. President Packer taught: "When any unworthy desires press into your mind, fight them, resist them, control them (see James 4:6–8; 2 Ne. 9:39; Mosiah 3:19). . . .

"That may be a struggle from which you will not be free in this life. If you do not act on temptations, you need feel no guilt. They may be extremely difficult to resist. But that is better than to yield and bring disappointment and unhappiness to you and those who love you."[10] Again, although resistance may be difficult, we must know that temptation to sin in various ways will always be a part of our mortal experience. We are imperfect. We are human. We are fallen mortals in a telestial world struggling mightily to live a celestial standard.

"Born That Way" vs. "God Made Me That Way"

A discussion of the nature of fallen man in the context of same-gender attraction naturally requires me to address the often-heard statements of some that "I was born that way" or "God made me that way." Even though these statements may sound similar in concept, there is a significant difference between the two.

"I was born that way." That some individuals may be "born that way"—born with natural inclinations or tendencies toward same-gender attraction—is quite possible. And it should be remembered that the passions or attractions we have that are contrary to the plan of God, or that make it a greater challenge to live the plan of God—whether they are homosexual or heterosexual or have nothing to do with sexuality at all—do not make us inherently evil. As Elder Jeffrey R. Holland suggested, they merely demonstrate that we are mortal and fallen. The natural desire to sin and to act upon those attractions—or any attraction contrary to

God's plan, for that matter—was sown in the flesh when we were conceived into mortality.

Elder Dallin H. Oaks of the Quorum of the Twelve Apostles stated: "We should distinguish between (1) homosexual . . . 'thoughts and feelings' . . . and (2) 'homosexual behavior.' . . . Some kinds of feelings seem to be inborn. Others are traceable to mortal experiences. Still other feelings seem to be acquired from a complex interaction of 'nature and nurture.' All of us have some feelings we did not choose, but the gospel of Jesus Christ teaches us that we still have the power to resist and reform our feelings (as needed) and to assure that they do not lead us to entertain inappropriate thoughts or to engage in sinful behavior.

"Different persons have different physical characteristics and different susceptibilities to the various physical and emotional pressures we may encounter in our childhood and adult environments. We did not choose these personal susceptibilities either, but we do choose and will be accountable for the attitudes, priorities, behavior, and 'lifestyle' we engraft upon them. . . .

"In each case . . . the feelings or other characteristics that increase susceptibility to certain behavior may have some relationship to inheritance. But the relationship is probably very complex. The inherited element may be nothing more than an increased likelihood that an individual will acquire certain feelings if he or she encounters particular influences during the developmental years. But regardless of our different susceptibilities or vulnerabilities . . . , we remain responsible for the exercise of our agency in the thoughts we entertain and the behavior we choose. . . .

"Most of us are born with [or develop] thorns in the flesh, some more visible, some more serious than others. We all seem to have susceptibilities to one disorder or another, but whatever our susceptibilities, we have the will and the power to control our thoughts and our actions. This must be so. God has said that he holds us accountable for what we do and what we think, so our thoughts and actions must be controllable by our agency. Once we have reached the age or condition of accountability, the claim 'I was born that way' does not excuse actions or thoughts that fail to conform to the commandments of God. We need to learn how to live so that a weakness that is mortal will not prevent us from achieving the goal that is eternal. . . .

" . . . Beware the argument that because a person has strong drives toward a particular act, he has no power of choice and therefore no responsibility for his actions. This contention runs counter to the most fundamental premises of the gospel of Jesus Christ. Satan would like us to believe that we are not responsible in this life. That is the result he tried to achieve by his contest in the pre-existence. A person who insists that he is not responsible for the exercise of his free agency because he was 'born that way' is trying to ignore the outcome of the War in Heaven. We are responsible, and if we argue otherwise, our efforts become part of the propaganda effort of the Adversary."[11]

"God made me that way." There is no doctrinal foundation for such a statement. That does not mean that same-gender attraction may not be legitimately among an individual's mortal challenges, but God did not create mortal, fallen man. As the Book of Mormon makes clear, man "brought upon himself" his own fall (Alma 42:12). If God had created mortal man, then death, sin, and all the other circumstances of mortality would be God's doing, and they would be eternal and permanent. Because man brought the Fall upon himself, he is the responsible moral agent, and it is therefore necessary that God rescue and redeem him from his fallen state.

Having brought about the Fall themselves, Adam and Eve became subject to punishment or reward for their actions. If we had been created by God in our mortal, fallen state, then there would be no justice in either punishment or reward, because our mortal state would be eternal and permanent, so that we "could not be agents unto [our]selves" (D&C 29:39). It has been made very clear that agents are precisely what we are to be. If it were not so, the eternal principle of agency would be invalidated, which cannot happen, or God would cease to be God. Agency was the principle fought over in the premortal war in heaven, and it is clear from our existence here on earth that God's purposes prevailed.

Furthermore, the Lord has explained that he does not create temporal or mortal conditions, nor does He function on a mortal level (see D&C 29:34).

With this understanding, it is important to put into context a statement made by President Spencer W. Kimball regarding homosexuality: "'God made me that way,' some say, as they rationalize and excuse themselves for their perversions. 'I can't help it,' they add. This is blasphemy. Is man not made in the image of God, and does he think God to be 'that way'? Man is responsible for his own sins. It is possible that he may rationalize and excuse himself until the groove is so deep he cannot get out without great difficulty, but this he can do. Temptations come to all people. The difference between the reprobate and the worthy person is generally that one yielded and the other resisted."[12]

The language President Kimball used may be hard, but the principle he taught is eternal and true. President Kimball's statement regarding the claim "God made me that way" is completely consistent with the possibility that some may be born with various factors influencing their attraction, but having inherent biological or psychological factors influencing their attraction does not mean "God made me that way." It is important to remember that that is not to say that God has no eternally valuable purposes in allowing us to experience whatever challenges, trials, attractions, temptations, or tendencies we have. He has allowed us to experience same-gender attraction—"to be this way"—and for some that attraction may very well be a part of their entire mortal sojourn. The purpose is that we may be tried in whatever way is necessary for us to learn the eternal lessons He would have us learn from our experiences here.

Latter-day Saint Worship of God

Because of our fallen nature, evidenced by our natural tendencies that are not in harmony with the plan, our only hope for salvation is through Jesus Christ. We know, without question, that the power to save us, to change us, to renew our souls, is in Christ, for God has declared: "Jesus Christ is the name which is given of the Father, and there is none other name given whereby man can be saved; Wherefore, all men must take upon them the name which is given of the Father, for in that name shall they be called at the last day" (D&C 18:23–24).

But for our fallen natures to be regenerated, for us to achieve our divine destiny of receiving all that our Father wants for His children, we must know Who we worship and how to worship Him. One of Jesus' purposes in His mortal mission was to teach those principles to His fallen brothers and sisters (D&C 93:7–20). Understanding and internalizing this concept has for me been one of great importance in coming to terms with same-gender attraction, for it is an attraction that commands devotion and feels so natural to me. I understood quickly, however, that if I did not deem my Father in Heaven worthy of greater devotion than my attraction, I would soon willfully submit. And in the society we live in today—especially with some of the political debates currently raging—one need not look far to know just how powerful a commander the attraction can be.

Elder James E. Talmage, in teaching the concept of worship, explained how the etymology of the word worship connotes worthy-ship. He then explicated the profoundness of the meaning of the word, saying, "The worship of which one is capable depends upon his comprehension of the worthiness characterizing the object of his reverence. Man's capacity for worship is a measure of his comprehension of God. The fuller the acquaintance and the closer the communion between the worshiper and Deity, the more thorough and sincere will be his homage. . . . True worship cannot exist where there is no reverence or love for the object. This reverence may be ill-founded; the adoration may be a species of idolatry; the object may be in fact unworthy; yet of the devotee it must be said that he worships if his conscience clothe the idol with the attribute of worthy-ship."[13]

Every human being worships. Each person has an innate desire to focus his affection and obey a master, even if that master is himself. The Savior's statement that He knew who He worshipped is powerful to me, because it took me a long time to figure out who I worship. Although I was raised a member of the Church, served a mission, attended Brigham Young University, taught at the Missionary Training Center in Provo, worked summers as a counselor for the Church's Especially for Youth program, studied in the Holy Land for a semester at BYU's Jerusalem Center, and was active in Church callings all along the way, it took the challenge of same-gender attraction to really pull me to my knees to decide Who it is that I want to command my allegiance. It took this challenge for me to begin asking questions I had never felt the need to ask before. Even though I learned about God and the scriptures and the Church through those experiences, and though I thought I loved the gospel of Christ and His Church, it took standing at a crossroads between two paths that felt very much a part of me—both of which were commanding loyalty—to really teach me about Who I worship and why I worship Him.

Just as it has been important for me to understand Who we worship, so it has also been important for me to learn how we worship. Again, Jesus has been my example. He worshipped the Father by diligently doing all that was asked of Him, and He did so willingly and with His full heart. He was perfectly obedient in putting first "the will of the Father in all things from the beginning" (3 Nephi 11:11). Our worship must be the same.

During Jesus' ministry in the Old World, a scribe said to Him, "I will follow thee whithersoever thou goest" (Matthew 8:19). Then another of His disciples said shortly thereafter, "Lord, suffer me first to go and bury my father." Jesus' bold response was "Follow me; and let the dead bury their dead" (Matthew 8:21–22). Desiring to bury a dead parent does not seem an unreasonable request, but the Savior was teaching a powerful lesson. The man was making even legitimate temporal matters and desires a priority over following the Lord. The desire for romantic love and companionship is a legitimate and holy desire, but we must be certain that we don't make our attractions and quest for companionship a priority over serving the Author of our salvation.

The commandment the Lord gave to worship the Father and to "seek ye first the kingdom of God and his righteousness" (3 Nephi 13:33) should be the desire and determination of our hearts, regardless of our circumstances. It should be our prime focus each day of our lives to worship the Lord in every capacity. As Elder James E. Talmage suggested, our willingness to live the commandments of our God is a direct measure of our comprehension of Him and His worthiness. That applies to every aspect of our lives, including how we use our agency to respond to the challenge of same-gender attraction. When our attractions—however natural and genuine—become a priority over the Father of our spirits, we have said something about our opinion of His worth as the object of our worship. But when we keep our focus on the Father and follow the commandments He has given us through His Son and His prophets, despite our challenges, we are heeding the required call to worship the Father— if that homage is sincere and is driven by love and a willing heart.

"Sanctify My Name"

During the time in my spiritual journey when I agonized over whether being faithful to the standards of the gospel was really worth it, and while struggling with conflicting desires about whether I really wanted for myself the things I knew God wanted for me, I was at one point sitting in church, praying for some sort of peace of mind and heart. I was touched by the words of a hymn I had heard many times but was now *hearing* for the first time:

> *May we who know the sacred Name*
> *From every sin depart.*
> *Then will the Spirit's constant flame*
> *Preserve us pure in heart.*[14]

I have reviewed those words often in my mind, and I still do not know exactly why they came with such force that morning, but they did, and I have continued to ponder their meaning. A verse I later read in the second book of Nephi helped me to better understand what I believe the Lord was trying to teach me. While teaching his people, Nephi, quoting Isaiah, said, "When he seeth his children, the work of my hands, in the midst of him, they shall *sanctify my name,* and *sanctify the Holy One of Jacob"* (2 Nephi 27:34; italics added).

If "Jesus Christ is the name which is given of the Father, and there is none other name given whereby man can be saved [and] all men must take upon them the name which is given of the Father" (D&C 18:23–24), then we who have taken that name upon us have the responsibility to sanctify that name and make it holy so that others will know that it is a name worthy of turning toward. The Book of Mormon prophet Samuel declared, "And if ye believe on his name ye will repent of all your sins, that thereby ye may have a remission of them through his merits" (Helaman 14:13).

The more I've studied the scriptures and pondered the words of the hymn that so impressed me in that sacrament meeting, the more strongly I've come to feel that we worship the Father and sanctify or glorify the name of His Only Begotten by the way we exercise our agency. In all things, Christ left us "an example, that [we] should follow his steps" (1 Peter 2:21), and that includes what it means to sanctify—or glorify— a name.

Christ glorified His Father by suffering His cross and by following "the will of the Father in all things" (3 Nephi 11:11). Likewise, we glorify Christ by obeying Jacob's exhortation to "believe in Christ, and view his death, and suffer his cross and bear the shame of the world" (Jacob 1:8). I doubt Jacob was being merely poetic in that poignant call to come unto Christ. As Christ glorified His Father, so must we glorify Christ by following His will in all things, those who experience same-gender attraction not exempted.

To understand how to glorify the name of Christ and make it holy, the prophet Ezekiel taught the importance God's people understanding the difference between the holy and the profane (Ezekiel 44:23). Understanding that distinction affects our acceptance of His atonement and the nature of our worship. As Paul taught, Christ will "be glorified in his saints" (2 Thessalonians 1:10). *Saints* means "holy ones" and is a title borne by members of the Church who, through the covenant of baptism, have taken upon them the name of Christ and solemnly promised to make His name holy by following His example and worshipping the Father. When dealing with a trial as powerful and as challenging as same-gender attraction, I have often thought that the most powerful way to sanctify the name of Jesus Christ is to dedicate our lives to wholly serving Him and fully living the teachings of the gospel. As we suffer this cross in a skeptical world that cries for sexual freedom, we glorify Christ, "for the preaching of the cross is to them that perish foolishness; but unto us which are saved it is the power of God. . . . The natural man receiveth not the things of the Spirit of God: for they are foolishness unto him: neither can he know them, because they are spiritually discerned" (1 Corinthians 1:18; 2:14). The idea that same-gender attraction could or even should be managed through submission to Christ is foolishness to those who do not understand the plan of salvation and His gospel in its restored fulness.

I freely admit that there is much I do not understand about the Atonement, but when the Savior said that He will enable me with power as I strive to suffer this cross with faith, live the gospel, and bear the shame of the world, I believe Him. We are here to glorify our God, and we dilute our power to receive His aid when we adopt the philosophies of men or give up in our fight. We, as the "holy ones" of God, cannot allow ourselves to become casualties in this war. We can glorify and sanctify him, or we can, as Paul said, "crucify to [our]selves the Son of God afresh, and put him to an open shame" (Hebrews 6:6) by disregarding His sacred laws.

When we live faithful to Him through the enabling grace of His atonement, we say something powerful about the glory of His name. The opposite is also true: Those who give in and submit to temptation, regardless of the challenge they experience, are also saying something about that name. That is the essential meaning of the other important concept Ezekiel declared was necessary for us to understand. To profane is to violate anything sacred or to treat it with irreverence or contempt; it is to be blasphemous, disrespectful, or sacrilegious; to profane something is to mark it with futility or ineffectualness. The principle of profanity is similar to vanity, and the third commandment written by the finger of God on Mount Sinai was "Thou shalt not take the name of the Lord thy God in vain; for the Lord will not hold him guiltless that taketh his name in vain" (Exodus 20:7). That under the Mosaic law the penalty for blaspheming the name of the Lord was death by stoning affirms the importance of the commandment (see Leviticus 24:16). The distinguishing principles of sanctity and holiness in contrast with vanity and profanity is something I've felt the Lord has been trying to help me understand in the last few years.

I had grown up with the understanding that a person profaned the name of the Lord or took it in vain only when he used the name of God inappropriately in speaking. I've come to understand a deeper and more profound meaning of that proclamation from Sinai. When we are baptized, we take upon us the name of Christ. To take the Lord's name in vain is not simply to swear; it is to use His name in any way that makes it empty or of little worth. Anytime we live contrary to His teachings, we make some statement about the value of that name.

Elder James E. Talmage said: "To take the name of God in vain . . . is to use that name lightly, to use it emptily, to use it without effect, so far as the intent is concerned. . . . We are apt to think that this has reference to the speaking of the name of God only . . . but beyond this there is profanity of action, which is of greater import than the spoken word, even as the prayer of the heart is greater than the prayer of the lips. . . . We take his name in vain whenever we wilfully do aught that is in defiance of his commandments, since we have taken his name upon ourselves."[15]

The lives we live bear testimony of Jesus and preserve His name. "Ye are the salt of the earth," the Savior said, "but if the salt have lost his savor, wherewith shall it be salted?" (Matthew 5:13; 3 Nephi 12:13). Salt is a preserver and does not lose its savor with age. Nor would those called to preserve righteousness and the name of Christ on the earth lose their preserving power through age or trial or tribulation. Only mixture with the elements of the world—with the doctrines and philosophies of men—will cause salt to lose its preserving effect. We, as Christ's covenant people, cannot make a difference in the world unless we are different from the world.

Elder John A. Widtsoe expounded the substance of worship and of making holy the name of our God: "We need, in this Church and Kingdom, for our own and the world's welfare a group of men and women in their individual lives who shall be as a light to the nations, and really standards for the world to follow. Such a people must be different from the world as it now is. . . . We are here to build Zion to Almighty God, for the blessing of all the world. In that aim we are unique and different from all other peoples. We must respect that obligation, and not be afraid of it. We cannot walk as other men, or talk as other men, or do as other men, for we have a different destiny, obligation, and responsibility placed upon us, and we must fit ourselves for that great destiny and obligation."[16] Those with feelings of same-gender attraction are just as desperately needed in this mission as are any other of God's children.

As sons and daughters of God and not of man (as Satan would have us believe) we have the seeds of divinity sown in our spirit, and I hope, despite my struggle with same-gender attraction, always to hearken to that call to be true to the Father, to strive daily to know more fully and worship more completely, and to glorify and make holy the name of His Son, the Savior in whose blood I can find mercy and redemption from my fallen nature.

Chapter 7

Paul, the Romans, and Homosexuality

With only a few scriptures in the Bible and none in the Book of Mormon or other Latter-day Saint scripture that refer to homosexuality explicitly, most discussions of homosexuality by those in the Church and other Christians outside it center on a statement made by Paul in his letter to the Roman Saints. In that letter the apostle Paul is getting to the core of a much subtler sin whose roots extend far beyond homosexuality, and he uses the homosexual behavior prevalent in Rome at that time as an example of a more profound principle. A latter-day apostle, Elder Richard G. Scott, has taught: "As you seek spiritual knowledge, search for principles. Carefully separate them from the detail used to explain them. Principles are concentrated truth, packaged for application to a wide variety of circumstances. A true principle makes decisions clear even under the most confusing and compelling circumstances. It is worth great effort to organize the truth we gather to simple statements of principle."[1]

Other biblical verses specifically condemn homosexual behavior, but Paul's epistle to the Romans is perhaps the most useful for placing that condemnation within a theological context. Examining statements from Romans 1 in a historical and doctrinal context, and according to the principle taught by Elder Scott, may shed greater light on the central truths that Paul focuses on in his discourse—that salvation is in Jesus Christ and that it is essential to place God at the center of our worship. My hope is that Romans 1 will cease to be a theological stick used to beat those who experience same-gender attraction and will instead become a way by which each child of God, regardless of what trials or attractions he or she experiences, may gain a deeper and broader perspective that will enhance their worship of our Father.

Though it is generally a few verses in chapter 1 of Paul's letter to the Roman Saints that are used to condemn homosexual behavior, those verses fall within the framework of a larger theological message. In verses 16 and 17 of the first chapter of his letter, Paul declares that God reveals His righteousness and power to the faithful who worship Him. In verses 18–32, in which Paul refers to homosexuality, he presents a negative formulation of that declaration: God withdraws His righteousness and power from the unfaithful who choose not to worship Him and who instead serve "the creature more than the Creator" (v. 25), those who worship idols. Verse 17 concludes with spiritual life for the faithful, and verse 32 concludes with spiritual death for the unfaithful.

A parallel principle taught in the Book of Mormon helps us understand more clearly Paul's overall message to the Romans. Speaking to Zeezrom, an initially contentious lawyer, Alma declares: "It is given unto many to know the mysteries of God; nevertheless they are laid under a strict command that they shall not impart only according to the portion of his word which he doth grant unto the children of men, according to the heed and diligence which they give unto him. . . . And he that will not harden his heart, to him is given the greater portion of the word, until it is given unto him to know the mysteries of God until he know them in full" (Alma 12:9–10).

As Paul does in Romans 1, Alma then presents the negative formulation of that thesis, saying, "They that will harden their hearts, to them is given the lesser portion of the word until they know nothing concerning his mysteries; and then they are taken captive by the devil, and led by his will down to destruction. Now this is what is meant by the chains of hell" (Alma 12:11).

As Paul declared, the gospel of Christ is "the power of God unto salvation" (Romans 1:17), and he meant that it is exactly that—the gospel of Jesus Christ is not just a message; it is also a power. The gospel is not simply a theological belief system that people can judge objectively and then decide whether they will accept or reject. It is not a world view that can be indifferently adopted or casually embraced, for it is a power that saves the souls of the Father's children and regenerates fallen man—*all* of fallen man, homosexual and heterosexual alike.

The gospel of Christ is the only eternal system leading to spiritual life. It is the power of salvation, but its power extends only to those who believe. The gospel is the power of salvation for those who exercise active trust in God—or who give "heed and diligence" (Alma 12:9), as Alma described it, to following the whole law of the gospel. As we exercise faith, God reveals more and more of His knowledge and righteousness to us.

As Paul begins the negative formulation of his initial declaration in Romans 1:18, he begins the theme in which his reference to homosexual behavior will fall. He speaks of the ungodly and the unrighteous who ignore their obligations to God and to other mortals. If the devotion we should be giving to God and others is misplaced, then we are committing idolatry, and this idolatry is the principle underlying Paul's discussion of the worship of God. He is speaking to all people, even through his reference to homosexual behavior.

The importance of placing God at the center of our worship is supreme to anything else we do in our lives. Our hearts have a natural capacity for affection and an instinctive desire to direct that affection toward something or someone. Elder James E. Talmage said that the manner in which one directs those affections "depends upon his comprehension of the worthiness characterizing the object of his reverence. . . . True worship cannot exist where there is no reverence or love for the object. This reverence may be ill-founded; the adoration may be a species of idolatry; the object may be in fact unworthy; yet of the devotee it must be said that he worships if his conscience clothe the idol with the attribute of worthy-ship."[2] If the devotion we should be giving to God and others is misplaced, then we are committing idolatry, and this idolatry is the principle underlying Paul's discussion of the worship of God.

Bearing in mind the principle of love, or "worthy-ship," we recall the

Prophet Joseph Smith's inspired translation of the phrase "who hold the truth in unrighteousness" (KJV Romans 1:18) to "who love not the truth, but remain in unrighteousness" (JST Romans 1:18), which helps us to understand what it means to hold the truth in unrighteousness. In our modern Western culture, we commonly think of the truth as something that can be believed or at least understood separately from our state of righteousness. For Paul and others of his time, however, truth is moral as well as factual: Truth is not truth to a person unless it is lived. A prime example of this connection in Greek thought is the word *apeitheo,* which can be translated both as "to disbelieve" and "to disobey," thus indicating that these people connected belief/disbelief with obedience/disobedience. Likewise, the degree to which we are unrighteous is the degree to which we fail to know and love Christ and the truths of His gospel. If we love the truths of the gospel of our God, then we do not seek to suppress it through our unrighteous worship of anything other than Him. Brigham Young once said, "Do you think that people will obey the truth because it is true, unless they love it? No, they will not. Truth is obeyed when it is loved."[3]

The next few verses in Paul's letter are especially important in helping us understand why Paul uses homosexual behavior as a type for idolatry in general. Paul speaks of two principal methods for understanding God's truth. The first is implied in the phrase "that which may be known of God is manifest in them" (Romans 1:19). The word translated "manifest" is especially significant. It can also be translated "to shine forth" and carries with it the idea of light.[4] This idea resonates with us as Latter-day Saints, especially, because of our understanding of the light of Christ, which, as Mormon taught, "is given to every man, that he may know good from evil" (Moroni 7:16).

Paul's second method for knowing truth is described in verse 20, where, in addition to the light of Christ, he appeals to the creation of the world as a model for knowing truth: "For God hath revealed unto them the invisible things of him, from the creation of the world, which are clearly seen; things which are not seen being understood by the things that are made, through his eternal power and Godhead; so that they are without excuse" (JST Romans 1:20). Paul is saying that implicit in the creation of the world, the visible things that God has made help us to understand what is not physically visible to us—namely, God's power and divinity—when we have truly contemplated them and sought to understand them.

Alma taught this same principle in his confrontation with Korihor, the anti-Christ: "All things denote there is a God; yea, even the earth, and all things that are upon the face of it, yea, and its motion, yea, and also all the planets which move in their regular form do witness that there is a Supreme Creator" (Alma 30:44).

Through the light of Christ and the creation of the world—two important ways for learning truth—every one of God's children is capable of, first, knowing the truths of God if they will honestly strive to obtain them, and, second, living the truths they do know. Every child of God has been given the capacity to distinguish between good and evil. The light of Christ is felt universally. Those not familiar with the truths of the gospel of Christ may be ignorant of the finer points of what the gospel requires of us, but if they are truly honest with themselves, they can discern the essentials of what is right and what is wrong.

One thing that we see by the light of Christ and that is implicit in the creation of the world concerning "the invisible things of [God]" is "his eternal power and Godhead." The Greek word translated "power" indicates not only sheer strength or power to overcome, as seems to be the case with the English word, but also ability to act—the eternal capacity to *create*. In God's creation we see the things that make Him God. His creative power distinguishes Him from the supposed divinity of the false gods, idols that are made and cannot make anything themselves. Understanding this idea is crucial to understanding homosexual behavior in a theological context. A central tenet of the fulness of the gospel of Christ is that creative power. The power to parent is a mark of true divinity.[5]

Speaking of the godly power of creation, Elder Jeffrey R. Holland said: "Physical intimacy is . . . symbolic of a shared relationship between them and their Father in Heaven. He is immortal and perfect. We are mortal and imperfect. Nevertheless we seek ways even in mortality whereby we can unite with Him spiritually. In so doing we gain some access to both the grace and the majesty of His power. . . . These are moments when we quite literally unite our will with God's will, our spirit with His Spirit, where communion through the veil becomes very real. At such moments we not only acknowledge His divinity but we quite literally take something of that divinity to ourselves. One aspect of that divinity given to virtually all men and women is the use of His power to create a human body, that wonder of all wonders, a genetically and spiritually unique being never before seen in the history of the world and never to be duplicated again in all the ages of eternity. A child, your child—with eyes and ears and fingers and toes and a future of unspeakable grandeur."[6]

On an earlier occasion, as president of Brigham Young University, he said: "Imagine that, if you will, . . . all of us . . . carrying daily, hourly, minute-to-minute, virtually every waking and sleeping moment of our lives, the power and the chemistry and the eternally transmitted seeds of life to grant someone else her second estate, someone else his next level of development in the divine plan of salvation. . . . I submit that we will never be more like God at any other time in this life than when we are expressing that particular power. Of all the titles He has chosen for Himself, Father is the one He declares, and *creation* is His watchword—especially human creation, creation in His image. His glory isn't a mountain, as stunning as mountains are. It isn't in sea or sky or snow or sunrise, as beautiful as they all are. It isn't in art or technology, be that a concerto or computer. No, His glory—and His grief—is in His children. We—you and I—are His prized possessions, and we are the earthly evidence, however inadequate, of what He truly is. Human life is the greatest of God's powers, the most mysterious and magnificent chemistry of it all, and you and I have been given it. . . . You and I—who can make neither mountain nor moonlight, not one rain-drop or a single rose—have this greater gift in an absolutely unlimited way. *And the only control placed on us is self-control—self-control born of respect for the divine sacramental power it is.*"[7]

God is a god of creation, and as partners in creation, we have the responsibility to honor that power and hold it sacred—and to use that power to further the purposes of God. Brigham Young said, "There are multitudes of pure and holy spirits waiting to take tabernacles, now what is our duty?—To prepare tabernacles for them; to take a course that will not tend to drive those spirits into the families of the wicked, where they will be trained in wickedness, debauchery, and every species of crime. It is the duty of every righteous man and woman to prepare tabernacles for all the spirits they can."[8]

As Paul refers to homosexual behavior in verses 26 and 27, he is making an important contrast. Richard Hays, a theologian from Duke University, writes that homosexual behavior provides a particularly graphic image of the way in which humanity, in their fallen state, often distort God's creative order in their idolatry: "[Paul's] reference to God as creator would certainly evoke for Paul as well as for his readers, immediate recollections of the creation story in Genesis 1–3. . . . The complementarity of male and female is given a theological grounding in God's creative activity: God has made them to become 'one flesh.' By way of sharp contrast, in Romans 1 Paul portrays homosexual behavior as a 'sacrament' (so to speak) of the anti-religion of human beings who refuse to honor God as creator: it is an outward and visible sign of an inward and spiritual reality. . . . Thus, Paul's choice of homosexuality as an illustration of human depravity is not merely random: it serves his rhetorical purposes by providing a vivid image of humanity's primal rejection of the sovereignty of God the creator."[9]

Remember, Paul is using homosexual sin as a type for all idolatry, much as Hosea in the Old Testament used heterosexual sin—a prophet marrying a harlot—to illustrate the same point. In the Old Testament, idolatry is almost always associated with sexual sin in general, in part because idolatry often involved sexual sin. Sexuality in and of itself is divine and is a part of what God made us to be. With the eternal nature of sexuality understood, Paul could have used any heterosexual sexual transgression as his example, but to a spiritually undiscerning and idolatrous people such as those in Rome, that particular contrast would not have been nearly as evocative as the example of homosexual behavior.

According to the Latter-day Saint understanding of the restored fulness of the gospel, eternal life is God's life—it is the kind of life that He lives. His glory and the mark of His Godhood is eternal increase, or "eternal lives." Therefore, in the eternities, eternal increase will be an essential part of the existence of all who become gods, for the highest glory of the heavens is that of exaltation in the celestial kingdom, and exaltation is eternal life.

The Prophet Joseph Smith taught: "Except a man and his wife enter into an everlasting covenant and be married for eternity . . . by the power and authority of the Holy Priesthood, they will cease to increase when they die; that is, they will not have any children after the resurrection."[10] The Prophet's grandnephew, President Joseph Fielding Smith, expounded on this important doctrine: "Some will gain celestial bodies with all the powers of exaltation and eternal increase. These bodies will shine like the sun as our Savior's does, as described by John.

"Those who enter the terrestrial kingdom will have terrestrial bodies, and they will not shine like the sun, but they will be more glorious than the bodies of those who receive the telestial glory. In both of these kingdoms there will be changes in the bodies and limitations. They will not have the power of increase, neither the power or nature to live as husbands and wives, for this will be denied them and they cannot increase.

"Those who receive the exaltation in the celestial kingdom will have the 'continuation of the seeds forever.' (D&C 132:19) They will live in the family relationship. In the terrestrial and in the telestial kingdoms there will be no marriage. Those who enter there will remain 'separately and singly' forever. (D&C 132:15–32)."[11]

Sexuality is a divine gift to each of God's literal offspring and is the ultimate symbol of divine creation. Since God is a god of creation, only those who hold sacred that divine gift of procreation will be granted use of it in the eternities. The divine Creator has ordained that the creative power he has temporarily granted us be expressed only within the bounds of the God-sanctioned institution of marriage between a man and a woman. Though the physical expression of intimate love between married couples is not solely for the purpose of creation, those sacred powers—and all expression of them—must be viewed with reverence. Perhaps the most meaningful way I have ever heard described the spirit of the law surrounding those powers is that when we use those powers in any form that is self-serving—whether married or unmarried or with another person or singly—we are abusing that sacred gift and must repent.

Irreverence for and abuse of sexual, procreative powers—whether that irreverence or abuse is homosexual or heterosexual—is placing the creation above the Creator, which is idolatry. And to the idol-worshiping people of the Greco-Roman world—many of whom, not coincidentally, esteemed homosexual practices—Paul uses homosexual sin as a type for all sexual sin because it clearly contrasts the creative power of God with the noncreative sin of homosexual actions. Paul ultimately teaches that "sexual sin [of all types] . . . makes sexuality into a lie; it makes it false and then worships that falseness. It mocks God profoundly, for it changes his glory—eternal increase, the creative power that marks His godhead—into something profane. For many, lust for the flesh, either heterosexual or homosexual, replaces godly desire."[12]

Considering Paul's letter to the Roman Saints, it is important to note that even though we can genuinely have a spiritual conviction that homosexual behavior is completely contrary to the Father's eternal purposes for His children—and have those feelings without any trace of bigotry or hatred toward those who participate in it—we must also remember that we cannot feel personal prejudice or hatred toward those who experience homosexual attraction (even those who participate in homosexual behavior) and use our religion to justify that prejudice and hatred. Dr. Hays of Duke University notes: "Certainly any discussion of the . . . application of Romans 1 must not neglect the powerful impact of Paul's rhetorical reversal in Romans 2:1: all of us stand 'without excuse' before God, Jews and Gentiles alike, heterosexuals and homosexuals alike. Thus, Romans 1 should decisively undercut any self-righteous condemnation of homosexual behavior. Those who follow the church's tradition by upholding the authority of Paul's teaching against the morality of homosexual acts must do so with due humility."[13]

Chapter 8

The Message of Paul to the World

I have pondered Paul's teachings about worship and idolatry again and again, continually reminding myself of their importance as I seek to deepen my communion with the Father and my worship of Him. Worship and idolatry have been recurring subjects in my discussions with other individuals who also experience feelings of same-gender attraction. I have thought deeply about their implications and applications in my life. With a deeper understanding of this broadly affecting principle, I have begun to see how those teachings relate to each one of us as children of God.

Worship and Idolatry

Our Father placed in the soul of each of His children the attribute of worship, but to fully worship God the Father, we must come to know Him, for there is no salvation in worshipping unknown gods. With the wondrous understanding of the gospel that we have because of the Restoration, we know how to better focus that divine instinct and use it for our salvation and eternal joy.

Idolatry is a sin against God, who is our Father, but its seriousness differs to some degree between those outside the Lord's Church and those within. This distinction applies to homosexual behavior as well. The contrast in seriousness could be compared to the sins of fornication and adultery. Fornication is a sin of serious magnitude, but for an individual who has entered into a covenant relationship with a spouse and who then engages in sexual relations outside that marriage covenant, that same act is adultery and becomes an even more serious sin.

That is how it is with idolatry of every form. Those who worship false gods outside a covenant relationship with God are sinning, but for those who worship false gods when they have made covenants to faithfully serve the God of Abraham, Isaac, and Jacob—and Him only—the sin of idolatry becomes spiritual adultery. In fact, in the Old Testament, the connection within covenant Israel between idolatry and adultery was so strong that they were often used as synonyms, whether the sins committed were sexual or not.

Throughout the Old Testament, the spiritual covenant between Jehovah and Israel is often symbolized by a marriage bond, and the imagery is continued in the New Testament between Christ and the Church. The Lord declared to covenant Israel: "I will betroth thee unto me in righteousness, and in judgment, and in lovingkindness, and in mercies. I will even betroth thee unto me in faithfulness" (Hosea 2:19–20). But as Andrew Skinner, dean of Religious Education at Brigham Young University, has said, "Nothing is more worthless or hurtful than false promises of fidelity."[1] Israel, after she had covenanted with the Lord, "decked herself with her earrings and her jewels, and she went after her lovers, and forgat me, saith the Lord" (Hosea 2:13).

Idolatry can come in many forms. Some blatantly reject God and any semblance of traditional morality and indulge in immoral behavior, sexual or otherwise. Others allow good and worthy things or genuine needs to take priority over Him. And there is the idolatry in which central principles of the true gospel—such as sexuality, knowledge, goodness, happiness, and family—can become corrupted. The chief point is that failing to keep God as the ultimate end and the only focus of our worship is to worship something else—to find something else to be more valuable than He is, even if that is something He longs for us to have through obedience to the laws of His gospel.

President Spencer W. Kimball defined idolatry as including "everything which entices a person away from duty, loyalty, and love for and service to God." He continued: "Modern idols or false gods can take such forms as clothes, homes, businesses, machines, automobiles, pleasure boats, and numerous other material deflectors from the path to godhood. What difference does it make that the item concerned is not shaped like an idol? Brigham Young said: 'I would as soon see a man worshipping a little god made of brass or of wood as to see him worshipping his property.' . . .

"Many worship the hunt, the fishing trip, the vacation, the weekend picnics and outings. Others have as their idols the games of sport, baseball, football, the bullfight, or golf. These pursuits more often than not interfere with the worship of the Lord and with giving service to the building up of the kingdom of God. To the participants this emphasis may not seem serious, yet it indicates where their allegiance and loyalty are."[2]

In speaking with those who experience feelings of same-gender attraction and who pursue homosexual relationships, common themes generally arise that are basically founded upon some species of idolatry, each of them a misguided application of principles central to the true gospel of Jesus Christ. Some powers, philosophies, institutions, and relationships are sacred to the true gospel and are part of God's purposes for the path toward godhood, but when they are put ahead of the Lord, or if God and religion are used as a *means* to obtain them as the desired *end,* they become idolatrous.

A prime example of a good and godly thing that can become vain and idolatrous if worshipped is sexuality. Our passions are God-instilled, but if they cease to become our servant and instead become our master, they are used in evil and destructive ways. President Spencer W. Kimball said: "We fear that never in the history of the world have there ever been so many more people bowing to the god of lust than there were bowing to golden calves and the images of wood and stone and metal. This idolatry, so closely associated with the destruction of mind and body, could inundate the world."[3] President Ezra Taft Benson expressed similar concern for the lack of reverence for intimate relations, resulting in the abundant "moral permissiveness that has taken root in our midst. Today sex is all but deified, and yet is promenaded before our youth in its most explicit, coarsest, and debasing forms."[4]

Marriage and intimacy and family are good and noble and godly things, but if we lose sight of the Master we serve, then our view of them becomes distorted and ultimately destructive to our relationship with the true and living God. In our popular culture that worships sex, sexuality, image, fashion, and almost all that is superficial, it is no wonder that so many in society fail to understand true intimacy, because eternal intimacy extends far beyond the sexual, and eternal love encompasses more than the romantic. When sexual attraction becomes the prime factor for seeking a companion with whom to share our hearts and lives, those who experience same-gender attraction have little motivation to seek a God-sanctioned marriage with a companion with whom they will spend eternity.

Another principle of godliness that we seek on our path to knowing God's goodness is just that—His goodness. There is a philosophy of moralism that consists of timeless moral principles. Most of the Judeo-Christian world holds the ancient injunction "Thou shalt not kill" to be a transcendent and absolute principle. To seek timeless principles of value to live by is a noble venture; to be moral is good; to be good is good—but if that is the only end we are seeking, then even goodness and morality can become idolatrous. There are good people everywhere. But there is a difference between living a Christlike life and being a Christian. Many Muslims, Buddhists, or atheists, for that matter, live Christlike lives. Many who live in homosexual relationships are wonderful people. But the call to Christ is not simply a call to be good and honorable. It is not simply a call to clothe the poor, feed the hungry, or to heal the sick. It is a call to be sanctified and holy—redeemed and regenerated—through the atoning blood of the Lord Jesus Christ and through faith on His name.

When the quest for principles and morals becomes our sole focus—and even our god—we encounter problems when a commandment is given that doesn't seem to have a foundational principle or moral we can immediately understand. For example, consider the commandment to Abraham to take Isaac into Moriah to be sacrificed or the commandment to Nephi to slay Laban. God sometimes gives commandments that don't make sense at a mortal, moralistic level. Lacking the understanding that "man doth not comprehend all the things which the Lord can comprehend" (Mosiah 4:9), individuals may cast aside a commandment in the belief that they can still be "good" without it. For the sake of goodness, they may be able to; but for the sake of Christ, discipleship, and holiness, they cannot. Those who try to find salvation simply in goodness are trying to build a latter-day tower of Babel. They rationalize that if there is a heaven, surely a "good" God wouldn't cast out His "good" children.

An idea similar to that of seeking goodness is that of seeking happiness. The scriptures and the words of modern prophets are laden with illustrations of "that happiness which is prepared for the saints" (2 Nephi 9:43). Book of Mormon prophets have declared that "men are that they might have joy" (2 Nephi 2:25) and have spoken of "the great plan of happiness" (Alma 42:8) and of "liv[ing] after the manner of happiness" (2 Nephi 5:27).

In the opening of this last dispensation, the Prophet Joseph Smith observed, "Happiness is the object and design of our existence; and will be the end thereof, if we pursue the path that leads to it; and this path is virtue, uprightness, faithfulness, holiness, and keeping all the commandments of God."[5] It is clear that happiness is God's "object and design" for us. To obtain it, our focus must be on Christ and the virtues He embodies. Often we hear only "happiness is the object and design of our existence," which may leave us with the misconception that the pursuit of happiness has preeminence above all else. This misconception is reminiscent of a counterfeit philosophy of the happiness that the Lord speaks of in the scriptures. That counterfeit philosophy, hedonism, is idolatry.

Although the word *hedonism* has many negative connotations—such as immediate physical gratification—it is primarily "the doctrine that pleasure or happiness is the sole or chief good in life."[6] To some, serving God is not an end in itself. It is the quest simply for "happiness," or possibly "treasures in heaven" (Matthew 6:20), and God and His gospel are viewed as the method for obtaining it. Although eternal happiness and glory will be by-products of our worship of the Father, to seek them by following Him as a means of obtaining them is idolatrous. We do not worship joy; we worship God. God is a giver of joy, but we must seek Him rather than simply seek what He has to offer us.

One biblical scholar stated that he has observed the phenomenon of hedonistic worship within the traditional Christian community: "The most basic truths of our faith have fallen victim to [a] self-centered theology. Many modern-day evangelists have reduced the gospel message to little more than a formula by which people can live a happy and more fulfilling life. Sin is now defined by how it affects man, not how it dishonors God. Salvation is often presented as a means of receiving what Christ offers without obeying what He commands. The focus has shifted from God's glory to man's benefit. The gospel of persevering faith has given way to a kind of religious hedonism. Jesus, contemporary theology implies, is your ticket to avoiding all of life's pains and experiencing all of life's pleasures."[7]

Failing to understand that God is the Great Eternal End we worship rather than simply a means for some other greater end of eternal happiness creates a problem for religious commitment when our faith is tried. If we see the gospel merely as a means to make us happy, and we are not happy, we begin to question the effectiveness of that means. If God is simply the Giver of Good Gifts—the Grand Rewarder and Punisher—then we will not understand why good people suffer and the wicked go free and unpunished. To hedonistic idolaters, mortal suffering may indicate that a person's commitment to a religious ideal is questionable, whereas pleasure-filled, pain-free lives indicate God's favor.

The happiness spoken of in scripture, unlike the hedonistic search for happiness, depends not upon circumstance but upon our relationship with God and cultivation of His Spirit—His Comforter. The Lord declared, "In this world your joy is not full, but in *me* your joy is full" (D&C 101:36; italics added). He is our happiness; He is our joy; and He will be our manna in the wilderness. The fundamental difference between hedonism and true happiness is that hedonism is centered in the self. The happiness described in scripture is the only happiness that will be eternal and comes only when we worship our Father and center our life on the redemption provided through His Son.

Even marriage—something sacred and central to the gospel of God—can be viewed hedonistically. Like the religious means-end relationship, with God as the means to a heavenly end, marriage is viewed as the cultural means to individual fulfillment. That is, people may pursue marriage because they believe it is necessary to a happy individual life. And just as people may leave the Church when they find that it doesn't meet their hedonistic expectations, so they may divorce when their marriage is no longer fulfilling their individual needs. Those with a hedonistic view who become unhappy in marriage then seek a relationship that will make them happy. For the hedonistic person, individual happiness trumps marital commitment.

President Ezra Taft Benson taught: "We must put God in the forefront of everything else in our lives. He must come first, just as He declares in the first of His Ten Commandments . . . When we put God first, all other things fall into their proper place or drop out of our lives. Our love of the Lord will govern the claims for our affection, the demands on our time, the interests we pursue, and the order of our priorities. We should put God ahead of *everyone else* in our lives."[8]

Idolatry and Homosexuality

For much of my life, even though I recognized my attraction to other men, I couldn't accept that attraction as real because I was different from what I had always understood homosexuals were like. I had bought into the misconception or the impression created by those who don't understand same-gender attraction that all homosexuals are bad people who care nothing for religion and perverts who only desire to satisfy the lusts of the flesh. The evils of bathhouses, nightclub dark rooms, promiscuity, pedophilia, and pornography are used to paint a picture of the evils of homosexuality. Yet that abhorrent view is an inaccurate representation. To be sure, those things are evils, but those same evils are indulged in by heterosexuals as well. The choice to participate in such things has as much to do with general morality as it does with sexuality. Not everyone fits the homosexual stereotype—although, of course, there most certainly are individuals who do represent it.

Another side to the homosexual "lifestyle" is given much less attention because it is far less sensational and scandalous. Those whose romantic and sexual attraction is naturally toward the same gender may recognize, and rightly, that it is human nature, not heterosexual nature, to desire romantic companionship and a family. Those without a correct understanding of God and His requirements for true, eternal happiness cannot understand why voices of society around them are shouting that their love is immoral. They cannot understand how it is immoral to want to connect with someone and spend their life with that person. There are couples who genuinely love each other and who want to live in a committed relationship away from the spotlights, clubs, and gay pride parades. Even love expressed in ways contrary to the Father's eternal purposes for His children still retains elements of love's grandeur. And although long-term homosexual relationships are much less common than long-term heterosexual relationships, they do exist. There are many who seek, as best they can, to live lives that are pleasing to God and of service to others.

The real plague of our nation and of the world in general is the pride that leads to idolatry.[9] Homosexual behavior is one manifestation of pride-caused idolatry when it is committed against the greater light the participating individuals possess. Although there are good and noble and respectable people everywhere—religious and nonreligious, heterosexual and homosexual—that is not what true Christianity is about. Christianity is not just about being "good," it is not just about being "moral," and it is not about being "happy" (referring to those qualities in the way society or popular theology and psychology would have us understand them). Christianity in its purest and restored sense is about being consecrated and sanctified; it is about being pure and holy; it is about "relying wholly upon the merits of him who is mighty to save" (2 Nephi 31:19); it is about becoming as God is and learning to live as He lives.

Concerning the restored truth the Lord has blessed us with as members of His Church, He said, "For of him unto whom much is given much is required; and he who sins against the greater light shall receive the greater condemnation" (D&C 82:3; see also Luke 12:48). As Latter-day Saints and stewards of the fulness of the gospel of Christ on the earth and as those who bear His name, we all—including those who experience same-gender attraction—should be more concerned with purifying our own lives and worshipping our God, especially when we have the perspective of the restored gospel from which to view life and the trials and challenges that accompany it.

With a true understanding of the plan of salvation and the nature of eternal life, one would clearly recognize that behavior toward a member of the same gender that is nonsexual but still romantic in its intent is contrary to the Father's plan for His children and requires sincere repentance. Loving another person and seeking romantic companionship is not a bad thing—it is a natural and divinely implanted instinct. What makes homosexual behavior wrong is not an evil inherent in being attracted to one of the same gender; what makes homosexual behavior wrong is the simple fact that it is contrary to the purposes of God, and when people serve the creature more than the Creator, they are guilty of the sin of idolatry.

That goes for any kind of sin. Heterosexual behavior, which is considered more "natural," is evil when individuals "[burn] in their lust one toward another" (Romans 1:27). The principal sin is in the root of homosexual behavior—the idolatry. The attraction is a challenge and a temptation—a cross to bear—but it is not in itself a sin. Although the challenges of those who experience same-gender attraction may be legitimate and unsolicited, we have been commanded "to act for [ourselves] and not to be acted upon" (2 Nephi 2:26), even by our very real and sometimes painful mortal trials.

If anyone ought to be less susceptible to the philosophies of men, with their limited light and understanding, it is the Saints of God. We have been given greater light and knowledge on which to base our choices. What media and gay political activists have to say about homosexuality should not be the philosophies upon which we base our attitudes and choices and lives. We understand that there is more to life—eternal life—than what we can fully comprehend in this mortal, fallen, second estate.

It is a given that appropriate heterosexual relationships are part of our ultimate exaltation in the eternities. Marriage and family are essential to the plan of God if we are to have a fulness of joy in the hereafter when we are fully redeemed from this fallen state. We must also remember that there are arguments both for and even against homosexuality that are nothing more than the philosophies of men. We must be careful to distinguish those philosophies from the spiritual and eternal truths of the gospel of Christ. Nephi declared: "O Lord, I have trusted in thee, and I will trust in thee forever. I will not put my trust in the arm of flesh; for I know that cursed is he that putteth his trust in the arm of flesh. Yea, cursed is he that putteth his trust in man or maketh flesh his arm" (2 Nephi 4:34).

Some who misunderstand the nature of same-gender attraction would argue that one cannot experience an attraction that is so "unnatural" and still be in God's full favor. Others may claim that one should focus on "changing" and doing all within his or her power to "overcome" same-gender attraction. Although our faith in God may require us to reconcile things in our life that may influence the attraction, putting an unbalanced and unhealthy emphasis and focus on "change" as a prerequisite to happiness or divine love and favor can be counterproductive, discouraging, and emotionally exhausting.

Just as we do not worship heterosexuality, so our salvation is not based upon the mortal realization of it. The ideal of a marriage and family may not be realized in mortality by some—or even many—of God's children for a variety of reasons, only one of them being same-gender attraction. The timing of the realization of those blessings is individual and must be worked through personally with the Lord. For those who experience same-gender attraction to use their attraction as a catch-all rationalization for failing to prepare and to strive for that eternal goal would be idolatrous.

Philosophies of pro-gay activists would draw some of the Saints of God into a life of homosexual activity—whether in promiscuous activity or in a committed, monogamous relationship—by claiming that one must follow one's attractions to be true to one's "real self." Monogamous relationships would obviously be better than promiscuous ones, but both are utterly forbidden by the Lord if we are to wholly follow His law necessary for eternal life. Others who promote homosexual activity say that it is unhealthy or deceptive to strive for marriage. They say that one cannot be true to himself and still have a healthy, successful, and fulfilling life in marriage and in being obedient to the commandments of God. True fulfillment and eternal happiness are not found in our sexual orientation. Yes, "men are, that they might have joy," but "in this world your joy is not full, but in *me* your joy is full" (D&C 101:36; italics added). Sexual expression, intelligence, goodness, joy, and happiness may be ours in harmony with our Father's plan and as the result of our relationship with Him and our worship of Him. They should not be sought at the expense of Him. Those who seek those things apart from God will be "ever learning, and never able to come to a knowledge of the truth" (2 Timothy 3:7). They will have "itching ears" (2 Timothy 4:3) and will be "tossed about by every wind of doctrine" (Ephesians 4:14). Finally, those who live contrary to faithful worship of the Father may find some "joy in their works [but] for a season" (3 Nephi 27:11).

Quoting Isaiah, Nephi said that those who "distress" Zion "shall be as a dream of a night vision; yea, it shall be unto them, even as unto a hungry man which dreameth, and behold he eateth but he awaketh and his soul is empty; or like unto a thirsty man which dreameth, and behold he drinketh but he awaketh and behold he is faint, and his soul hath appetite" (2 Nephi 27:3). Without the Spirit, we in our finite minds cannot really comprehend what will bring us eternal happiness and fulfillment. Only God knows what will do that. Contrary to popular theology, sometimes war is the only means to peace, and sometimes pain, tragedy, challenge, or sacrifice is the only means to true joy, fulfillment, and eternal happiness.

As Jacob said, "Our lives passed away like as it were unto us a dream" (Jacob 7:26). Trying to find happiness in mortality outside the ways the Lord has prescribed may result in a measure of temporary happiness and people may find "joy in their works for a season" (3 Nephi 27:11), but once this life passes and they are awakened to the Lord's reality, they will find their souls faint and hungry. They will find that after seeking happiness in the ways of the world or in the ways our fallen natures have prescribed, they have lost the very thing they spent their lives seeking. Ultimately, their works must come to an end, and "every tongue should confess that Jesus Christ is Lord, to the glory of God the Father" (Philippians 2:11).

Chapter 9

According to the Lord's Own Will and Pleasure

"Faith is hoping for things which are not seen, which are true." For years this was my typical response to an inquiry about the meaning of faith. It seemed fairly standard and accurate, and it is in the scriptures. In the last few years, though, as I've come to terms with my experience with same-gender attraction, I've had to rediscover the meaning of faith. I've had to search it out and seek to understand it on an entirely new level. Shortly after I started being honest about my feelings, I came across a particular verse of scripture in the Book of Mormon. As I read the words, "never did any passage of scripture come with more power to the heart of man than this did at this time to mine. It seemed to enter with great force into every feeling of my heart. I reflected on it again and again" (Joseph Smith–History 1:12). It has since become a theme scripture, whose words I look to again and again for comfort and perspective: "But if ye will turn to the Lord with full purpose of heart, and put your trust in him, and serve him with all diligence of mind, if ye do this, he will, according to his own will and pleasure, deliver you out of bondage" (Mosiah 7:33).

"Thy Timing Be Done"

For the longest time, I thought of the bondage referred to in Mosiah 7:33 as my feelings of same-gender attraction. I now believe that is only partly true. I believe a large part of the bondage I have experienced is my lack of vision of the purposes of God, which has caused my faith to waver. I believe that if I will turn to Him with full purpose of heart and serve

Him with all diligence of mind, He will deliver me. First, He will deliver me from the darkness of mind and heart and wavering of faith I've experienced by revealing to me His mysteries and helping me to don "the armour of [His] light" (Romans 13:12) as I give greater heed and diligence to His word. Then, He will deliver me from the same-gender attraction I experience, "according to his own will and pleasure" (Mosiah 7:33). I don't know when that will happen; I don't know whether it will even happen in mortality. But I do know that having faith in Christ requires me to believe it *will* happen. "My words are sure and shall not fail," the Lord taught, "but all things must come to pass in their time" (D&C 64:31–32).

"The issue for us," Elder Neal A. Maxwell taught, "is trusting God enough to trust also His timing. If we can truly believe He has our welfare at heart, may we not let His plans unfold as He thinks best? The same is true with the second coming and with all those matters wherein our faith needs to include faith in the Lord's timing for us personally, not just in His overall plans and purposes."[1] On another occasion, he said, "Since faith in the timing of the Lord may be tried, let us learn to say not only, 'Thy will be done,' but patiently also, 'Thy timing be done.'"[2]

Professor Robert L. Millet shared an experience concerning faith and timing and the Lord's enabling power: "I had occasion to work with a young man who was struggling with same-sex attraction. He had violated his temple covenants but sincerely wanted to change. Church disciplinary measures were taken, and he began to work toward change. He spoke often of how difficult it was for him to be active in the Church, to attend all the activities, and in general to be a typical Latter-day Saint when he felt so very atypical. He committed to avoid inappropriate sexual activity but wrestled with his same-sex attraction. One day he asked me: 'If I do the things you have asked me to do—go to Church, read the scriptures, fast and pray, plead for divine help, receive priesthood blessings when necessary, and be chaste—can you assure me that the Lord will take away these desires, these attractions? Can you promise me they will go away?' It was a tough question.

"As I recall, I said something like this: 'I know that the Lord can indeed change you, change your heart. I know that He can do that instantaneously if He chooses to do so. I know that the power of change is in Jesus Christ, and that dramatic and rapid change can take place. I do not know, however, whether the Lord will change you right away. I know this: If you do what you have been asked to do, and if you do it regularly and consistently, from now on, God will change you, either here or hereafter. You may be required to deal with these feelings until the day you die. But I can promise you two things—first, these feelings will eventually be transformed; and second, if God does not choose to bring about a major change in your nature in this life, he will strengthen and empower you to deal with the temptations you will face. You don't need to face this on your own.'"[3]

The Foundation of Faith

Because of my experience with same-gender attraction, everything I understood faith to be has been called into question. This trial has caused me to think about just how deep my spiritual roots were—and, as it has been with many other things, I found I was wanting. I have come to understand that for true faith to exist, the untruths we believe concerning ourselves, the nature of our challenges, and the gospel must cease to exist.

My first reaction when confronting my feelings of same-gender attraction was discouragement and loss of faith, for the truth of my experience defied what I had understood of the gospel truths taught in the Church. As I grew in the Spirit, my attractions became more intense, and that was completely inconsistent with my understanding of truth—with what "should" have been happening. Because all authentic truth is faith promoting, the problem was not in the gospel or the teachings of the Church but rather in my understanding of them. Authentic truth promotes authentic faith, and if authentic truth shakes our faith, then our faith is ill-founded and we must ask ourselves deeper questions. Truth, even difficult truth, will only deepen and give breadth of vision to authentic and saving faith.

From the time we are in Primary, we sing the words: "The wise man built his house upon the rock." Whether our house is built upon the rock or upon the sand doesn't matter until "the rains [come] down, and the floods [come] up."[4] It is when the rains and the floods come that the nature and strength of our spiritual foundation are tried. It is often said that trials perfect us, but it is Christ and His atonement that perfect us. Our trials simply reveal to us our true natures, so we can then turn to Christ for His perfection and for His regenerating grace and power. Mormon reflected, "Except the Lord doth chasten his people with many afflictions, yea, except he doth visit them with death and with terror, and with famine and with all manner of pestilence, they will not remember him" (Helaman 12:3).

Only oversimplified or ill-founded faith will easily break or be shaken when confronted with difficult truths—and the experience of same-gender attraction is one of them. Although confronting the truth of my experience with same-gender attraction at first shook my faith and my testimony, my quest for spiritual understanding has not ended in my giving up my faith in the gospel of Christ and His latter-day Church. Rather, it has been a means of developing and strengthening my faith. The process has been painful at times, and I've received a few scars along the way, but the process has given my faith more solidity and more breadth.

Faith is the principle by which the worlds were organized. It is the very essence of religion. It is faith that saves. Or, rather, it is not faith that saves but faith in Jesus Christ. Faith is the trust in the Lord that motivates us to do His will. The object of our faith and prayer is not to align the will of God to ours but to align our will to His. Faith is not the power of positive thinking, nor is it the same as simple belief. It is not the power to force change upon our circumstances or upon the agency of others.

On my mission I had a companion who would become extremely discouraged when others rejected the message we shared. We were serving together in a predominantly Catholic area when he said to me one night in a voice filled with frustration, "I used to think that if I could have the faith to move a mountain, then surely I could convert a Catholic."

Mormon notes: "O how great is the nothingness of the children of men; yea, even they are less than the dust of the earth. For behold, the dust of the earth moveth hither and thither, to the dividing asunder, at the command of our great and everlasting God" (Helaman 12:7–8). Our faith will never be strong enough to force others to use their agency the way we want them to. The Father has perfect faith, and yet a third of His children rejected Him completely. Likewise, His Only Begotten in the flesh has perfect faith, and yet while He was in mortality, His message was rejected by most who heard it. Our faith can only be strong enough to affect the way we exercise our own agency. Paul was a man of faith, and yet consider the thorn he pleaded with the Lord to remove. Despite his aching petitions, it was not taken away. The Lord often has purpose in allowing us to experience pain, and the perfect manifestation of our faith is to seek to understand that purpose and then humbly accept it.

Faith calls for our utmost diligence and greatest confidence—not confidence in ourselves, but rather confidence in Christ. Faith in the institutions of the world or in ourselves cannot save us. Faith unto salvation requires service to Him and to Him only. "No man can serve two masters" (Matthew 6:24). If I am serving my attractions—myself—then I am not serving God. If I am the master of my ship, then Christ cannot be my Master.

A scriptural story that expresses the importance of a proper foundation of faith is Lehi's vision of the tree of life. Many people never made it to the path, and others made it to the path but did not grasp the rod and eventually wandered off. Of real interest is the difference between the two groups of people who grasped the rod and who actually partook of the fruit of the tree of life—one group fell away after partaking of the fruit, and the other did not.

Once as I was reading the account quite closely, certain words that I had never before noticed caught my attention. Those who fell away, the record tells us, caught hold of the iron rod and "did press forward through the mist of darkness, *clinging* to the rod of iron, even until they did come forth and partake of the fruit of the tree," only to afterwards walk away from the tree in shame, because those in the great and spacious building scoffed at them (1 Nephi 8:24; italics added). In subtle contrast, those who partook of the fruit and stayed true caught hold of the rod of iron and "did press their way forward, *continually holding fast* to the rod of iron, until they came forth and fell down and partook of the fruit of the tree" (1 Nephi 8:30; italics added).

My experience with feelings of same-gender attraction and associations with others who share this challenge have made the difference between these two groups of people more clear for me. The word *clinging* seems to carry with it a connotation of fear or desperation. It almost seems as if these individuals were "clinging" because they were afraid of something, scared to admit or talk about the source of their fear. So it is with many who experience the challenge of same-gender attraction. Because of the negative rhetoric voiced in society, some who have this challenge remain fearfully quiet, dreading the possibility of rejection or the withdrawal of love.

They may fear other implications as well. In light of the continual emphasis on family in the Church, some are deathly afraid of what this attraction means for their faith and for a future marriage and family that they have been taught their entire life to treasure. Some individuals quietly and at times tragically marry in the desperate hope that the attraction will eventually extinguish itself if they do the right thing. Some experience self-hatred and self-loathing. To be fair, is it perhaps only natural for them to fear or hate themselves or their attraction when they perceive that so much of their surrounding world fears or hates them?

Many pray and plead and fast and covenant with God that they will do anything if He will only take these "evil" feelings from them. And when He doesn't, so many—too many—wander from the tree of life, despite previous lives of diligent activity in the Church. Either out of discouragement or misunderstanding or because their hearts are more set upon the things of the world, they leave the tree. Often they leave in spite of their testimonies of the gospel and the love they have felt for and from God. Then they head toward the "great and spacious building" and fall "away into forbidden paths and [are] lost" (1 Nephi 8:26, 28).

The second group, on the other hand, "continually [held] fast" to the rod. They saw something more in their experience than the other group did. They did not fear. They knew what they believed, they knew what they wanted, and they went forward in faith—faith in the Lord's timing for them and in His infinite redeeming and enabling atonement. They maintained an eternal perspective, sensing there was more to life than the world around them would have them believe. They didn't ask the Lord why they had to experience the trials they had but rather asked what He would have them learn from them, if it was His will that they bear their particular crosses.

They did not glory in their challenges but gloried in the Lord, and they understood the necessity of refining adversity. They understood that He allowed them to experience challenges through which He could teach them and tutor them—mold them—so they might become what He wants them to become. It wasn't easy. The mists of darkness still swirled around them, and people still mocked, but they "heeded them not" (1 Nephi 8:33). These are the men and women whose lives, even today, are lived not in quiet desperation but in quiet inspiration. They steadfastly maintain their faith and continual focus on God and His purposes and His love.

Faith, Change, and the "Mark" of Christ

A million voices cry out for our attention, but we must learn to recognize the voice of the Shepherd. I've felt for a long time that the people who experience same-gender attraction and who remain active in the Church—with peace and hope and faith and a feeling of joy intact—are those who believe in the truth of the gospel and in the divine mission of the Church and also love truth and honestly seek it. They who remain faithful not only believe in God but love God and seek diligently to develop a personal communication with Him to acknowledge the hand

and face of God in their individual lives. They cultivate His Spirit, the eternal Comforter, in their hearts. They are able to keep their focus on the Master.

There are many good things we could focus on, but if we are not focusing on "the mark"—who is Christ—our faith can easily be shaken (Jacob 4:14). People who experience same-gender attraction may often feel overwhelming pressure to "change" the nature of their attractions, or their sexuality—and they'll do anything to make it happen. There is a strong tendency to feel that no matter what our challenges may be, if we pray more, fast more, read scripture more, or attend church and the temple more, then we can and will "change." Yet, despite how often or how deeply and sincerely many have prayed, fasted, read scripture, or attended the temple, they have continued to experience feelings of same-gender attraction with little or no change in intensity.

President Ezra Taft Benson made a statement that caused me to think a lot about this idea. He said, "When you choose to follow Christ, you choose to be changed." That is a powerful statement, and I have come to believe that the key words are "*be* changed." It implies an outside force or power—I believe it implies the regenerating grace of Christ. I also believe that the foremost "change" he is referring to is a change in our hearts rather than in our sexuality—our affections rather than our attractions. President Benson continued: "The Lord works from the inside out. The world works from the outside in. The world would take people out of the slums. Christ takes the slums out of people, and then they take themselves out of the slums. The world would mold men by changing their environment. Christ changes men, who then change their environment. *The world would shape human behavior, but Christ can change human nature.*"[5]

In my own fight to "change," I thought often of these words. When I first read them, I was sure President Benson meant that if I were truly to choose to follow Christ and be a true Christian, I would first have to choose to change the nature of my attractions. But after years of trying to "change," which included counseling and support groups and personal efforts to alter circumstances in my life that I was led to believe might have influenced the attraction, the intensity of my attraction remained the same.

It is true that in the eternal scheme the nature of those attractions must be changed, but as I further contemplated the words of President Ezra Taft Benson, the eyes of my understanding were opened. I saw that first and foremost, President Benson was referring to the nature of our hearts. Salvation is based upon whether our hearts have been turned to Christ. There are some things we simply cannot force change upon through our own efforts, no matter how hard we try or how diligently we continue those efforts.

The fact remains that there are certain things we will never be able to change, and those we will have to leave completely in the hands of the Savior and His infinite atonement. If someone loses a leg in this mortal, fallen world, no amount of fasting or prayer or scripture study or temple attendance is going to bring that leg back unless the Lord wills it to be so. With some things—most importantly, the things pertaining to our salvation—we can only do in faith what He has asked, so that the Spirit and the power of His atoning sacrifice can work in us. We can choose to follow Christ so that we can then "*be* changed" by *Him* "according to His own will and pleasure" (Mosiah 7:33).

The actions of prayer, fasting, scripture reading, and temple and church attendance don't change us. But each of these things does play an essential role in change, because if we are doing them sincerely and properly, they will be, in part, the means by which our hearts will be turned to Him as our great Eternal End. Christ is the Eternal End; if we put too much focus on the means, we may lose sight of Him. Christ is the Qualifier for change and salvation. If we instead view the actions of missionary work, prayer, fasting, scripture reading, or temple and church attendance as the qualifier for change, or salvation (and they become our "mark," or our focus), then we are "looking beyond the mark" of Christ and will be "blinded" (Jacob 4:14).

Those actions of faith do have an important purpose. They give us strength, provide necessary ordinances, help us to invite the Spirit, and turn our hearts to Christ, but it is He who ultimately changes and delivers us. He has promised that He will deliver us both spiritually and physically, but He didn't say when. He has not promised that it will happen by Monday, and He has never promised it will happen in its entirety even in mortality. I hope He does deliver me from the physical bondage of this challenge while I am in this second estate, but even if He doesn't, I will rejoice in His name and stand as His witness. For the time being, I continue to pray and am striving to live so that the part of my nature that is important for salvation now may be more fully changed—so that I may be more fully delivered from spiritual bondage.

Those who feel that counseling or therapy can help them come to terms with or overcome or diminish feelings of same-gender attraction here in mortality may be required by their faith in the Messiah to take those measures, for "faith without works is dead" (James 2:26). A powerful story of the effects of faith combined with works has been told by President Thomas S. Monson: "Heartwarming is the example of the mother in America who prayed for her son's well-being as the vessel on which he served sailed into the bloody cauldron known as the Pacific theatre of war. Each morning she would arise from kneeling in prayer and serve as a volunteer on those production lines which became lifelines to men in battle. Could it be that a mother's own handiwork might somehow directly affect the life of a loved one? All who knew her and her family cherished the actual account of her sailor son, Elgin Staples, whose ship went down off Guadalcanal. Staples was swept over the side; but he survived, thanks to a life belt that proved, on later examination, to have been inspected, packed, and stamped back home in Akron, Ohio, by his own mother!"[6]

Brigham Young taught that when the Lord has blessed us with light and knowledge, it is our responsibility in our faith in Christ to do all we can to apply it and then ask the Lord to consecrate that application to our good. He said, "You may go to some people here, and ask what ails them, and they answer, 'I don't know, but we feel a dreadful distress in the stomach and in the back; we feel all out of order, and we wish you to lay hands upon us.' 'Have you used any remedies?' 'No. We wish the Elders to lay hands upon us, and we have faith that we shall be healed.' That is very inconsistent according to my faith. If we are sick, and ask the Lord to heal us, and to do all for us that is necessary to be done, according to my understanding of the Gospel of salvation, I might as well ask the Lord to cause my wheat and corn to grow, without my plowing the ground and casting in the seed. It appears consistent to me to apply every remedy that comes within the range of my knowledge, and to ask my Father in heaven, in the name of Jesus Christ, to sanctify that application to the healing of my body."[7]

We who have the challenge of same-gender attraction have a responsibility to do all we can to understand our feelings or attractions and work to alter anything that may have influenced the attraction, but it is also important to remember that those things in and of themselves cannot alter our natures in any saving way: only Christ can do that.

Works without faith are dead as well. Our eternal salvation isn't based upon mortal heterosexual attraction. President Howard W. Hunter taught, "I am aware that life presents many challenges, but with the help of the Lord, we need not fear. If our lives and our faith are centered on Jesus Christ and his restored gospel, nothing can ever go permanently wrong. On the other hand, if our lives are not centered on the Savior and his teachings, no other success can ever be permanently right."[8]

"No other success" could include the potential success of changing our sexual attractions through counseling or therapy—and yet that success will not exalt us if our lives are not centered on Christ and His restored gospel. A faithless person who "changed" his homosexual attraction would end up just as faithless an individual but with heterosexual attraction. As I slowly learn to center my life in Christ, I am discovering that I become like that which I have put my faith in. If I focus on heterosexuality and center my faith in it, I may or may not gain greater heterosexual attraction in mortality, but if I center my faith in the Messiah, I will be redeemed and regenerated: I will become a "new creature" in

Christ (2 Corinthians 5:17)—and the nature of my sexual attraction will be changed "according to his own will and pleasure" (Mosiah 7:33).

The focus we need to have on Christ was demonstrated by Peter's walking on the water toward the Savior. Only when his gaze was fixed firmly upon the Son of God did he have the faith necessary to walk upon the water. And it was only when he took his eyes off the Savior and "saw the wind boisterous" that he began to sink (Matthew 14:30). I have at times felt the boisterous winds of frustration when I've read of the sociological and political debates concerning the possibilities and impossibilities and the shoulds and shouldn'ts of changing a person's orientation. I've often felt frustration (and heard from others that they experience similar feelings) as a result of comments made by many inside and outside the Church about those who deal with same-gender attraction. But I've also learned that I must never let the societal storms of individuals who are biased or ignorant or naïve pull my focus from the One who saves and thus allow myself to sink or fall away from the truth. Those who will survive are those who are willing to forgive and be patient with others—both inside the Church and outside it—because they too are growing and learning.

Each of us, whether we experience same-gender attraction or some other challenge, is a divine work in progress, and the Lord is working with us individually. In the meantime, we are going to inflict our weaknesses and our misunderstandings and our ignorance upon one another, and we must learn patience and forgiveness. We are each growing spiritually on different levels, and God is passionately interested in the salvation and growth of each of His children.

Commitment to the Lord's Church and His Prophets

In addition to the actions of prayer, fasting, and scripture reading, the institutional Church of Jesus Christ and the prophets whom He has called to lead and guide it are another essential means that God has provided His children to help us return to Him. But if the Church and His prophets are not viewed from that perspective, they could become barriers to our developing authentic faith in Jesus Christ rather than serving the purpose for which they were organized or called: to witness for His name and to enhance our faith in Him. The Church was organized for the purpose of spreading and promoting the restored gospel of Christ and its standards. The Church itself is a vehicle—a means.

To be active in the Church of Jesus Christ does not necessarily mean actively applying the gospel of Christ or the atoning blood He shed for us (see Mosiah 4:2). Gospel activity includes Church activity, but the converse of that may not necessarily be true. Elder M. Russell Ballard has stated that the Church has been placed on earth as "scaffolding that helps support and strengthen the family."[9] Understanding Elder Ballard's use of the word *scaffolding,* meaning a temporary structure, is vital in helping us understand that the Church is the Lord's authorized, earthly means of assisting us in creating eternal families and in turning our hearts and lives to Him.

Concerning the possible detrimental effects of focusing too much on the institutional Church, Elder Bruce R. McConkie taught the regional representatives of the Church in 1982: "Our tendency—it is an almost universal practice among most Church members—is to get so involved with the operation of the institutional Church that we never gain faith like the ancients, simply because we do not involve ourselves in the basic gospel matters that were the center of their lives.

"We are so wound up in programs and statistics and trends, in properties, lands, and mammon, and in achieving goals that will highlight the excellence of our work, that we 'have omitted the weightier matters of the law.' And as Jesus would have said: 'These [weightier things] ought ye to have done, and not to leave the other undone' (Matt. 23:23).

"Let us be reminded of the great basic verities upon which all Church programs and all Church organization rest.

"We are not saved by Church programs as such, by Church organizations alone, or even by the Church itself. It is the gospel that saves. The gospel is 'the power of God unto salvation' (Rom. 1:16)."[10]

The "mark" of our salvation is Jesus of Nazareth (Jacob 4:14). He is the Messiah. The Church is built upon the Rock but is not the Rock itself (see Matthew 7:24–25; 16:15–18). We do not—and should not—worship the institution or focus upon it as if it were the end. The saving power the Church has is in its divinely authorized ordinances, but they are empty and meaningless if our gaze is not fixed firmly upon the Son of God.

The Church of Jesus Christ of Latter-day Saints is God's Church on the earth, and it is the only vehicle He has authorized to promulgate His gospel. Though the Church and the gospel could be considered two distinct entities, trying to separate them is analogous to trying to separate the doctrines of grace and works. Anyone who truly understands the gospel of Christ knows that salvation is obtained fully and completely through the grace of Christ alone. But that does not eliminate the requirement for us to covenant with Him that we will give our lives completely to Him and live as He has commanded through His prophets and His Spirit. It was never intended that the doctrines of grace and works be separated, for there is an intricate covenant relationship between our God and His children. The effort to separate them is spiritually dangerous and inevitably fruitless. So it is also with the Lord's Church and His saving gospel message.

"The Church of Jesus Christ is the custodian of the gospel of Jesus Christ and thus the only place where the ordinances of salvation may be found. When the kingdom of God is established on earth; when the Church has been restored; when the necessary priesthoods and keys and authorities have been bestowed—when these conditions are obtained, mankind will come unto Christ (and thus unto salvation) through the statutes and ordinances of the Church or they will not enjoy the blessings of heaven. Though the Church is but the means to an end (Christ is the end), a person deceives himself who supposes that he can enjoy the benefits and privileges of the gospel in his life without being active and involved in the living Church."[11]

President Gordon B. Hinckley declared: "This Church, I submit, is far more than a social organization where we gather together to enjoy one another's company. It is more than Sunday School and Relief Society and priesthood meeting. It is more than sacrament meeting, more even than temple service. It is the kingdom of God in the earth. It behooves us to act in a manner befitting membership in that kingdom."[12]

One of the duties of the kingdom of God on the earth, an organization that is "far more than a social organization," is to safeguard the institution or organization of marriage, an organization that is also "far more than a social organization." Eternal marriage is a prerequisite to eternal life, the kind of life God lives. Marriage is more than tax credits and medical benefits; it is even more than a symbol of commitment between two people who genuinely love one another. It is quite likely that there are some homosexual relationships that are more committed and loving than some heterosexual relationships, but that doesn't change the fact that marriage, when organized by the priesthood, is an eternal organization of godhood and is strictly reserved for the joining of a man and a woman. Any union on earth—whether between those of the same or opposite genders—that is not sealed by the holy priesthood will end with mortal death.

Those who are critical of the Church or who are simply waiting around for leaders of the Church to "see the light" and allow homosexuals to marry or to condone legal civil unions do not have a sound spiritual understanding of the place of marriage within the doctrine of the gospel. The Church does not support the traditional marriage of a man and a woman simply because it is traditional. The Church supports traditional marriage because it is divine—it is the eternal order of godhood.

Elder Boyk K. Packer stated: "Some work through political, social, and legal channels to redefine morality and marriage into something unrestrained, unnatural, and forbidden. But they never can change the design which has governed human life and happiness from the beginning."[13] Though the specific circumstances were different, the apostles in the meridian Church had similar concerns regarding those who were trying to alter or redefine aspects of the gospel. Paul, with his trademark boldness, warned of those who would "pervert the gospel of Christ" by preaching "another Jesus" or "any other gospel" than the one preached by those apostles who had had hands laid upon their heads and were set apart by the priesthood of heaven to preach the message of salvation (Galatians 1:7–9; 2 Corinthians 11:4). Paul worried that their "minds should be corrupted from the simplicity that is in Christ" (2 Corinthians 11:3). In addition, Peter and Alma both warned against those who "wrest" the word of God, whether it be from the scriptures or the living oracles, for if they did, it would only be "to [their] own destruction" (2 Peter 3:16; Alma 13:20; see also Psalm 56:5; D&C 10:63).

Concerning those who experience same-gender attraction, President Gordon B. Hinckley stated in an October general conference address in 1998: "We want to help these people, to strengthen them, to assist them with their problems and to help them with their difficulties. But we cannot stand idle if they indulge in immoral activity, if they try to uphold and defend and live in a so-called same-sex marriage situation. To permit such would be to make light of the very serious and sacred foundation of God-sanctioned marriage and its very purpose, the rearing of families."[14]

The following year, in reference to Proposition 22 (or the Knight Initiative) in California that aimed to preserve traditional marriage, President Gordon B. Hinckley said: "We deal only with those legislative matters which are of a strictly moral nature or which directly affect the welfare of the Church. . . . Such is currently the case in California, where Latter-day Saints are working as part of a coalition to safeguard traditional marriage from forces in our society which are attempting to redefine that sacred institution. God-sanctioned marriage between a man and a woman has been the basis of civilization for thousands of years. There is no justification to redefine what marriage is. Such is not our right, and those who try will find themselves answerable to God.

"Some portray legalization of so-called same-sex marriage as a civil right. This is not a matter of civil rights; it is a matter of morality. Others question our constitutional right as a church to raise our voice on an issue that is of critical importance to the future of the family. We believe that defending this sacred institution by working to preserve traditional marriage lies clearly within our religious and constitutional prerogatives. Indeed, we are compelled by our doctrine to speak out."

But he again reemphasized that opposition to the "attempts to legalize same-sex marriage should never be interpreted as justification for hatred, intolerance, or abuse of those who profess homosexual tendencies, either individually or as a group. As I said from this pulpit one year ago, our hearts reach out to those who refer to themselves as gays and lesbians. We love and honor them as sons and daughters of God. They are welcome in the Church. It is expected, however, that they follow the same God-given rules of conduct that apply to everyone else, whether single or married."[15]

With that having been said years ago, the nation is again in a political uproar over this same issue. There has been mass lobbying for same-gender marriage rights in Massachusetts, New York, California, and Oregon, among other places. There has been picketing for and against it. Some carry signs and tote bumper stickers that read, "Your Religion Is Not My Government!" Others cruelly and wrongly declare, "God hates homosexuals!" In this time of confusion and turmoil, when the mists of darkness threaten on every side (see 1 Nephi 8:23), it is imperative that the Saints of God recognize and closely follow those whom the Almighty has called to guide His covenant people in these last days.

There are those who criticize Church leaders for lacking understanding of those who experience feelings of same-gender attraction. Elder Boyd K. Packer acknowledged: "We are sometimes told that leaders in the Church do not really understand these problems. Perhaps we don't. There are many 'whys' for which we just do not have simple answers. But we *do* understand temptation, each of us, from personal experience. Nobody is free from temptations of one kind or another. That is the test of life. That is part of our mortal probation. Temptation of some kind goes with the territory."[16]

Unless the prophets and apostles have experienced this challenge themselves, they won't understand it perfectly, and they may not understand perfectly how to help. It is imperative to understand, however, that their call to the apostleship was not a call to perfectly understand every problem, trial, or challenge the members of the Church face. I believe they do sincerely strive to understand members' needs so that they can better serve those needs. They may not understand same-gender attraction perfectly, but they do understand Christ's word and His plan for our redemption and salvation. They do understand His love, mercy, judgment, and justice, and they were called to be "special witnesses of the name of Christ in all the world" (D&C 107:23)—to bear witness of the name of Him who does understand us perfectly, of Him who took upon Himself our infirmities "that his bowels may be filled with mercy, according to the flesh, that he may know according to the flesh how to succor his people according to [our] infirmities" (Alma 7:12). Christ is the one who does understand perfectly every problem and every pain His people experience, and He will succor us in our extremity. The prophets and apostles are a means called to turn us to the *End,* so that *He* can heal us— so that He can "bind up the broken-hearted [and] proclaim liberty to the captives" (D&C 138:42).

If the prophets did understand our infirmities perfectly and could succor us perfectly, we might be tempted to view them as an end for our welfare and salvation rather than heeding their call to come to the only One in whom there is the power to be redeemed and regenerated from our fallen state. Christ is our Redeemer, through whose blood we may obtain salvation, but His word is dispensed through His prophets. Through prophets, the nature of Christ and His atonement are revealed to us. Through prophets, we learn how we must live and what we must do to "apply [His] atoning blood" (Mosiah 4:2).

Speaking to his apostles, Christ said, "I am the vine, ye are the branches" (John 15:5). When Lehi partook of the fruit of the tree of life, it was from the branches that the fruit was plucked. These branches (prophets and apostles) in Lehi's dream were connected to the true vine (Christ). The vine provided the life and the nourishment so that the fruit of eternal life could be dispensed through the branches (see 1 Nephi 8). Likewise today, it is through the living branches—those connected to the living and true Vine—that we receive His eternally binding word, which applies to *all* of *His* children, homosexually or heterosexually attracted alike.

Through the grace of Christ and his atonement, those who are reborn through Christ become the "seed" of Christ. Abinadi, in the sermon given to King Noah that resulted in Abinadi's death, taught a powerful truth connecting rebirth in Christ to obedience to the prophets He calls:

"When [Christ's] soul has been made an offering for sin he shall see his seed. . . . And who shall be his seed?

"Behold I say unto you, that whosoever has heard the words of the prophets, yea, all the holy prophets who have prophesied concerning the coming of the Lord—I say unto you, that all those who have hearkened unto their words, . . . that these are his seed, or they are the heirs of the kingdom of God.

"For these are they whose sins he has borne; these are they for whom he has died, to redeem them from their transgressions" (Mosiah 15:10–12). Those who have not only "heard the words of the prophets" but who have also "hearkened unto their words" are those who shall be counted as the seed of Christ. These are "they whose sins he has borne"— these are they who will be cleansed by His blood. We must exercise authentic faith in the authentic truth that God has called these men to lead His Church, and He will bless us if we have faith in and strictly heed their counsel. President Ezra Taft Benson put it most poignantly: "When obedience ceases to be an irritant and becomes our quest, in that moment God will endow us with power."[17]

If our salvation depends upon our hearkening to the word of the Lord as given through His prophets, it seems reasonable that we should take every opportunity to partake of the living waters dispensed through them. It is important that Latter-day Saints be diligent in their efforts to hear the words of the Lord's servants. For those with a testimony of living prophets, the level of our urgency to hear and to hearken to them is a measure of our dedication to Christ and His gospel.

These perilous and confusing last days—when men "call evil good, and good evil; [and] put darkness for light, and light for darkness; [and] put bitter for sweet, and sweet for bitter" (Isaiah 5:20)—are probably the most crucial time in all of history for mankind to watch closely the Lord's chosen servants. I believe that issues discussed and debated in our modern culture will be major sifters in the Church. Many will divide members of the Church on one level or another. What the prophets of God speak on various matters will divide those who believe that the Lord leads us today through His prophets from those who do not. When the Lord commanded Nephi to separate himself from his brothers, he said, "And all those who would go with me were those who believed in the warnings and the revelations of God; wherefore, they did hearken unto my words" (2 Nephi 5:6).

Those who insist on criticizing the leaders of the Church on matters of one kind or another, including same-gender attraction, should carefully consider the following counsel by President George Q. Cannon: "If any of you have indulged in the spirit of murmuring and fault-finding and have allowed your tongues to give utterance to thoughts and words that were wrong and not in accordance with the spirit of the Gospel, . . . you ought to repent of it with all your hearts and get down into the depths of humility and implore Him for the forgiveness of that sin—for it is a most deadly sin. The men who hold the Priesthood are but mortal men; they are fallible men. . . . No human being that ever trod this earth was free from sin, excepting the Son of God. . . .

"Nevertheless, God has chosen these men. He has singled them out. . . . He has selected them, and He has placed upon them the authority of the Holy Priesthood, and they have become His representatives in the earth. He places them as shepherds over the flock of Christ, and as watchmen upon the walls of Zion. And He holds them to a strict accountability . . . for the authority which He has given to them, and in the day of the Lord Jesus they will have to stand and be judged for . . . the manner in which they have exercised this authority. If they have exercised it wrongfully and against the interests of His work and the salvation of

His people, woe unto them in the day of the Lord Jesus! He will judge them. . . .

"God has chosen His servants. He claims it as His prerogative to condemn them, if they need condemnation. He has not given it to us individually to censure and condemn them. No man, however strong he may be in the faith, however high in the Priesthood, can speak evil of the Lord's anointed and find fault with God's authority on the earth without incurring His displeasure. The Holy Spirit will withdraw itself from such a man, and he will go into darkness . . . However difficult it may be for us to understand the reason for any action of the authorities of the Church, we should not too hastily call their acts in question and pronounce them wrong."[18]

Faith, Marriage, and Timing

Another of the means that we can place too much focus on—one that can be frustrating and disheartening to many who experience same-gender attraction—is marriage. If we keep our focus on Christ, marriage will come when we are ready and when He feels it is time for us, individually. I've had to learn to place my life completely in His hands, trusting that He knows what is best for me. Until I learned to do that, I got depressed whenever I heard a talk on marriage, which—because I was living in a singles ward at Brigham Young University—was all the time. But I now understand that He will work with me, nurture me, and prepare me so that I can eventually be ready for it when it is right, whether that be in this life or the next.

The topic of marriage for many who experience same-gender attraction is one that often carries great concerns. But, in all honesty, in a day of increasing selfishness, infidelity, and divorce, many of my friends who do not experience same-gender attraction in any degree also worry greatly about the prospect of marriage. I believe there is great reason for anyone, regardless of their challenges, to be cautious and prayerful about the "who, what, when, where, why, and how" of marriage. In this Church, focused as it is on marriage and the family, there is an abundance of literature from Church leaders and others that can help individuals prepare themselves to be successful and happy within marriage—again, regardless of what challenges, temptations, or attractions they experience. I would like to share some insights that I feel are important for those who experience the challenge of same-gender attraction to at least consider.

Never having been married, I can share very little on this topic from my own experience. But I can share some things I have learned from the Lord's prophets on principles that apply to this issue. There are also things I've learned from observing and speaking with others who experience same-gender attraction—some for as long as nearly forty years—but who also have successful and happy marriages and children and grandchildren. I share these brief thoughts only as ideas to consider and then to take to the Lord. The nature of same-gender attraction is different for different individuals, and the decision of when and who to marry and how to go about it in relation to this challenge is a very personal one that should be made only with guidance from priesthood leaders and in intimate communion with our Father in Heaven.

I believe strongly that God does want every one of us to prepare and strive for a "celestial" marriage, which is, of course, much more than simply being married in the temple. Whether or not that marriage happens in this life may be something we have no control over, but I believe our willingness to strive for it and prepare for it says something to God about our commitment to His eternal principles and His desires for us as His children. It is important to remember, however, that a commandment such as marriage, which requires the exercise of another's agency for it to be kept, is not something that can be planned with precision or forced through "faith." Our faith is manifest in the diligence with which we prepare and strive for it—and then we must allow it to happen in the Lord's own time.

Elder Dallin H. Oaks taught: "Because of things over which we have no control, we cannot plan and bring to pass everything we desire in our lives. . . . Even our most righteous desires may elude us, or come in different ways or at different times than we have sought to plan. For example, we cannot be sure that we will marry as soon as we desire. A marriage that is timely in our view may be our blessing or it may not."

He then shared an example from the life of his second wife, Kristen, whom he married after his first wife died of cancer. "Older singles have some interesting experiences. While [Kristen] was at her sister's place to celebrate her fiftieth birthday, her sister's husband shared something he had just read in a newspaper. 'Kristen,' he said, 'now that you are a single woman over 50, your chances of marrying are not as good as your chances of being killed by a terrorist.'

"The timing of marriage is perhaps the best example of an extremely important event in our lives that is almost impossible to plan. Like other important mortal events that depend on the agency of others or the will and timing of the Lord, marriage cannot be anticipated or planned with certainty. We can and should work for and pray for our righteous desires, but, despite this, many will remain single well beyond their desired time for marriage."[19]

It seems that many who experience this challenge have varying attitudes about how one who has feelings of same-gender attraction should approach marriage or whether one should even approach it at all. In my conversations with men who are skeptical of someone with this challenge marrying a woman, I have received a fairly typical response: "It would be unhealthy, selfish, and deceitful to attempt to marry a woman. It's not fair to her. And the 'just get married and it will go away approach' has ruined families and turned out horribly in almost every single case. A daughter of God who is worthy to marry in the temple deserves to be with a man who can love her and only her completely."

I've thought a lot about this and similar statements. I'm not naïve enough to think that marriage for one who experiences same-gender attraction would be easy, but, in truth, is marriage ever easy? Even when each marriage partner feels a strong heterosexual attraction for the other? To make a blanket statement that marriage for a person who experiences this challenge is "unhealthy" or "deceitful" or "unfair" is erroneous. There are certainly ways to approach marriage that would be healthy, honest, and fair to the potential spouse.

It is most important for individuals to remember that marriage should most certainly not be viewed as a "cure" for same-gender attraction. A person with same-gender attraction is deceiving himself if he marries with that expectation. President Gordon B. Hinckley taught: "The Lord has proclaimed that marriage between a man and a woman is ordained of God and is intended to be an eternal relationship bonded by trust and fidelity. Latter-day Saints, of all people, should marry with this sacred objective in mind. Marriage should not be viewed as a therapeutic step to solve problems such as homosexual inclinations or practices, which first should clearly be overcome with a firm and fixed determination never to slip to such practices again."[20] It is important to note here that President Hinckley is saying that behavior must be overcome before marriage, not necessarily the attraction.

If individuals who recognize the implications of their attraction marry as therapy or in the expectation of being "cured"—and then confide in their spouse only after they realize they had deceived themselves with this expectation, that certainly is dishonest and unfair to the spouse. Does that mean that the idea of marriage should be entirely abandoned? I don't believe so. Every fallen, mortal being who marries enters marriage with challenges or temptations or problems or tendencies of one form or another. That is normal. But it is important to consider that different individuals may be either more capable or more willing to work with different challenges.

In the case of a man, as long as he is spiritually clean and worthy to marry and emotionally healthy—for to be truly happy in marriage, we must first learn to be truly happy single—the decision of what is "fair" to the woman should be her decision. There is certainly the risk that she may not feel she can marry a man who experiences same-gender attraction. Her decision might be difficult to accept when feelings are deep, but it is her decision and she should have the opportunity to make it. Other women may be willing and able to healthily marry someone who experiences this attraction. If past transgression is involved, whether an individual feels it important to share that transgression with a future spouse is individual and may depend on circumstance and the promptings of the Spirit, but past transgressions and present challenges are two different issues.

Those with feelings of same-gender attraction should always be open and honest with a potential spouse about their attraction, so that the potential spouse can understand the implications and difficulties associated with it. As with any challenge, if we refuse to allow someone else to see us and love us for who we really are—a faithful child of God who happens to experience a difficult trial—how are we to obtain the love and support that we so desperately need and desire? With openness and honesty, we can allow a potential spouse to decide whether or not the challenge of same-gender attraction is a burden he or she feels both willing and capable of bearing with us. In addition, the potential spouse should not just know about the challenge; it is important for that individual to have time to understand it as much as possible—to study and ponder and prayerfully consider potential individual implications.

When those of us who experience same-gender attraction take it upon ourselves to decide what is "fair" for a potential spouse, we must not play the martyr with our own challenge. Many other marital situations might be considered more "unfair" to a wife, for example, than having a husband who is attracted to other men but who does not act on his attraction. Consider the rising numbers of adult males in the United States—both homosexual and heterosexual—who are addicted to pornography. Is it "fair" for any woman to have to live with that spiritual poison or to compete with a porn star, male or female? Is not pornography in and of itself—again, whether heterosexual or homosexual—a killer of spirituality and marriage? What about all the heterosexual "fatherless" or "husbandless" families in the world where the marriage is seemingly intact, but the man eats and sleeps by remote control or is rarely home because of work or some other reason? What about the emotional and physical abuse that takes place in homes as the result of an uncontrolled temper or addiction to drugs or alcohol? What about heterosexual men who are attracted to their wife but who choose not to temper their desires for other women and are thus unfaithful? Are any of these situations "fair" to the women or children involved?

The longer I live and the more closely I observe the world around me, the more I have come to feel that to love another person completely has little to do with our sexual orientation but rather entirely to do with our hearts and our commitment to our spouse and to Christ—regardless of the nature of our attractions. The more I think about the things the Lord has taught me through my experience with this attraction, in addition to other gifts and talents the Lord has blessed me with, the more I feel that they will strengthen, rather than weaken, my future marriage.

A young woman I know who has had close relationships with men who experience this attraction shared with me her feelings about the possibility of marrying someone with this challenge. She said, "I think, regardless of whether a man experiences same-gender attraction, he must be attracted to the woman he wants to be with—and attraction is more than just physical. What I'm trying to say is that as long as my husband is committed to the Lord and to me, I don't care if he has feelings of attraction to other men. Other married men may feel attracted to other women and not act on those feelings—this just happens to be a different challenge. I would hope he could look to the heart of me—my soul, my personality, my mind, and, yes, some physical attributes as well—and see me as beautiful as a whole and as a companion he would want to be with forever. I'd want a man to love me as a person and not because I am a woman. Yes, the road will be hard, and there will probably be weak moments, but isn't it the same for someone who has never had thoughts or feelings of attraction toward the same gender? Obviously an immeasurable amount of trust would have to be present for both people in the relationship, but that is true for any relationship."

A friend of mine who is married to a man who experiences same-gender attraction shared with me some of her feelings concerning her relationship with her husband. "One of the greatest blessings in our relationship has been our openness with each other, and that openness with each other and with the Lord has been the foundation of our relationship to this day. I am an inquisitive person. Asking questions helps me get to know people better. I wanted to better understand some of his previous experiences with this challenge in his life before because I wanted to better understand who he is now. I also know there are limits to what I need to know, and he has always been open and honest about answering my questions.

"I am not naïve enough to think that because he is attracted to me he has found the mysterious cure for same-gender attraction and will never be attracted to another man again. But I do know he is attracted to me, and that is enough. No married person ever becomes so blinded by love that they no longer recognize the beauty of another person. The kind of man I was attracted to before I married is still attractive to me. I just don't look a little too long now or flirt or do any of the kinds of things I did when I was still single. My heart and my covenants are toward my Heavenly Father and my husband. That standard should be true for anyone who is married—whether they have feelings of same-gender attraction or not."

The most important thing we can do is to stay faithful to the things we know to be true and to seek the Lord's Spirit in helping us go forward with what we know He would have us do. And we should recognize that though sexual attraction is an important part of marriage, a man needs only feel it for one woman and not all or even many women. The most important aspects of a marriage, however, extend beyond physical intimacy to spiritual and emotional intimacy. Contrary to what we may perceive from popular culture, marriage and intimacy should not be based upon sex or sexuality or physical image. Marriage should be based on mutual love, respect, strong friendship, and eternal commitment.

A good male friend of mine who experiences same-gender attraction and who is also married shared with me his feelings concerning his marriage, saying, "Marriage is difficult, and many struggling with same-gender attraction may feel that it is an impossible undertaking, but for my wife and me, marriage is working—for both of us. I agree that marriage should never be viewed as a 'cure' for anything, but it should likewise never be viewed as an impossible feat, hopelessly out of reach for someone who is naturally attracted to others of the same gender. Recently, another man who similarly struggles with same-gender attraction asked me the main reason I feel my marriage works. My first response was simply that I enjoy spending time with my wife more than anyone else in the world. It's true. We have a wonderful time together. She is so beautiful to me—very striking with a dramatic flair, and she is probably one of the funniest people in the world without even trying to be. She is talented and passionate and so spiritually mature and in tune. She is caring and compassionate. My wife is a prize.

"In my eyes, my wife is my special gift from Heavenly Father—a gift that He sent me after I had told myself for a long time that it was all right to be alone as long as He was the primary focus in my life. For a period in my life I was without the influence of the Church and was involved in relationships with other men, but when I finally decided to give my life to the Lord, I accepted in my heart that I would probably never marry, and I was okay with that. I also knew, however, that if I was obedient to the laws and ordinances of the gospel, I would have that chance at some time. I just figured that for the time being I would focus on being a good uncle and brother and son. I would take care of my parents when they got old. I would be that quirky single guy in a family ward that everyone knew but just did not know much about. That was me, and that was fine. Then along came the woman who was to become my wife.

"The Lord always knows best—and what a blessing it is that He does not get distracted by all of our planning and plotting. He never lets our 'expertise' get in the way of His eternal plan for us. I thank my Heavenly Father for my wife each time I pray. I thank Him that He has blessed me with someone who wants to make our marriage work as much as I do. Our sights are set on the eternities—together. And we talk about everything—everything—even my challenge with same-gender attraction. When I met my wife, I was still attracted to other men, and I believe that attraction will probably always be there to some extent. But I try not to focus on it too much, for I believe the necessary 'change' is not in the attraction but in the behavior. I have an honest and intense attraction to my wife, but that is not to say that I am suddenly now attracted to other women in the same fashion or that I am no longer attracted to men.

"Early on, we decided that a commitment to openness was imperative to the success of our life together. I have joked with my wife about her never having to worry about me being a 'skirt chaser.' I have committed to always being faithful to my dear wife, and I have promised my Heavenly Father and Savior that I will never participate in immoral behavior with men again. My greatest concern has always been the 'discovery' of details relating to past transgressions creeping in and ruining our marriage, so I told my wife about my challenges within days of meeting her. I knew that I cared deeply for her, and I felt that I had to be honest from the beginning if things were going to work out. It was a leap of faith that I believed had to be taken in order for her and my Heavenly Father to know of my sincerity. My wife does not love me 'in spite' of my challenge—she loves me 'because' of my challenge.

"One of the most important things for us in making our marriage work is that my wife and I are very much focused on each other's happiness. That is not to say that our relationship is perfect, and that we do not have our own selfish motives from time to time. We are infinitely 'human,' but at the core of our relationship is the desire to do whatever we can to make the other person happy. Our relationship with each other, and our relationship with our Heavenly Father, as individuals and as a couple, is the foundation of our relationship. We pray and study the scriptures together every day—even if we are unhappy with each other at the time. It is difficult to remain unhappy with another person when you are kneeling in prayer together, thanking your Father in Heaven for His mercy and love, and asking Him for assistance in your life together."

When we are searching for an eternal companion, we should consider what is most important and what we are really looking for. We should not look for someone who "completes" us, for the only Person who can do that is the Lord. But we do need to find someone whom we love and are romantically and sexually attracted to and with whom we are compatible. Same-gender attraction does not have to be an automatic death sentence to a relationship. The suggestion that all marriages with this challenge fail is false. We do hear more about the marriages that fail, but I believe that is at least partially because those who have successful marriages are quietly and faithfully serving each other and their God.

The following is an experience of another friend of mine with this attraction. I thought his words were quite profound: "I feel God has been very merciful to me in regards to finding my wife. I despised dating; it made me feel awkward. God knew this, so I think he blessed me with a good friend I could just be with. We didn't have to go on 'dates.' We did things together and enjoyed each other; we had many of the same interests. One night I was praying about our relationship because I was contemplating taking it further, but I wanted to feel attracted to her in a more complete way.

"During and after that prayer, I remember feeling one of the most wonderful things I've ever felt. I felt the beautiful desire of being with her. I never thought I could have felt that way. It seemed like I couldn't stop smiling all night. My whole body felt good. It was in contrast to the feelings of desire or attraction I've felt for other men. Beyond just being free of lust and covetousness, there was together with it a unique inimitable feeling of truth that I can't explain. I think it was just untainted love flowing through me. All I could do was lie in my bed pondering the sacred feelings and thanking God.

"This is the way I interpreted this experience: God, in His remarkable mercies, allowed me, if just for that moment, to see the vision of the future (and present)—a vision of celestial love—a vision of what I, as an eternal man, am capable of despite all of my earthly obstacles. That night, I feel I had a sacred, true vision of things as they really are, 'for the Spirit speaketh the truth and lieth not. Wherefore, it speaketh of things as they really are, and of things as they really will be; wherefore, these things are manifested unto us plainly, for the salvation of our souls' (Jacob 4:13). I knew that for me personally, God wanted me to be married in this life, and now I wanted it too.

"We eventually married and now have a son. I love both of them very much. I am attracted to my wife, but I am also still attracted to other men. It's a battle I have to fight every day, but I am still winning the fight. I don't think I am doing my wife any injustice by being married to her; she loves me too, and we both agree that we are better off now than we were before we were married. I pray that I will have the Spirit with me every day to help me to continue see things as they 'really are,' because when I don't see things as they really are, it is easier to be subjected to temptation and lose the vision of eternal life I am striving for. To maintain that vision, I do what I can to keep myself spiritually nourished."

It is worth noting again that our continual focus should be on Christ and not on marriage. Marriage may be a very real and healthy possibility for some, but what works for one may not work for all. Likewise, it should not be construed that because marriage did not work for one it will not work for anyone. We are all different, and the nature of our experience with same-gender attraction and the factors that have influenced it are different as well. Because some with same-gender attraction have been successful in marriage, it may be tempting to misplace our focus, become obsessed with the idea of whether or not we personally can marry, and thus lose the proper eternal perspective. For some, no matter how valiant or faithful or sincere they may be in doing everything right and living according to God's will, marriage may not be a part of their mortal experience. We have to learn through the Spirit what God's plan is for us individually within His overall plan for our salvation and exaltation.

I know testimony-bearing, faithful individuals who love the Lord, who desire to live according to His divine will, and who want to marry but who are currently inadvertently repulsed by the idea of being physically intimate with someone of the opposite gender. These individuals should in no way feel pressured or forced into marriage in order to do the "right thing" or to be "cured" or to follow a cultural standard or someone's example because "they did it, and it works for them, so you can do it too." The truly right thing to do is to stay close to our Father in Heaven, maintain an intimate communion with Him, and follow the Spirit that He will bless us with if we are faithful. His Spirit will help us to know individually what we can do to more fully prepare ourselves to eventually—capably, healthily, and willingly—make that eternally binding covenant with the Lord and our eternal companion. We must be willing to put our will on the altar and allow God to direct the affairs of our life. The possibility of marriage must be left in the Lord's hands. Even though we may not all find our eternal companion and marry in this mortal probation, we all can find genuine fulfillment in faithfulness to Christ and His laws, if we will seek Him and draw on His enabling grace.

In my spiritual journey through the wilderness of mortality, I have learned much and expect to learn much more concerning faith. My initial, simple understanding of faith in God has evolved. Certainly, faith is hoping for things which are not seen, which are true. But it is in hoping enough and trusting enough in those things which are not seen, which are true, that we show our willingness to offer our whole soul as an offering unto him (see Omni 1:26). Faith is the willingness to take what we value most into the land of Moriah and place it on the altar there (see Genesis 22:2).

Faith is trusting in the Lord enough to believe that He sees a much larger picture than the one we currently see and that He has a purpose for us in all that we go through. It is believing in and trusting His prophets to teach us what we need to know in order to stay on the straight and narrow path toward eternal life. It is trusting in His timing as well as in His reality. Faith is hoping for Him enough to give our life for Him and to live our life for Him. It is believing that if we "will turn to the Lord with full purpose of heart, and put [our] trust in him, and serve him with all diligence of mind," He will, "according to his own will and pleasure, deliver [us] out of bondage" (Mosiah 7:33).

Chapter 10

To Mourn and to Comfort

I was baptized a member of the Church when I was eight years old, and I made the covenant then that I would be "willing to bear one another's burdens, that they may be light; yea, and . . . willing to mourn with those that mourn; yea, and comfort those that stand in need of comfort" (Mosiah 18:8–9). But I am only now beginning to learn the significance of that covenant—I am only now beginning to understand the love and the mercy God has called on us to bestow upon each other. I have always believed in the Atonement, and I have always believed in the importance of the second great commandment, to "love thy neighbour as thyself" (Matthew 22:39), but it is only now that I am beginning to internalize them and to realize their true significance.

I've never fully understood what it means to have genuine compassion, and I don't think I yet know how to express Christlike love. But my feelings of same-gender attraction have driven me to my knees in prayer for His mercy and enabling power, which have helped me to understand more about His love than I did previously. And although I'm a fairly slow learner, which means He will be teaching me for a long time, I'm grateful that I am now at least beginning to comprehend.

For much of my life, I had it relatively easy. When people had problems, my first response—even if I didn't vocalize it—was to tell them to get over it, that everyone has problems, and if they would get outside themselves, their problems wouldn't seem so significant. Looking back, I see how arrogant, self-righteous, and close-minded I was toward views or problems others experienced that differed from my own.

It was easy for me to judge others for weaknesses I couldn't relate to—to shout exhortations to those on the front line, while I myself stood in ease and safety, a mere spectator guarded from the field of battle. But now that I have finally recognized the seriousness of my own weaknesses, which have been brought to light because of this challenge, I feel the beam being taken from my own eyes and am able to see beyond the myopic view I've held for so long regarding others' pains and challenges. As I stood at a crossroads with a torn heart, shortly after I first started talking with others who experience this challenge, I met a young man who mistakenly felt I was more emotionally and spiritually solid than he was. He worried that I would judge him for choices he had made and was still struggling with. He said a couple of times that he hoped I wouldn't judge him, and it surprised me that he would say something like that, because I had never had the slightest inclination to think negatively of him, regardless of his past choices.

What startled me even more was that I did *not* have such an inclination to judge, as I frequently had in the past. At the same time, it felt really good not to have that predisposition. My experience with feelings of same-gender attraction has taught me profound lessons about some of the "weightier matters" (Matthew 23:23)—namely, judgment, mercy, faith, and charity—for which I am extremely grateful and about which I might not have learned without being tried the way that I am. What is most important to me is that I am learning those things, and I feel closer to the Lord for it.

An instance in the life of the Savior has taught me an insightful lesson about the commandment to "mourn with those that mourn . . . and comfort those that stand in need of comfort" (Mosiah 18:9). When Lazarus became ill, Jesus explained that there was purpose to this experience. He said to Mary and Martha, "This sickness is not unto death, but for the glory of God, that the Son of God might be glorified thereby." He remained for a short time and then called His disciples to return with

Him to Judea, for, said He, "Our friend Lazarus sleepeth; but I go, that I may awake him out of sleep." When Jesus came into Judea, Mary approached Him, weeping, fell to His feet, and said, "Lord, if thou hadst been here, my brother had not died." He watched her as the tears fell from her cheeks, and He wept with her (John 11:4, 11, 32, 35). He didn't tell Lazarus's sisters that everything was all right, for in their eyes it wasn't. Lazarus was dead, and they were in pain. Although Christ knew that Lazarus would live—that their loss was temporary—and that there was a glorious purpose to the tragedy, He didn't belittle His friends' grief. Their pain was still pain, and their tears were still tears. He didn't try to explain it away, and He didn't try to rationalize away their tears. He wept with them, and He loved them.

So it is with us. Christ suffered beyond all mortal comprehension; He "hath descended below them all" (D&C 122:8)—our trials and anguish will never be anything near the degree that He experienced—but the Great Almighty is still descending, for He weeps when we weep, cries when we cry, aches when we ache, mourns when we mourn. And He comforts us when we stand in need of comfort.

I am just now beginning to understand the significance of my calling to do the same—to mourn with those who weep and to comfort those whose eyes are wet and whose arms are heavy. Judgment is not mine; it is His, and His alone. I have been called to love others and to weep with them. We should not have to bear our crosses alone, and we should not have to fear the judgment of others—especially that of the Saints of God, who bear His name—in our pain. It feels unbelievably good to talk with others about their pains, challenges, trials, and even transgressions and not feel to condemn or belittle. It feels good to have a greater sense of compassion as I learn to look more upon the heart of men and women and less upon their behavior. I have come to care more about individuals regardless of their beliefs or lifestyle.

The Prophet Joseph Smith taught: "Nothing is so much calculated to lead people to forsake sin as to take them by the hand, and watch over them with tenderness. When persons manifest the least kindness and love to me, O what power it has over my mind, while the opposite course has a tendency to harrow up all the harsh feelings and depress the human mind."[1] The power of patient and eternal love should never be underestimated.

It is also important for us as Saints to remember that many individuals who experience same-gender attraction—whether or not they have testimonies of the truthfulness of the gospel of Christ and of the divine role of His Church—will choose not to remain faithful. They may have lost their testimony or their desire to remain faithful, or they may just be treading a thorny path as they seek to understand their personal experience and reconcile it with what they have been taught to believe. It may be wise to heed the example of Jesus in his response to the woman taken in adultery. He did not condemn her, neither did He condone her sins, but He told her to "go, and sin no more" (John 8:11). Like the Savior, we also must love and comfort and refrain from condemning those who have chosen paths contrary to His teachings. We must love them and embrace the good that is in them, regardless of some of their current choices. Until the day—whether in this life or the next—when "that spark of divinity in each of them will ignite, [and] they . . . assert their agency as sons and daughters created in the image of God and renounce the destroyer," we can do as Alma and Mosiah did for their sons. [2] We can pray to the Father in the name of His Son that their loved ones will "be brought to the knowledge of the truth" (Mosiah 27:14).

Regarding those who wish to be affiliated with the Saints, even while they are struggling with submission to their attraction, the resurrected Lord taught the Saints at Bountiful: "Ye shall meet together oft; and ye shall not forbid any man from coming unto you when ye shall meet together, but suffer them that they may come unto you and forbid them not; but ye shall pray for them, and shall not cast them out; and if it so be that they come unto you oft ye shall pray for them unto the Father, in my name" (3 Nephi 18:22–23).

In a speech given while serving as president of Brigham Young University, Jeffrey R. Holland connected the attitude with which we respond to the needs and pains of others with our understanding of the Atonement. He said: "I want to suggest to you that it is your relationship with other people, including your husband or wife and your children that gives you your best chance to say what you believe about the Atonement. Your most important beliefs are not going to be statements made in a classroom. They certainly aren't going to be statements made in a symposium. What you will say best about your understanding of the Atonement, about love and repentance and forgiveness, will come in your human relationships with people who have problems, people who make mistakes, who haven't in every hour of every day done all that he or she could have done in righteousness. You know I'm describing you and me."[3]

As I am learning to place my life and my weaknesses and my imperfections completely in the hands of God, I am learning to do the same with the lives and weaknesses and imperfections of others. I'm learning to put more faith in the love and mercy and understanding of God's judgment and less in my own. I have greater compassion for how difficult trials can be, but I don't think I would have learned the lessons I have had I not been blessed with this trial. Yes, as crazy as it might sound, I have come to feel that on some level my experience with same-gender attraction has been an important blessing for my life. That recognition doesn't make the trial any easier, and there are still times when I weep, wondering when the fight will end, but at least I am beginning to recognize the incredible good that has resulted from my experience.

We all have struggles; we all experience tragedy; we all suffer from varying trials, challenges, and temptations common to our mortal, fallen state. But the cleansing, redeeming power of the Lord's atoning blood has made it possible for us to overcome—for all of us to overcome. The way we manifest compassion and mourn with others and comfort them in their own challenges—even if they, like Mary and Martha, do not immediately sense the greater purpose and vision—says something about our internalized understanding of the Lord's merciful nature and the love that motivated His atoning sacrifice.

"Through a Glass Darkly"

One of the many different groups of people that need the kind of outreach, compassion, and charity the Savior taught and exemplified is those who experience same-gender attraction. A slow evolution is taking place in the understanding of homosexuality both in society and in the Church, although in diverging directions. As society and popular culture become increasingly licentious, I believe the members of the Church, as Saints of the Most High, will evolve toward the "mind of Christ" (1 Corinthians 2:16) with respect to those who experience this attraction.

In 1991, the First Presidency of the Church declared: "Sexual relations are proper only between husband and wife appropriately expressed within the bonds of marriage. Any other sexual contact, including fornication, adultery, and homosexual and lesbian behavior, is sinful."[4] Church members should not embrace or condone homosexual behavior in any form, nor should they wish for the Church to change its position on the matter, but the members of Christ's Church must grow in Christlike compassion and acceptance of those who experience same-gender attraction. In so doing they will become a light to the world.

The First Presidency's statement is the word of the Lord on the matter of sexual morality. That word will not change, particularly concerning something as eternal and sacred and godly as the nature of sexuality. We must become more open-minded in our approach to same-gender attraction, but in doing so we need not stray from revealed truth. Rather, in our approach we must move beyond myopic views concerning the nature of this challenge to support in a Christlike manner those who experience it and who sometimes find it painful to conform their lives to the truth.

It is important to realize that our own knowledge of eternal truths—of God's nature, of love or any other principle of the gospel—is not absolute but relative to our capacity, experience, and position. Our understanding is partial, restricted, and complex, and one who is guided by reason alone, without the faith and hope and charity spoken of by Paul, may actually be guided by misunderstanding, bigotry, cynicism, fear, and even hatred. It is necessary that the Saints of God seek to understand as well as to be understood.

We do not comprehend, as God does, the end from the beginning, and the minds of many of the Lord's covenant people often seem as prejudiced as they were anciently. Too often Saints have walked and reacted in darkness, not heeding the Light that is in them. We have neither the mind nor the full knowledge of God, and until we do, it is crucial that we do as Paul taught and abide in faith and hope and charity. It is through the gifts of charity and the grace of Christ that we have the capacity to imagine what it is like to suffer as another person suffers.

"That They Might Be Remembered and Nourished"

The Church of Jesus Christ was designed by God to be a haven where those who experience mortal challenges, including same-gender attraction, can come for love and strength and compassion and understanding. It is His people who can and must create that haven. The Church is a "hospital for sinners"—the treatment being the gospel of grace and redemption and regeneration—not a "country club for Saints."[5] It was designed to be a place where those who are weak but loved of God can come to be "remembered and nourished by the good word of God, to keep them in the right way, to keep them continually watchful unto prayer, relying alone upon the merits of Christ, who was the author and the finisher of their faith" (Moroni 6:4).

Too often among the Saints those who experience same-gender attraction learn to feel that they are inherently evil, wicked, degenerate, and selfish because those in a position to teach often do not distinguish between the person with homosexual attractions and the homosexual behaviors the attractions may sometimes lead to. Confucius taught: "To study without thinking is futile. To think without studying is dangerous."[6] With an issue as sensitive and complicated and often controversial as same-gender attraction, we must be especially careful about what we study and teach and the way in which we teach it. As individuals with same-gender attraction grow up in an environment of misinformation and misunderstanding, they learn to hate themselves. Some learn to see themselves as inherently an enemy to all that is good and virtuous, and consequently they lose their sense of worth and value in the eyes of God. Under this pressure a few—and any is too many—take their own lives.

The way the Saints of God teach and reach out toward those who experience this and other challenges—and even those entangled in sin—should be more representative of the way our Savior taught and ministered. One evangelical author discussed the relationship Christ had with those who most needed His succoring in contrast to the relationship we as Christ's people often have with those who need succoring. Although he was speaking of the evangelical Christian community, a parallel can be drawn to what may occur in the Latter-day Saint community if we are not wise. He said: "The more unsavory the characters, the more at ease they seemed to feel around Jesus. People like these found Jesus appealing: a Samaritan social outcast, a military officer of the tyrant Herod, a quisling tax collector, a recent hostess to seven demons. In contrast, Jesus got a chilly response from more respectable types. Pious Pharisees thought him uncouth and worldly, a rich young ruler walked away shaking his head, and even the open-minded Nicodemus sought a meeting under the cover of darkness. . . . Somehow we have created a community of respectability in the church. The down-and-out, who flocked to Jesus when he lived on earth, do not feel welcome. How did Jesus, the only perfect person in history, manage to attract the notoriously imperfect? And what keeps us from following in his steps today?"[7]

God loves and desires to reach out to every one of His children, and at baptism we covenanted to do the same—"to mourn with those that mourn; yea, and comfort those that stand in need of comfort" (Mosiah 18:9). That is our stewardship, and a most important part of our call to holiness. If we as members of His Church do not seek out those who need Him most, we may alienate those who most desperately long for the Savior's loving embrace and healing grace. In this situation, we may alienate those who experience same-gender attraction and want to remain faithful to Christ and active in His Church but who find less comfort in the Church and among the Saints than they otherwise might. Elder Neal A. Maxwell stated, "The hands which hang down and most need to be lifted up belong to those too discouraged even to reach out anymore."[8]

Saints of the meridian Church provide an example for us today, for despite the thorn in Paul's flesh, he said he found comfort among the people of the Lord: "And my temptation which was in my flesh ye despised not, nor rejected; but received me as an angel of God, even as Christ Jesus" (Galatians 4:14). The meridian Saints had a large portion of the charity Christ exemplified. Charity is not simply alms or good deeds; it is a very real Godlike love that those of the world cannot comprehend. If we truly have charity, we see from the perspective of eternity—we see others as God sees them, and we strive to help them and build them as God would strive to help and build them. That is the "pure love of Christ, and it endureth forever. . . . Wherefore, my beloved brethren, pray unto the Father with all the energy of heart, that ye may be filled with this love" (Moroni 7:47–48).

One thing is clear. It is important that the Saints of God avoid treating those who experience same-gender attraction as if they were in open rebellion against God and deserve to be shunned or socially "stoned." Rather, they should be treated with the kind and loving attitude exemplified by the Master. Most individuals who experience same-gender attraction, if given a choice, would likely prefer not to experience such an attraction, if for no other reason than their life would be easier.

There have been times when I have wept because of the difficulty of this challenge, and there have been times when I have wept with gratitude, knowing how much more difficult it could be if I didn't have friends and leaders and family who love me unconditionally and support me. It is only recently—because of that love and support—that I have been able to finally begin to open up and allow myself to truly be loved and to learn to truly love myself as well. For years I bore the burden alone in fear and self-hatred. For years I was certain I could never tell another soul my feelings because of how "evil" those forbidden feelings were.

But when I could no longer bear my suppressed burden alone, I was grateful for those who were so filled with charity and compassion for all people that I did not fear their judgment and dared venture to ask for their support and confidence. After prayerfully selecting those I initially told and gauging their response, I began to feel much more comfortable with who I am as an individual and with the attraction I experience. If their response had not been so compassionate, I might never have trusted another person and would still be hiding in fear and my own self-homophobia.

As I have felt comfort in sharing my feelings with others who did not judge but instead reached out in compassion, I have often thought of the response of Joseph Smith after he was finally allowed to reveal the plates to others. After returning home from his experience with the Three Witnesses, "Joseph threw himself down beside [his mother], and exclaimed, 'Father, mother, you do not know how happy I am: the Lord has now caused the plates to be shown to three more besides myself . . . and I feel as if I was relieved of a burden which was almost too heavy for me to bear, and it rejoices my soul, that I am not any longer to be entirely alone in the world.'"⁹

When I first told my family, they embraced me and told me that they loved me. I was still their son, I was still their brother—and their affection was unchanged. I felt so liberated, and that evening I lay in bed with tears in my eyes as I expressed my gratitude to my Father in Heaven for their loving response. A difficult situation could have been made more difficult by their reaction, but what they said and did was exactly what I needed. Their hearts and arms were still open to me, they loved me, and they would be there for me when I needed them. For many, that may be all that is really needed.

In my journey through the experience of having feelings of same-gender attraction, and as I have encountered various responses to the issue of homosexuality in general, I have noticed that those who have known individuals who experience the attraction (most often someone close to them or someone they love a great deal)—whether or not those individuals act on that attraction—have been much more compassionate and loving. That kind of response does not mean such individuals acknowledge homosexual behavior as theologically or morally acceptable, but they handle the issue in a sympathetic and kindhearted manner. They give greater place in their hearts for understanding and for the love of God.

Elder Alexander B. Morrison, in an address to individuals who experience same-gender attraction, said: "The struggle with same-gender attraction is one of the most trying, difficult and painful challenges faced by God's children. I can never forget sitting up most of the night with a young American doing charitable work in Eastern Nigeria. He had struggled for many years with same-gender attraction, from adolescence through his mission, and his time thereafter in university studies. Though in great personal pain, he had endured in faithfulness, but finally came to me in despair, not knowing how to proceed, hoping only that if he wandered the dangerous roads of Nigeria at night he could be killed and put out of his misery. My heart ached for him.

"Same-gender attraction . . . entails great spiritual struggle and may require years and even a lifetime of prayer, tears, repentance and diligence . . . [Some], despite valiant and prayerful effort, continue to struggle with the challenge of same-gender attraction. Their burdens are heavy, and their tears many. As I counseled my young friend in Nigeria, they can, however, struggle on in faith, keeping the commandments of God, with the assurance He will strengthen and sustain them. It is not easy, but perhaps it is not intended to be so."[10]

As homosexuality becomes more visible in our society, more individuals will be willing to acknowledge their same-gender attraction and cease suppressing their feelings. If there is support, spiritual warmth and nourishment, and a haven for them in Christ's kingdom, there is a much greater probability that they will seek that haven. President Howard W. Hunter taught, "In the gospel view, no man is alien. No one is to be denied. There is no underlying excuse for smugness, arrogance, or pride."[11]

The Prophet Joseph Smith said: "While one portion of the human race is judging and condemning the other without mercy, the Great Parent of the universe looks upon the whole of the human family with a fatherly care and paternal regard; He views them as His offspring, and without any of those contracted feelings that influence the children of men, causes 'His sun to rise on the evil and on the good, and sendeth rain on the just and on the unjust' [Matthew 5:45]. He holds the reins of judgment in His hands; He is a wise Lawgiver, and will judge all men, not according to the narrow, contracted notions of men, but, 'according to the deeds done in the body whether they be good or evil,' or whether these deeds were done in England, America, Spain, Turkey, or India."[12]

The nature of homosexual attraction is still greatly misunderstood, but hopefully, as time and truth tell their story, the loving arms of compassion can be extended to help individuals through their challenge. If there is only coldness, cynicism, fear, misunderstanding, and suspicion, those who are weak in faith will go where they can find the love and acceptance they desperately need and long for. It is my hope that the growth of God's kingdom will foster growth in understanding those who have challenges, who live daily through trials that seem unbearable, and that with growth in understanding will come a greater willingness for God's people "to mourn with those that mourn . . . and comfort those that stand in need of comfort" (Mosiah 18:9).

Chapter 11

A Place in the Kingdom

Where? The word has been ever-present in my heart as I have pleaded with God to know my place in the Church and kingdom of God. My whole life and perceived place in the Church had been built partly upon my aspirations for a future family. When I finally confronted the hard reality that my lifelong desire might not be realized in this life, I became completely despondent. I believed that my place in the kingdom was nothing more than a fading dream, and I was bound to leave what I had always loved most. I became discouraged and hopeless. It was not until I gained a better understanding and conviction of the real Rock and His purpose for me in mortality that my hope and determination was renewed and I began to better understand what my place in the kingdom would be. That place may be vastly different from what I had always hoped and imagined, but now my hope is simply in Christ—I will ever strive to let Him lead my life wherever He may.

Even though family is a critical part of the gospel and an important part of the mortal Church, our faith and conviction should not be built entirely upon having our own family here in this life. The Church's focus on eternal marriage and family may not apply to me at this time. Although I hope to marry and have a family, I have to leave that to Him. It is something that I, with my struggle with same-gender attraction, have had to place completely in His hands.

But whether marriage is to be a part of my mortal experience or not, I have wondered what my role in the Church family is to be. As I've read

Paul's counsel to the Corinthian Saints, I've come to know that there is a place for me within the Church and kingdom of Christ. He said: "For as the body is one, and hath many members, and all the members of that one body, being many, are one body: so also is Christ. For by one Spirit are we all baptized into one body, whether we be Jews or Gentiles, whether we be bond or free; and have been all made to drink into one Spirit.

"For the body is not one member, but many. If the foot shall say, Because I am not the hand, I am not of the body; is it therefore not of the body? And if the ear shall say, Because I am not the eye, I am not of the body; is it therefore not of the body? If the whole body were an eye, where were the hearing? If the whole were hearing, where were the smelling? But now hath God set the members every one of them in the body, as it hath pleased him. And if they were all one member, where were the body? But now are they many members, yet but one body.

"And the eye cannot say unto the hand, I have no need of thee: nor again the head to the feet, I have no need of you. Nay, much more those members of the body, which seem to be more feeble, are necessary: And those members of the body, which we think to be less honourable, upon these we bestow more abundant honour . . . Now ye are the body of Christ, and members in particular" (1 Corinthians 12:12–27).

Unfortunately, a portion of Paul's powerful analogy of the body as type for Christ's Church and kingdom is sometimes a heartrending reality. Sometimes the foot really does say, "Because I am not the hand, I am not of the body." And sometimes the eye does say to the hand, and the hand to the feet, "I have no need of you." Sometimes those with homosexual attraction feel that because they are "different," they are not welcome in the Church, Sometimes that unwelcome feeling is caused, tragically, by the myopic "eye" or ignorant "hand" that made him or her feel that way.

But the living Spirit of the living God has helped me to know that I do have a place in His kingdom—that I and every child of God who is willing to make and keep covenants, despite our differences, are desperately needed as part of His "body" if it is truly to be whole. Although it may be difficult for someone with same-gender attraction to stay in the Church and remain faithful to its standards, if we have true faith that there is something more after this life, we are assured that the faith and sacrifice will be worth it. In the meantime, however, we have to find an individual role in the Church family. I've often asked myself why I must experience a trial and temptation that is so unnatural and yet feels so natural? Why couldn't my mortal challenge at least be something "normal"?

One day while I was pondering my feelings of attraction to other men and what that might entail for my life, I had a strong impression that has since proved to be very significant in my life. The words of Jacob in the Book of Mormon came to my mind: "We would to God . . . that all men would believe in Christ, and view his death, and suffer his cross and bear the shame of the world" (Jacob 1:8). I believe we need to bear the cross of Christ, but why this cross? Then, as the prophecy of Alma to the Saints in Gideon concerning the long-awaited Messiah again impressed itself upon me, I gained a small insight into the answer to this question. The Spirit rested upon me, teaching me: "He will take upon him their infirmities, that his bowels may be filled with mercy, according to the flesh, *that he may know according to the flesh how to succor his people according to their infirmities*" (Alma 7:12; italics added).

The Lord has said that His people are to be the saviors of men in the sense that they help the Savior in His work and turn people to Him (see D&C 103:9–10). The Savior understands us and can succor us because He suffered trial and temptation beyond what we will ever suffer. For members of the Church to fulfill their baptismal covenant to "mourn with those that mourn . . . and comfort those that stand in need of comfort" (Mosiah 18:9), they must have some idea of how to succor others in their afflictions. Those who have suffered similar trials are often more compassionate and understanding and hence more able to point those in mourning to their Savior, who can completely understand their pain.

The number of people experiencing same-gender attraction—or at least those willing to be open with it—seems to be increasing, and the trend will likely continue. As the Church spreads throughout the world, it is almost certain there will be an increased number of Church members who experience same-gender attraction. The feeling I had was that I must taste a little of the pain of this trial in order to "succor" others in the future—inside and outside the Church—that they may know they can turn to Christ for hope, redemption, and spiritual healing.

I do not know what the individual purposes for others who experience same-gender attraction may be or whether their individual place and mission within the kingdom is similar to mine. But this much I do know: they are loved by their literal and divine Father in Heaven, who wants them Home, and there is most certainly a place for them within the kingdom of God and within the body of Christ. The place that they fit may not be the one traditionally viewed or the ideal sought for, but our God and His Christ have placed each of us here for a reason. There is much for us to learn and to teach others that we may not have been able to do in any other way.

There is much that those who experience same-gender attraction and who desire to stay faithful to the Church and to Christ can do to enrich the lives of other Church members. A number of close friends and others have told me that their relationship with me has helped them grow in their understanding of those who experience this attraction—that the issue was for the first time made an intensely personal one, which caused them to think more deeply about their attitudes toward it. We need to help people move beyond the misunderstandings and the myopia so that this issue can be addressed in a more positive and healthy manner. I know many individuals who deal with same-gender attraction who, because of it, seem to have grasped some of the "weightier matters" of the law (Matthew 23:23)—namely, mercy, compassion, and grace. I have grown from knowing such individuals and learning from them, and I feel they have much to offer the world and the kingdom. If they remain faithful to Christ, they will be powerful instruments in His hands to lead people to Him.

An Instrument in the Hand of the Lord

As for me, I am just beginning to see the fulfillment of that spiritual witness I received as I was pondering this challenge and its relation to the gospel. I have felt on a few occasions that the Lord has been able to use me as an instrument in a small way to help people better understand this challenge—or to help others who experience it better understand the redeeming and enabling power of their Deliverer. While I was teaching at the Missionary Training Center, on my first day with a group of elders I discussed, as usual, the importance of seeing beyond common "labels" in missionary work—"nonmember," "investigator," "less-active," "convert," etc. I told the elders that their teaching would be much different, much more powerful and sincere, if they would learn early to look to the souls of individuals and truly see them as literal children of our Father in Heaven with divine potential and individual needs.

I had taught this principle numerous times in the years I had taught at the MTC, but for the first time ever I was impressed to share an insight I had gained while working on my mission with the men who were living in a homosexual relationship. I wasn't sure I wanted to, though, because I didn't want to give an awkward impression to these elders. I didn't want them to suspect anything about me or feel awkward discussing this topic, which in my previous experience had almost always seemed to attract derogation or discomfort. But the impression was there, nonetheless, so I shared the experience, and I wondered for the rest of the night what that impression implied.

The next class period, however, I felt I knew the reason the impression had been given to me. Randomly, I chose one of the elders from the district to take out of class and individually evaluate his teaching skills. While the elder was presenting a principle from the discussions, I had the distinct impression that he was the reason I had been prompted to share my experience. Toward the end of that district's stay in the MTC, he approached me with a concern that had been weighing on his mind. He wanted to know how he should respond if people asked him about a Church doctrine or position on which he disagreed with the prophets.

Noting his sincerity and the seriousness of the question, we went into a private room where he began to explain. He mentioned that he had some friends who were homosexual and he couldn't see anything wrong with two people being together who loved each other. At that moment, I knew that he wasn't concerned just for his "friends." Understanding what he was really asking, I responded to his "real" concern while, for the sake of his comfort, keeping it in the context of what he had actually asked me. We had a positive and enlightening conversation—in which I did not reveal my own struggle—and that seemed to be the end of it.

But he did leave me a private note before he left the MTC, thanking me for helping him with his concerns regarding homosexuality and affirming that he would continue to seek personal revelation on the matter. And then he was gone.

Several months later, I received a letter from him in which he again thanked me for our conversation and referred to his earlier concern, noting that his experience in the MTC had been really difficult for him but that he was slowly coming to understand things better as he sought personal revelation in his life. I responded, noting that I hadn't realized he had struggled so much, other than the concern he had approached me with at the very end of his stay at the MTC. He wrote back to me, confiding his struggle with same-gender attraction.

With his consent, I have decided to disclose our exchanges for two purposes. One is that the experience with my missionary friend has helped me to better understand the Lord's purpose in allowing me to experience this attraction. The other reason is that I believe our exchange shows to some degree the experience of this other son of God as he has been slowly coming to understand the importance of his own experience with this challenge and of the value of his own place in the kingdom.

He wrote: "As far as the MTC goes, I was having a really hard time. I trust you a great deal, so I feel I can tell you what was going on. I went into the mission field with a 'clean slate,' but inside I thought I was gay.

So, here I was wondering how I was going to teach about the wonderful plan of salvation when I felt I didn't have a chance at the greatest goal myself. I remember thinking, 'How can I teach about eternal marriage when I don't think I'll have the opportunity?' So inside I was torn apart. I didn't know how I was going to be able to testify of something that I didn't feel (at the time) pertained to me.

"I know that is one of the reasons I came to you with my concerns. I can remember the time you told of the experience talking with LDS men with the same struggle I have, and the genuine Christlike love you showed toward them (Because I'm not sure if you know this, but many Latter-day Saints don't react well to non-heterosexuality!). I remember your advice those last few days, and I can remember your profound words of counsel.

"You asked in your letter if things have changed at all since I've been out on my mission. It's amazing the changes that have taken place in my life. I went into the MTC with the mind frame that I would never get married, and I'd try to live the way God would want me to, and that would be that—perhaps buy a cat . . . Yeah, basically goals and dreams that scratch the surface of what I have the potential of achieving. Now, at this time, I actually have eternity in my mind frame, and it is on my top list of goals, dreams, and desires. Obviously, it's not like it's 'POOF!'—all my troubles and struggles are gone, but looking at life in an eternal perspective, it makes the struggles not as hard and helps me rely more on our Father in Heaven and the ones who want to see me succeed in this life and beyond, such as family and friends. So it's great. I hope you weren't weirded out by me dropping that info on you, but I think you can handle it.

"As far as the homosexuality issue on a mission, I've had the opportunity to use my experience to help other people out. There was a time we went into the city to contact people, and we came across a man who was about twenty-two, who was a member of the Church, and gay. The reason he left the Church was that he didn't feel welcome. After we talked with him for a while, he had a greater understanding of the gospel of Jesus

Christ and how he is loved. I'm not sure where he is now, but I know he walked away from that conversation with a greater outlook on his faith in Jesus Christ and how he felt about the Church. To be honest, I'm not going to hide my experience if I can use it to help. (On the other hand, I'm not going to tell everyone just for conversational purposes!) I have rebuked several missionaries, though, after hearing them discuss how God hates homosexuals. It's interesting! Whoa!"

As I read about this elder's feelings, wondering if he would ever have an opportunity to receive one of the greatest blessings of the gospel, I ached for him because I understood. When I responded—still not revealing to him my own struggle with same-gender attraction because of the nature of my relationship with him as teacher and student—I shared with him some of the thoughts, principles, and doctrines of the gospel of Christ that I thought might be helpful for him in his struggle, knowing how difficult things had been for me personally.

He responded almost immediately with the following:

"It is so comforting to know that there are others out there who have such a balance of compassion toward people with homosexual feelings and, at the same time, have such a strong conviction of the gospel of Jesus Christ. I can relate completely to the things you shared about Stuart Matis. I've had these feelings since middle school, and I naturally assumed going to church more, praying more, reading scripture more, etc., would change me. Although it gave me a wonderful knowledge of the gospel, it didn't change me. I even expected change when I went through the temple, and when I entered the MTC. I guess that's one of the reasons I was so down in the MTC. I had expected all my problems to somehow disappear as soon as I put on that badge, but they didn't.

"And like others, I've been depressed and felt isolated to the point I thought taking my life would solve it all. Obviously I didn't go though with it, but up until your letter, I still felt like I needed to work harder, or maybe prove myself, and perhaps I'd overcome my personal battles. But what you said—that it isn't about 'change'; it's about Christ—hit me so hard, and once again I felt an immense sense of hope, and I felt my love and faith in Christ increase. I've come to realize that I'm not a bad person for having these feelings and inclinations, and I shouldn't wait to be 'changed' because I'm doing my scripture study every morning or tracting for so many hours a day. It will happen according to His own will and pleasure.

"Jesus Christ loves me and wants what's best for me—I just have to have faith in Him, trust and serve Him, and He'll do what He knows is best for me. I'm really coming to understand the importance of focusing on Christ. The example of Peter's faith to walk on the water really touched me. I gained a lot of insight I never before realized. It's great because whenever I doubt or feel like I'm not adequate, I think of seeing Christ off in the distance on the water—a light amidst a dark and troubled situation—and it gives me hope. I have to keep my focus on Christ and everything else will fall into place.

"In my patriarchal blessing it says that I will pass through certain experiences to fortify my life and glorify my Father in Heaven. As far as the homosexuality thing goes, I look back on what I was told by Church leaders and family, and I know that they wanted what was best for me, and because of them I am where I am today."

In awe of his deepened understanding of the gospel and of his relationship to Christ and the Father, I cried as I read his letter. I cried as I read of his renewed and strengthened faith and hope in Jesus Christ—the Son of God I have grown reverence so deeply. It was at this point that I started to understand the significance of what my mission in mortality may be—simply to stand as a witness for Christ, despite this challenge.

My missionary friend shared something in that letter that seems appropriate and important to expand upon here: it was his adherence to the counsel of his family and Church leaders that helped him to get to the mission field. Even though we have all covenanted to mourn for and comfort and be the saviors of men for each other, the kingdom of God is a kingdom of order, and those who have stewardship over us—primarily our parents and ecclesiastical leaders—should be our first line of resource for guidance and counsel. The most recent edition of the *"For the Strength of Youth*" pamphlet reads: "Homosexual activity is a serious sin. If you find yourself struggling with same-gender attraction, seek counsel from your parents and bishop. They will help you."[1]

The stewardship of our parents and leaders is something we must be willing to put trust and faith in. Though they are not perfect—and they do not pretend to be—they have been called by God to lead and watch over us as His children. He will qualify those whom He calls, and if they make mistakes of judgment, we must not take it upon ourselves to "steady the ark" (see 2 Samuel 6:6–7; D&C 85:8). Rather, we must have the proper faith in God to allow Him to judge them with the justice and mercy of His eternal righteousness.

Fulfilling Our Stewardships in the Kingdom of God

Elder M. Russell Ballard gave an address in a recent priesthood session of general conference concerning stewardship and how the Lord has ordered His kingdom to ideally work. His address was about preparing missionaries to serve, but it could also be applied to the concept of stewardship as a whole and, hence, to how the issue of same-gender attraction should ideally be addressed within the order of Christ's earthly kingdom. He said: "Now, fathers, you have a vital role in this preparation process. We know that the most profound influence on helping young men prepare for the Melchizedek Priesthood, marriage, and fatherhood is the family. If your sons understand the basic doctrines required to become a faithful father, they will surely be ready to serve as a full-time missionary. Unfortunately, far too many fathers abdicate this eternal responsibility. You may assume that the bishop and the seminary, Sunday School, and Young Men teachers and leaders are in a better position to motivate and inspire your sons than you are. That simply is not the case. While ecclesiastical leaders are important to your son's priesthood and missionary preparation, the Church exists as a resource to you. It is not a substitute for your inspired teaching, guidance, and correction.

"Consequently, if we are 'raising the bar' for your sons to serve as missionaries, that means we are also 'raising the bar' for you. If we expect more of them, that means we expect more of you and your wife as well. Remember, Helaman's 2,000 stripling warriors were faithful because 'they had been taught to keep the commandments of God and to walk uprightly before him' (Alma 53:21)—and that instruction came in their homes.

"Some fathers don't think they have the right to ask worthiness questions of their children. They think that is the purview of the bishop alone. Fathers, not only do you have the right to know the worthiness of your children, you have the responsibility. It is your duty to know how your children are doing with regards to their spiritual well-being and progression. You need to monitor carefully the issues and concerns they share with you. Ask specific questions of your children regarding their worthiness, and refuse to settle for anything less than specific answers.

"Too often our bishops have to instruct youth to talk to their parents about problems they are having. That procedure should actually flow the other direction. Parents should be so intimately aware of what is going on in their children's lives that they know about the problems before the bishop does. They should be counseling with their children and going with them to their bishops if that becomes necessary for complete repentance. As divinely appointed judges in Israel, the bishop and the stake president determine worthiness and resolve concerns on behalf of the Church; but, fathers, you have an eternal responsibility for the spiritual welfare of your children. Please assume your rightful place as counselor, adviser, and priesthood leader in preparing your sons to bear the Melchizedek Priesthood and to serve as missionaries."[2]

Although same-gender attraction in and of itself is not a worthiness issue in the least degree, it is a concern that can affect the spiritual welfare of the individual who experiences it, depending on how that individual responds to the attraction. The fatherhood responsibility Elder Ballard speaks of—knowing the concerns of their children so they might better provide guidance, strength, and encouragement—applies as much to the challenge of same-gender attraction as it does to any other challenge, trial, or concern individuals may face. Of course, we should always seek the counsel of the Lord and follow the Spirit, and, as the Proclamation on the Family states, "circumstances may necessitate individual adaptation," but confiding in our parents concerning the feelings or attractions we struggle with and allowing them to be a support to us should be the general rule—that is the order of the kingdom.[3]

Our stewards—parents and ecclesiastical leaders alike—may be humble, and we may think we know more than they, but we must seek their counsel and follow it. Concerning working with ecclesiastical leaders specifically, President George Q. Cannon taught: "Many of the people think, 'I know more about this matter than my Bishop does,' when some temporal matter is agitated. That feeling is running through the minds of numbers of the people; and while this is the case, your Bishops will probably not be as wise as they might be; they have not your faith to sustain them. But when the time comes that you have implicit faith and confidence in God and in those whom He appoints to preside over you, in things temporal as well as spiritual, your Bishops will have all the wisdom needed to give you the counsel you require."[4]

In continuing my exchange with the young missionary but still not feeling it appropriate to reveal my own struggle, I wrote more of the ideas I had learned concerning Christ and the Atonement in the hope that his faith would continue to be strengthened. And because in his previous letter he had also explained that at one point in his struggle he had planned to take his life and offered to share the story at another time, I inquired about it.

He responded:

"During college, in one of my classes there was this guy I was getting to be pretty good friends with who just happened to be in the same situation I was with this attraction. Anyway, to spare the details, he was beautiful inside and out, and it ended up that I had to decide whether I wanted to pursue a relationship with him or whether I was going to pursue a mission.

"Nothing inappropriate ever happened with him, but I still had to decide. It was one of the hardest decisions I've ever had to make. Most of my family knew about him and were naturally upset, so I felt like I was torn between my family and what I felt inside. My friend would always tell me to be true to myself, and my family would always tell me that I knew what was right—and inside my mind I couldn't be true to myself and do what was right. It just seemed like a lose-lose situation.

"So one night, I picked up the keys, went out the front door, and had every intention to end my life. I got in my car, threw in my favorite CD (thinking it would be the last time I'd listen to it), and drove south on the Interstate. I kept driving, wondering where and how to do it—I wanted to wreck my car with me inside, but I just kept driving. Tears were streaming down my face, and I felt there was no hope. Out of the corner of my eye I saw this bright building—a temple. I decided to check it out. I got off at the next exit and drove through the side streets trying to find this temple. Luckily it was a really dark night, so I could tell which way I had to go by the soft glow.

"Well, I was a few blocks away, and this thick fog started to drape over the streets. I got on this road that seemed to be going nowhere—but it was right there in front of me before I knew it. I was literally in awe at the sight of this magnificent building, and the tears came flooding down again. After a quick drive around the grounds, I realized it was the Mt. Timpanogos Temple. I sat there in the parking lot and poured out my soul to my Father in Heaven, letting Him know everything I was feeling—and I knew He was there. Something inside me told me to go home and sleep—so I did, and when I woke up I felt so much better about everything. I ended up choosing to trust in the counsel of my family—and here I am. I feel as though that temple in all reality literally saved my life. It holds a special place in my heart and is a symbol of life to me—and for that reason it is also there that I received my endowments.

"I also wanted to share with you an experience I had recently. There is a member around this area who is really good family friends with my old companion. I got to know him, and we get along really well. Well, he came on exchanges the other week, and after talking quite a bit, he told me he was gay. This man is in his late forties, active in the Church, has a temple recommend and all that, but he is struggling because of the comments and snide remarks from his ward. He loves the gospel of Jesus Christ but is burnt out on the Church (meaning many of the people in it). I say this because I've been able to share with him some of the things you've shared with me, and it has helped out a lot. He told me once that he thinks God might not love him as much because of some of the things he's been through (three engagements). I just looked at him and said, 'You don't really believe that, do you?' And then I proceeded to explain how much God loves each and every one of us.

"Ever since I first saw him, I thought that he was one of the reasons I was called here on my mission. I told him that when I get back from my mission that he and I will do a temple session together. There is nothing I love more than being in the celestial room knowing that I'm doing all right—and knowing that, yes, I can make it here someday. I think you said it best when you wrote, 'Our eternal salvation isn't based upon our mortal heterosexuality.' It all goes down to that change of heart and to be able to have our focus in the right direction—on our Lord and Savior Jesus Christ. Granted, I'm far from perfect, and I need help every day, but knowing that my Father in Heaven does love me and that He and Jesus Christ truly understand me gives me such peace. I feel so blessed to have the understanding of the things I do."

In another letter, my friend shared with me a difficult experience that occurred on his mission and how he not only grew from it but also how through it he was able to see his own growth—both in his relationship to God and in his understanding of this issue in his life:

"I've recently had a strong witness testify to me that I was blessed with these trials to help me help others—I only hope I can have the faith and strength to do what the Lord would have me do. Recently in this mission, there were rumors going around that I might be gay—and some of my closest friends out here were worried if it was true and how I might react to people speculating (man, you keep an apartment clean and dress well and BAM! the speculations start!! Go figure . . .) Anyway, I confronted someone to see if there were any rumors going around about me, and he had the decency to be honest with me and tell me that people think that I might be gay. He then asked me if there was any truth to the rumors—I said yes and we talked about it for about ten minutes.

"Instantly, his understanding was broadened and his misconceptions cleared somewhat in regards to people who struggle with these attractions. Of course, word spreads fast out here in the mission field among other missionaries—but you know what? I don't mind. Maybe that's what it's all about. There are so many people who don't understand—just like I didn't before I came on this mission. Hopefully I might be an instrument in the Lord's hands to help people realize I'm not the spawn of Satan because I have these inclinations—but to help them understand, to a greater extent, God's love for each of us individually, Christ's love for us and the power of His Atonement—and all the eternal principles that apply to everyone, despite our trials and tribulations.

"It took quite a long time for me to understand that I'm not an evil person because of this attraction. I mean, homosexuality is a part of me, but it doesn't define me, ya know? It's strange to look back on my life and remember how I used to feel. It was almost like having a ball and chain attached to my ankle or something. This trial was something that weighed me down and was something I thought hindered my progress in becoming a better person. I didn't think there was any way I could turn this trial around and actually use my experience and feelings to help bring me closer to my Father in Heaven—and at the same time, help others come closer to Him as well. What an amazing blessing it's been!

"Isn't it funny that there are rumors flying around this mission about me being gay? Once again, if this type of thing had happened a year and a half ago, I probably would've packed my bags and cried all the way home just because I didn't understand then what a great blessing this trial truly is! I think it's good for other missionaries to understand that members of the Church who have these attractions aren't bad people just because they have those attractions—and if missionaries look at me and use me as an example to come to that conclusion, then so be it. I'm not about to latch another ball and chain onto myself and let these rumors hold me down."

Through my experience with this elder—both watching him grow in Christ and gain a greater perspective of his place in the gospel kingdom and at the same time realizing to a greater degree at least a portion of my own mission in mortality—I have grown tremendously, and I have felt greater love for my Father and my Redeemer. I have had similar conversations and experiences with others with whom I have developed close and lasting friendships—others who have touched my life and kindled in my heart a greater desire to stand as a witness for my God both to the world and to many who are members of Christ's Church but who live with misunderstanding, ignorance, suspicion, or fear of those who experience same-gender attraction.

Standing as a Witness for God

When I was given the opportunity to write about this issue, I saw it as chance to further educate people about some of the things I feel the Lord has taught me in regard to what I believe is the true nature of this challenge. I was initially very wary. First of all, writing has never been one of my talents, and I doubted my capacity to put something so sensitive and personal into words in a way that would help others understand why I believe and feel the way I do. Also, I had some idea of the nature of the various responses that were sure to come—I expected criticism from those whose beliefs vary from my own concerning the nature of this attraction and the appropriate response to it.

Second, I'm only twenty-six years old—a mere babe in arms, in the eyes of some—and my experience and understanding are minimal compared to the wide range of others' experiences. I worried about being as comprehensive as possible but still keeping the ideas and doctrines general enough so they could apply to those whose experiences have been distinctly different from my own.

With the encouragement and support of others close to me, once I made the decision to attempt to translate my convictions and passions onto paper, I was confronted with the difficult decision of whether or not I would attach my real name to the book. With a topic so widely misunderstood—and one in which there is such passionate controversy and divergence of belief—I was initially extremely hesitant. Although this volume contains a record of my spiritual journey and of the doctrinal understanding I've gained as I've experienced this trial, I had to consider the implications putting my name on the work would have. In addition to my own concerns, it seemed like everyone around me had a few of their own to throw into the already scorching internal fire.

Some worried about my "labeling" myself. And what about a potential future family? How would this affect them? How would those critical of the Church and its resolute stand on this issue respond? How would they treat my name and the convictions and doctrines I hold so dear? These and other questions forced me to do a lot of pondering and internal searching—and, most important, I had to turn to my God in prayer for guidance. Only He knows me perfectly, and only He could give me the heavenly confirmation and peace I would need to go forward with whatever became the final decision.

One thought that often came to my mind as I pondered and studied the scriptures was what it means to stand as a witness for God. I really feel the Lord has been merciful to me in helping me to understand the things I do, because so many others I know who experience this attraction leave the Church out of discouragement or frustration, feeling there is no place for them in it. I have come to feel strongly that the challenge of same-gender attraction is nothing to be ashamed of. It is a challenge—nothing more. There may be sin in how I respond to it, but the sin is not in the attraction itself. I felt that if I were to stand as a witness for Christ and discuss the nature of this challenge—and its relation to the gospel—with the potency with which it needed to be said, I would have to associate my real name with it.

I believe in Christ and in the fulness of the gospel, and when it comes to proclaiming both the redeeming and enabling power of His name, with this specific book and in this particular situation, I could not stand behind "Name Withheld." Because I'm not married, I had to take into consideration how it could affect my potential future family but, nevertheless, as I continued to ponder and pray, I knew what I needed to do, and I felt the Lord's peace with that decision. That is the only thing that matters to me. So, regardless of what happens in the future concerning a family or the societal response to the convictions recorded on these pages, I know the Lord is with me and will provide a way for me to do whatever it is that He would have me do. I must allow Him to be the Author of my life, and I will leave it in His hands.

I hope to stand with the faith of the ancient apostles who "rejoic[ed] that they were counted worthy to suffer shame for his name" (Acts 5:41). If people feel there is shame in exercising faith in Jesus Christ through a trial of this nature that I didn't choose, then so be it! I will glory in His name. With the misunderstanding and homophobia that exists in society and among many members of the Church, I felt strongly that if the only voices heard on this issue were those of political rights activists, gay sitcoms, and pride parades, this issue would never be understood and accepted within a gospel framework and in the most Christ-centered and faithful way.

I do not believe it appropriate for those of us who have feelings of same-gender attraction to casually announce our challenge from the pulpit or to share it with anyone other than those who have stewardship over us or with whom we feel the Lord has guided us to share it. But I do believe that unless we who experience this challenge—and who desire to live faithful to God and refuse to suppress our feelings in quiet desperation—are willing to discuss our feelings with those who love us and who can bless and help and strengthen and support us, the misperceptions of society and those closest to us will never change. In addition, we cannot healthily and submissively lay our whole souls on God's altar and be reformed through the power and grace of Christ's atonement as long as parts of ourselves are compartmentalized and shamefully locked away in a "closet." For true healing and redemption to take place, we must be able to take out our feelings, hold them up before our God, lay them humbly on His altar, and, as Elder Jeffrey R. Holland stated, "kneel there in silent submission, and willingly walk away."[5]

As for me, it will be impossible to keep my experience with feelings of same-gender attraction as private as I would have liked, but I hope, nevertheless, to move forward with my life in other ways and with my many other passions and interests. Life is about Christ and salvation and sharing the gospel with others. Though I am not ashamed of my attraction, the attraction itself is not me—it is only a small part of who I am in this world. I know who I am—a literal child of my literal and eternal Father in Heaven—and although I have no problem with the terms *gay* or *same-gender attracted* or other terms people use to refer to those who have these feelings, there are a hundred other ways I would describe myself before I would use any of them. I am a son and a brother. I am an uncle and a nephew. I am a student and a friend. Even more important, I hope to be called a Christian and a Latter-day Saint, a member of the house of Israel and of the seed of Abraham. I am a god "in embryo" with "unlimited potential for progress and attainment" of a divine destiny in the celestial realms of my Father in Heaven.[6]

Shortly after returning home from my missionary service, I began working at the temple. One day while I was sitting in one of those sacred rooms waiting for the next session, I was reading about Israel after they had been called to build a tabernacle to the Lord. The Lord commanded Israel: "Take ye from among you an offering unto the Lord: whosoever is of a willing heart, let him bring it, an offering of the Lord; gold, and silver, and brass." He continued with the list of all that was needed to build His house: "And they came, every one whose heart stirred him up, and every one whom his spirit made willing, and they brought the Lord's offering to the work of the tabernacle of the congregation, and for all his service, and for the holy garments" (Exodus 35:5, 21).

As I sat in the temple reading these verses concerning ancient Israel—the people whom I had always thought of as being profoundly stubborn and ignorant—I was touched with understanding and compassion for their desire to worship and to serve the Lord despite their shortcomings, for they did have that which was most important—willing hearts. Their desire to serve and their willingness to sacrifice was so great, in fact, that those who had been called by Moses to receive their offering "spake unto Moses, saying, The people bring much more than enough for the service of the work, which the Lord commanded to make. And Moses gave commandment, and they caused it to be proclaimed throughout the camp, saying, Let neither man nor woman make any more work for the offering of the sanctuary. So the people were restrained from bringing. For the stuff they had was sufficient for all the work to make it, and too much" (Exodus 36:5–7).

Touched by their willingness and their faith, I pondered these verses recording the lives of my ancestors. As I did so, I had a strong spiritual impression. It was as if the Lord were saying to me, "Ancient Israel was called to build a tabernacle. Despite their shortcomings and their weaknesses, their hearts were willing, and they heeded my call. You, my son, have likewise been called to a responsibility of great magnitude, for you have been called to build a kingdom. Are you willing to sacrifice, to serve, and to build?" The feeling was poignant, and I wondered if I did have the same willingness to serve—to serve until the Lord would say that my efforts were "sufficient for all the work to make it, and too much."

My heart is willing, and though I am weak and have challenges and trials, I believe that there is a place for me in God's kingdom. This particular challenge is still not over for me, nor do I know whether it will be in mortality. But with a "perfect brightness of hope" (2 Nephi 31:20), I will strive to live for God and proclaim His gospel. My feelings concerning the gospel of Christ and His earthly Church and kingdom echo the bold proclamation of President Brigham Young: "I wanted to thunder and roar out the Gospel to the nations. It burned in my bones like fire pent up . . . [and] nothing would satisfy me but to cry abroad in the world, what the Lord was doing in the latter days. . . . I had to go out and preach, lest my bones should consume within me."[7]

The word of God is in my heart as a burning fire shut up in my bones. I believe that the latter-day restoration of the gospel of Christ is the work of the Almighty. I feel it! Although I do not fully understand what my place is in the body of Christ and the full implications of what will be required of me in this life to build His kingdom, I continue to seek to better understand that place. But at least this much I know: The Lord is my God, and He loves me. He is holy and full of grace and truth, and He wants me Home, and for that reason a ransom was made; for that reason did He say, "I will be merciful unto them, . . . if they will repent and come unto me; for mine arm is lengthened out all the day long" (2 Nephi 28:32).

I love Him and want to give my life to Him. I am eternally grateful for the peace and perspective and purpose I have felt as He has helped me through His Holy Spirit of truth to better understand the divine purpose in my mortal challenges. "I glory in plainness; I glory in truth; I glory in my Jesus, for he hath redeemed my soul from hell" (2 Nephi 33:6).

Notes

Part 1
A Parent's Spiritual Journey toward Understanding

Chapter 9
The Love of the Brethren

1. *"For the Strength of Youth"* (1990), 15; ibid. (2001), 28.
2. Packer, "'Ye Are the Temple of God,'" 74.
3. Nelson, "How Firm Our Foundation," 76.
4. Morrison, "Some Gospel Perspectives on Same-Gender Attraction."

Chapter 10
Submitting to God's Will

1. Holland, "Will of the Father in All Things," 78.

Chapter 11
Reaching Out in Christlike Love

1. Eyring, "'Feed My Lambs,'" 83.

Part 2
A Young Adult's Search for Purpose and Peace

Chapter 2
Facing Reality

1. Lewis, *Mere Christianity,* 189.
2. Roberts, "Book of Mormon Translation," 9.
3. Smith, *Gospel Doctrine,* 3–4.
4. Widtsoe, *Evidences and Reconciliations,* 16.
5. Nibley, *World and the Prophets,* 134.
6. Packer, "Little Children," 17.
7. Cowdery, "Letter,"112.
8. McConkie, "Purifying Power of Gethsemane," 9.

Chapter 3
A God of Miracles

1. Oaks, "Miracles," 6.
2. Holland, "Cast Not Away Therefore Your Confidence," 10.
3. Ibid.
4. Ibid.
5. Young, *Journal of Discourses,* 4:216.

Chapter 4
"That I May Prove Them"

1. As cited in Taylor, *Journal of Discourses,* 24:264.
2. Ibid., 24:197.
3. Smith, *Teachings of the Prophet Joseph Smith,* 150.
4. Dahl, "Abrahamic Test," 62.
5. Millet, "Healing Our Wounded Souls."
6. Dahl, "Abrahamic Test," 63.
7. As cited in Dahl, "Abrahamic Test," 62.
8. Young, *Journal of Discourses,* 3:266.
9. Lewis, *Mere Christianity,* 174.
10. Dahl, "Abrahamic Test," 58.
11. Kimball, *Faith Precedes the Miracle,* 96.
12. Millet, "God and Human Tragedy."
13. Lewis, *Problem of Pain,* 35–36.
14. John G. Stackhouse, *Can God Be Trusted? Faith and the Challenge of Evil* (New York: Oxford, 1998), 13, as cited in Millet, "God and Human Tragedy."
15. Maxwell, "Why Not Now?" 13.
16. Millet, "God and Human Tragedy."
17. Packer, *The Play and the Plan,* 2–3.
18. Cited in Kimball, *Miracle of Forgiveness,* 105.
19. Frankl, *Man's Search for Meaning,* 104.
20. Benson, *Teachings of Ezra Taft Benson,* 21.
21. Lewis, *Problem of Pain,* 35–36, 38.
22. Packer, "Choice," 21.
23. Cited in McKay, "Pioneer Women," 8.
24. Featherstone, "Self-Inflicted Purging," 99; italics in original.
25. Smith, *Lectures on Faith,* 6:7, 11.
26. "Lord, I Would Follow Thee," *Hymns,* 220.
27. McConkie, "How and Why of Faith-Promoting Stories," 5.
28. Cited in Maxwell, "Response to a Call," 112.
29. Ballard, "Like a Flame Unquenchable," 86.
30. Maxwell, *If Thou Endure It Well,* 54.
31. Maxwell, "Applying the Atoning Blood of Christ," 23.
32. Kimball, "Absolute Truth," *Ensign,* September 1978, 8.
33. Smith, *Teachings of the Prophet Joseph Smith,* 332.
34. Holland, "Will of the Father in All Things," 76–78.

Chapter 5
Hope through the Atonement

1. Holland, "Missionary Work and the Atonement," 24–25.
2. Ibid.
3. Lewis, *Mere Christianity,* 126.
4. Maxwell, "Shine as Lights in the World," 11.
5. Millet, "God and Human Tragedy."
6. Scott, "Trust in the Lord," 17.
7. Maxwell, *Neal A. Maxwell Quote Book,* 261.
8. Maxwell, *Deposition of a Disciple,* 52.
9. Kimball, "Give Me This Mountain," 79.
10. Hafen, *Disciple's Life,* 562.
11. Britsch, "Trusting God When Things Go Wrong," 30.
12. As cited in Madsen, *Joseph Smith the Prophet,* 92.
13. Maxwell, "More Determined Discipleship," 73.
14. Hunter, "Reading the Scriptures," 65.
15. Packer, "Candle of the Lord," 54.
16. Holland, "'Come unto Me,'" 19.
17. Packer, "Standard of Truth," 25–26.
18. Millet, "God and Human Tragedy."
19. Robinson, *Believing Christ,* 95–97.

Chapter 6
Son of Man or Son of God?

1. Benson, *Teachings of Ezra Taft Benson,* 21.
2. Kimball, "Circles of Exaltation," 23; italics in original.
3. Benson, *Witness and a Warning,* 33.
4. Millet, "Regeneration of Fallen Man," in *Selected Writings of Robert L. Millet,* 171.
5. Robinson, *Following Christ,* 52–59.
6. Holland, *Christ and the New Covenant,* 206–7.
7. Ibid., 203–4.
8. Young, *Journal of Discourses,* 8:160.
9. Ibid., 10:173.
10. Packer, "'Ye Are the Temple of God,'" 74.
11. Oaks, "Same-Gender Attraction," 9.
12. Kimball, *Teachings of Spencer W. Kimball,* 276.
13. Talmage, *Articles of Faith,* 395–96.
14. "Sweet Is the Peace the Gospel Brings," *Hymns,* no. 14.
15. Talmage, Conference Report, October 1931, 50–53.
16. Widtsoe, Conference Report, April 1940, 36.

Chapter 7
Paul, the Romans, and Homosexuality

1. Scott, "Acquiring Spiritual Knowledge," 86.
2. Talmage, *Articles of Faith,* 395–96.
3. Young, *Journal of Discourses,* 7:55.

4. See Faulconer, *Romans 1,* 77. I appreciate Professor Faulconer's review of a number of the ideas in this chapter that rely on his work.

5. Ibid., 79.

6. Holland, "Personal Purity," 77.

7. Holland, *Of Souls, Symbols, and Sacraments,* 30–32; italics added.

8. Young, *Discourses of Brigham Young,* 197.

9. Hays, "Relations Natural and Unnatural," 191.

10. Smith, *Teachings of the Prophet Joseph Smith,* 300.

11. Smith, *Doctrines of Salvation,* 2:287–88.

12. Faulconer, *Romans 1,* 89.

13. Hays, "Relations Natural and Unnatural," 210.

Chapter 8

The Message of Paul to the World

1. Skinner, "Israel and Judah in the Ninth and Eighth Centuries Before Christ," 44.

2. Kimball, *Miracle of Forgiveness,* 40–42.

3. Kimball, "Why Call Me Lord, Lord, and Do Not the Things Which I Say?" 7.

4. Benson, *This Nation Shall Endure,* 126.

5. Smith, *Teachings of the Prophet Joseph Smith,* 255–56.

6. *Merriam-Webster's Collegiate Dictionary,* 10th ed., s.v. "hedonism."

7. John MacArthur Jr., *Our Sufficiency in Christ* (Dallas: Word Publishing, 1991), 154–55, as cited in Judd, "Hedonism, Asceticism, and the Great Plan of Happiness," 205.

8. Benson, "The Great Commandment—Love the Lord," 4; italics in original.

9. See Benson, "Beware of Pride," 4.

Chapter 9

According to the Lord's Own Will and Pleasure

1. Maxwell, *Even As I Am,* 93.

2. Maxwell, "Plow in Hope," 59.

3. Millet, "Doctrine of Merit," 121–22.

4. "The Wise Man and the Foolish Man," *Children's Songbook,* 281.

5. Benson, "Born of God," 6; italics added.

6. Monson, "Prayer of Faith," 21.

7. Young, *Journal of Discourses,* 4:24.

8. Hunter, *Teachings of Howard W. Hunter,* 40.

9. Ballard, "Feasting at the Lord's Table," *Ensign,* 81.

10. McConkie, "Holy Writ Published Anew," 236–38.

11. McConkie and Millet, *Doctrinal Commentary on the Book of Mormon,* 3:3.

12. Hinckley, "Ensign to the Nations," 84.

13. Packer, "Standard of Truth," 25.

14. Hinckley, "What Are People Asking about Us?" 71.

15. Hinckley, "Why We Do Some of the Things We Do," 54; italics added.

16. Packer, "Covenants," 85; italics in original.

17. Staheli, "Obedience—Life's Great Challenge," 82.

18. Cannon, *Gospel Truth,* 215, 217.

19. Oaks, "Timing," 190–91.
20. Hinckley, "Reverence and Morality," 47.

Chapter 10
To Mourn and to Comfort

1. Smith, *Teachings of the Prophet Joseph Smith,* 240.
2. Packer, "Standard of Truth," 25.
3. Holland, CES Symposium address.
4. First Presidency letter, 14 November 1991, as cited in Oaks, "Same-Gender Attraction."
5. Buckner, "Many Are Called," 55.
6. Confucius, *Analects of Confucius,* 8.
7. Philip Yancey, *The Jesus I Never Knew* (Grand Rapids, Mich.: Zondervan, 1995), 147–48; as cited in Millet, "God and Human Tragedy."
8. Maxwell, "Swallowed Up in the Will of the Father," 23.
9. Smith, *History of Joseph Smith by His Mother,* 152–53.
10. Morrison, "Some Gospel Perspectives on Same-Gender Attraction."
11. Hunter, "The Gospel—A Global Faith," 18.
12. Smith, *History of the Church,* 4:595–96.

Chapter 11
A Place in the Kingdom

1. *"For the Strength of Youth"* (2001), 28.
2. Ballard, "Greatest Generation of Missionaries," 46.
3. First Presidency and the Council of the Twelve Apostles, "The Family: A Proclamation to the World," 102.
4. Cannon, *Gospel Truth,* 274.
5. Holland, "Will of the Father in All Things," 78.
6. Benson, *Teachings of Ezra Taft Benson,* 21.
7. Young, *Journal of Discourses,* 1:313–14.

Sources

Ballard, M. Russell. "Feasting at the Lord's Table." *Ensign,* May 1996.

———. "The Greatest Generation of Missionaries." *Ensign,* November 2002.

———. "Like a Flame Unquenchable." *Ensign,* May 1999.

Benson, Ezra Taft. "Beware of Pride." *Ensign,* May 1989.

———. "Born of God." *Ensign,* November 1985.

———. "The Great Commandment—Love the Lord." *Ensign,* May 1988.

———. *The Teachings of Ezra Taft Benson.* Salt Lake City: Bookcraft, 1988.

———. *This Nation Shall Endure.* Salt Lake City: Deseret Book, 1977.

———. *A Witness and a Warning: A Modern-day Prophet Testifies of the Book of Mormon.* Salt Lake City: Deseret Book, 1988.

Britsch, Todd A. "Trusting God When Things Go Wrong." *Brigham Young University 1997–98 Speeches.* Provo, Utah: Brigham Young University, 1998.

Buckner, David L. "Many Are Called, but Who Is Chosen?" In *Serving with Strength throughout the World.* Salt Lake City: Deseret Book, 1994.

Cannon, George Q. *Gospel Truth: Discourses and Writings of President George Q. Cannon.* Edited by Jerreld L. Newquist. 2 vols. in 1. Salt Lake City: Deseret Book, 1987.

Children's Songbook. Salt Lake City: The Church of Jesus Christ of Latter-day Saints, 1989.

Confucius. *The Analects of Confucius.* Translated by Simon Leys. New York: W. W. Norton, 1997.

Cowdery, Oliver. Letter. *Messenger and Advocate* 1, no. 7 (April 1835): 112.

Dahl, Larry E. "Abrahamic Test." In *A Witness of Jesus Christ: The 1989 Sperry Symposium on the Old Testament.* Edited by Richard D. Draper. Salt Lake City: Deseret Book, 1990.

Eyring, Henry B. " 'Feed My Lambs.' " *Ensign,* November 1997.

Faulconer, James E. *Romans 1: Notes and Reflections.* Provo, Utah: FARMS, 1999.

Featherstone, Vaughn J. "A Self-Inflicted Purging." *Ensign,* May 1975.

First Presidency and the Council of the Twelve Apostles. "The Family: A Proclamation to the World." *Ensign,* November 1995.

"For the Strength of Youth" [pamphlet]. Salt Lake City: The Church of Jesus Christ of Latter-day Saints, 1990.

"For the Strength of Youth" [pamphlet]. Salt Lake City: The Church of Jesus Christ of Latter-day Saints, 2001.

Frankl, Viktor E. *Man's Search for Ultimate Meaning.* New York: Washington Square Press, 1985.

Hafen, Bruce C. *A Disciple's Life: The Biography of Neal A. Maxwell.* Salt Lake City: Deseret Book, 2002.

Hays, Richard B. "Relations Natural and Unnatural: A Response to John Boswell's Exegesis of Romans 1." *Journal of Religious Ethics,* Spring 1986.

Hinckley, Gordon B. "An Ensign to the Nations, a Light to the World." *Ensign,* November 2003.

———. "Reverence and Morality." *Ensign,* May 1987.

———. "What Are People Asking about Us?" *Ensign,* November 1998.

———. "Why We Do Some of the Things We Do." *Ensign,* November 1999.

Holland, Jeffrey R. "Cast Not Away Therefore Your Confidence," *Ensign,* March 2000.

———. CES Symposium address, August 1980.

———. *Christ and the New Covenant.* Salt Lake City: Deseret Book, 1997.

———. " 'Come unto Me.' " *Ensign,* April 1998.

———. "Missionary Work and the Atonement." *Ensign,* March 2001.

———. *Of Souls, Symbols, and Sacraments.* Salt Lake City: Deseret Book, 2001. Originally presented as an address at Brigham Young University, Provo, Utah, January 12, 1998.

———. "Personal Purity." *Ensign,* November 1998.

———. "The Will of the Father in All Things." *Brigham Young University 1988–89 Devotional and Fireside Speeches.* Provo, Utah: Brigham Young University, 1989.

Hunter, Howard W. "The Gospel—A Global Faith." *Ensign,* November 1991.

———. "Reading the Scriptures." *Ensign,* November 1979.

———. *The Teachings of Howard W. Hunter.* Edited by Clyde J. Williams. Salt Lake City: Bookcraft, 1997.

Hymns of The Church of Jesus Christ of Latter-day Saints. Salt Lake City: The Church of Jesus Christ of Latter-day Saints, 1985.

Journal of Discourses. 26 vols. London: Latter-day Saints' Book Depot, 1854–86.

Judd, Daniel K. "Hedonism, Asceticism, and the Great Plan of Happiness." *The Fulness of the Gospel: Foundational Teachings from the Book of Mormon.* Salt Lake City: Deseret Book and Religious Studies Center, 2003.

Kimball, Spencer W. "Absolute Truth." *Ensign,* September 1978.

———. "Circles of Exaltation." *Charge to Religious Educators.* 2d ed. Salt Lake City: The Church of Jesus Christ of Latter-day Saints, 1979.

———. *Faith Precedes the Miracle.* Salt Lake City: Deseret Book, 1977.

———. "Give Me This Mountain." *Ensign,* November 1979.

———. "Marriage Is Honorable." In *Speeches of the Year, 1973.* Provo, Utah: Brigham Young University, 1974.

———. *The Miracle of Forgiveness.* Salt Lake City: Bookcraft, 1969.

———. *Teachings of Spencer W. Kimball.* Edited by Edward L. Kimball. Salt Lake City: Bookcraft, 1982

———. "Why Call Me Lord, Lord, and Do Not the Things Which I Say?" *Ensign,* May 1975.

Lewis, C. S. *Mere Christianity.* New York: Macmillan, 1943.

———. *The Problem of Pain.* New York: Macmillan, 1962.

Madsen, Truman G. *Joseph Smith, the Prophet.* Salt Lake City: Bookcraft, 1989.

Maxwell, Neal A. "Applying the Atoning Blood of Christ." *Ensign,* November 1997.

———. *Deposition of a Disciple.* Salt Lake City: Deseret Book, 1976.

———. *Even As I Am.* Salt Lake City: Deseret Book, 1982.

———. *If Thou Endure It Well.* Salt Lake City: Bookcraft, 1996.

———. "A More Determined Discipleship." *Ensign,* February 1979.

———. *The Neal A. Maxwell Quote Book.* Edited by Cory H. Maxwell. Salt Lake City: Bookcraft, 1997.

———. "Plow in Hope." *Ensign,* May 2001.

———. "Response to a Call." *Ensign,* May 1974.

———. "Shine as Lights in the World." *Ensign,* May 1983.

———. "Swallowed Up in the Will of the Father." *Ensign,* November 1995.

———. "Why Not Now?" *Ensign,* November 1974.

McConkie, Bruce R. "Holy Writ Published Anew." In *Doctrines of the Restoration: Sermons and Writings of Bruce R. McConkie.* Edited by Mark L. McConkie. Salt Lake City: Bookcraft, 1989.

———. "The How and Why of Faith-Promoting Stories." *New Era,* July 1978.

———. "The Purifying Power of Gethsemane." *Ensign,* May 1985.

McConkie, Joseph Fielding, and Robert L. Millet. *Alma through Helaman.* Vol. 3 of *Doctrinal Commentary on the Book of Mormon.* Salt Lake City: Bookcraft, 1996.

McKay, David O. "Pioneer Women." *Relief Society Magazine,* January 1948.

Millet, Robert L. *Alive in Christ: The Miracle of Spiritual Rebirth.* Salt Lake City: Deseret Book, 1997.

———. "The Doctrine of Merit." *The Fulness of the Gospel: Foundational Teachings from the Book of Mormon.* Salt Lake City: Deseret Book and Religious Studies Center, 2003.

———. "God and Human Tragedy: How the Lord Can Transform Tragedy into Triumph." Address delivered at Brigham Young University Education Week, 18 August 2003.

———. "Healing Our Wounded Souls." Address delivered in Salt Lake City, Utah, September 2000.

———. "The Regeneration of Fallen Man." In *Selected Writings of Robert L. Millet,* a volume in *Gospel Scholars Series.* Salt Lake City: Deseret Book, 2000.

Monson, Thomas S. "The Prayer of Faith." *Ensign,* May 1978.

Morrison, Alexander B. "Some Gospel Perspectives on Same-Gender Attraction." Address delivered in Salt Lake City, Utah, 16 September 2000.

Nibley, Hugh. *The World and the Prophets.* 3d ed. Salt Lake City and Provo: Deseret Book and FARMS, 1987.

Nelson, Russell M. "How Firm Our Foundation." *Ensign,* May 2002.

Oaks, Dallin H. *The Lord's Way.* Salt Lake City: Deseret Book, 1991.

———. "Miracles." *Ensign,* June 2001.

———. "Same-Gender Attraction." *Ensign,* October 1995.

———. "Timing." *Brigham Young University Devotional and Fireside Speeches, 2001–2002.* Provo, Utah: Brigham Young University, 2002.

Packer, Boyd K. "The Candle of the Lord." *Ensign,* January 1983.

———. "The Choice." *Ensign,* November 1980.

———. "Covenants." *Ensign,* November 1990.

———. "Little Children," *Ensign,* November 1986.

———. *The Play and the Plan.* Salt Lake City: The Church of Jesus Christ of Latter-day Saints, 1997.

———. "The Standard of Truth Has Been Erected." *Ensign,* November 2003.

———. "'Ye Are the Temple of God.'" *Ensign,* November 2000.

Roberts, B. H. "Book of Mormon Translation." *Improvement Era,* July 1906.

Robinson, Stephen E. *Believing Christ: The Parable of the Bicycle and Other Good News.* Salt Lake City: Deseret Book, 1992.

———. *Following Christ: The Parable of the Divers and More Good News.* Salt Lake City: Deseret Book, 1995.

Scott, Richard G. "Acquiring Spiritual Knowledge." *Ensign,* November 1993.

———. "Trust in the Lord." *Ensign,* November 1995.

Skinner, Andrew C. "Israel and Judah in the Ninth and Eighth Centuries Before Christ." In *1 Kings to Malachi.* Edited by Kent P. Jackson. Vol. 4 of *Studies in Scripture* series. Salt Lake City: Deseret Book, 1993.

Smith, Joseph. *History of The Church of Jesus Christ of Latter-day Saints.* Edited by B. H. Roberts. 2d ed. rev. 7 vols. Salt Lake City: The Church of Jesus Christ of Latter-day Saints, 1952–51.

———. *Lectures on Faith.* Salt Lake City: Deseret Book, 1985.

———. *Teachings of the Prophet Joseph Smith.* Selected by Joseph Fielding Smith. Salt Lake City: Deseret Book, 1976.

Smith, Joseph F. *Gospel Doctrine.* 5th ed. Salt Lake City: Deseret Book, 1939.

Smith, Joseph Fielding. *Doctrines of Salvation.* Compiled by Bruce R. McConkie. 3 vols. Salt Lake City: Bookcraft, 1954–56.

Smith, Lucy Mack. *History of Joseph Smith by His Mother.* Edited by Preston Nibley. Salt Lake City: Bookcraft, 1958.

Staheli, Donald L. "Obedience—Life's Great Challenge." *Ensign,* May 1998.

Talmage, James E. *The Articles of Faith.* 12th ed. Salt Lake City: The Church of Jesus Christ of Latter-day Saints, 1924.

———. Conference Report, October 1931.

Widtsoe, John A. Conference Report, April 1940.

———. *Evidences and Reconciliations.* Compiled by G. Homer Durham. 3 vols. in 1. Salt Lake City: Bookcraft, 1987.

Young, Brigham. *Discourses of Brigham Young.* Compiled by John A. Widtsoe. Salt Lake City: Deseret Book, 1998.

Index